SIGNS IN THE WILDERNESS

Signs in the Wilderness

Intertextuality and the Testing of Nicodemus

DANIEL H. FLETCHER

WIPF & STOCK · Eugene, Oregon

SIGNS IN THE WILDERNESS
Intertextuality and the Testing of Nicodemus

Copyright © 2014 Daniel H. Fletcher. All rights reserved. Except for brief quotations in critical publications or reviews, no part of this book may be reproduced in any manner without prior written permission from the publisher. Write: Permissions. Wipf and Stock Publishers, 199 W. 8th Ave., Suite 3, Eugene, OR 97401.

Wipf and Stock
An Imprint of Wipf and Stock Publishers
199 W. 8th Ave., Suite 3
Eugene, OR 97401

www.wipfandstock.com

ISBN 13: 978-1-62564-915-7

Manufactured in the U.S.A. 09/17/2014

Most Scripture quotations have been translated by the author unless indicated otherwise.

Scripture quotations from The Holy Bible, English Standard Version, are copyright © 2001 by Crossway Bibles, a division of Good News Publishers. Used by permission. All rights reserved.

Scripture quotations from the New Revised Standard Version Bible, are copyright © 1989 by the Division of Christian Education of the National Council of Churches of Christ in the U.S.A. Used by permission. All rights reserved.

Scripture quotations from the NEW AMERICAN STANDARD BIBLE, are copyright © 1962, 1962, 1963, 1968, 1971, 1972, 1973, 1975, 1977, 1988, 1995 by the Lockman Foundation. Used by permission.

Scripture Quotations designated (NIV) are from THE HOLY BIBLE: NEW INTERNATIONAL VERSION®. NIV®. Copyright © 1973, 1978, 1984, 2011 by International Bible Society, www.ibs.org. All rights reserved worldwide.

Scripture quotations taken from the *Holy Bible,* New Living Translation, are copyright © 1996, 2004, 2007. Used by permission of Tyndale House Publishers, Inc., Carol Stream, Illinois 60188. All rights reserved.

Critical editions of original language texts used include: Nestle-Aland, *Novum Testamentum,* copyright @ 1993 by Deutsche Bibelgesellschaft, *Biblia Hebraica Stuttgartensia, copyright* @ 1997 by Deutsche Bibelgesellschaft, and Rahls-Hanhart, *Septuaginta,* copyright @ 2006 by Deutsche Bibelgesellschaft.

To my family for their sacrifice and support:
mercy, peace, and love in abundance.

CONTENTS

List of Tables and Figures | viii
Acknowledgments | ix
Abbreviations | xi
Introduction | xiii

Chapter 1: History of Research | 1

Chapter 2: Methodological Approach | 30

Chapter 3: Seeing Is Not Always Believing | 71

Chapter 4: Eyes of Faith | 125

Conclusions | 183

APPENDIX 1: ΕΡΗΜΟΣ IN THE NEW TESTAMENT | 187
APPENDIX 2: BAPTISM AND "WATER AND SPIRIT" IN JOHN 3:5 | 190
APPENDIX 3: NICODEMUS'S CONFUSION AT BEING BORN FROM ABOVE | 192

Bibliography | 195

TABLES AND FIGURES

Tables

1. Johannine echoes of Numbers | 59
2. Johannine allusions to Numbers | 60
3. Johannine allusions to Deuteronomy | 61
4. Linguistic comparison between Num 21:8–9 and John 3:14–15 | 152
5. Seeing is believing | 163

Figures

1. Eschatological Spirit rooted in wilderness | 120
2. Triad of eschatological Spirit | 121
3. Interrelation of Suffering Servant, Son of Man, and Jesus Messiah | 149

ACKNOWLEDGMENTS

I FIRMLY BELIEVE IN the importance of community for faith formation. No one reads Scripture in isolation. No piece of literature—whether an academic tome or a daily devotional guide—is the product of an individual interpreter. It is in this spirit that I recognize those who have laid stone upon stone for the building up of the community of faith that surrounds me.

Signs in the Wilderness is a revision of my PhD dissertation at Westminster Theological Seminary originally entitled, "The Wilderness Motif in John 3:1–21 and Its Impact on Johannine Signs and Faith: An Intertextual Case Study" (2012), and I would be remiss if I did not extend a heartfelt thanks to Westminster's biblical studies faculty for surrounding me with a spirit of fellowship while pursuing my doctorate. Thanks especially to my dissertation advisor, Brandon Crowe, and to my second reader, Vern Poythress, for offering words of encouragement and exhortation during the writing process. I am indebted to Steve Taylor for graciously allowing me to serve as a Greek Teaching Fellow while pursuing doctoral studies at Westminster. I owe a word of thanks to Doug Green for introducing me to the "echo chamber" of Scripture. Pete Enns and Dan McCartney opened up to me the vast world of Second Temple hermeneutics, which plays a substantial role in this study. I appreciate Mike Kelly's willingness to provide a listening ear, which proved priceless as I navigated various interpretive issues, not to mention the intricacies of classic rock music. I am beholden to the blessed memory of J. Alan Groves (1952–2007), who advocated bold readings, which reflect the living and active character of Scripture. I value the input of Gary Manning at Biola University and appreciate his willingness to serve as the external reader for my dissertation, and for his advice on readying this manuscript for publication. I am grateful for the support of Michael Turner, Stanley Patterson, and Rodney Cloud at Amridge University. To the Bible faculty at Lipscomb University, who cultivated my passion for biblical studies during my years there (1997–2002): I continually remember your work produced by faith and your labor prompted by love. While my interest in intertextuality did not occur until doctoral studies at Westminster, my love for the Gospel of John began at Lipscomb under the direction of Michael Moss and John Mark Hicks, the former textually, the latter theologically.

Not only have professors watered the word in my heart, but also pastors, especially Joel Dalrymple, whose partnership in the gospel is central to my edification and enlightenment. Adam Hill and Ray Patton, who are as close as brothers to me, have generously given from their storehouses of wisdom. Their friendship has remained constant from our days together at Lipscomb, even unto today, as we have pursued our respective ministries and advanced degrees. I greatly appreciate the editorial efforts of Lauren Daniel and Kim Graefe. My thanks to Matthew Wimer at Wipf & Stock for a smooth publication process.

Most importantly, I give sincere thanks to and for my family for their love and loyalty, patience and perseverance, and for being a continual source of motivation and faithfulness.

Daniel H. Fletcher
May 29, 2014

ABBREVIATIONS

ABD	*Anchor Bible Dictionary*
ANE	Ancient Near East
Ant.	Josephus, *Jewish Antiquities*
ʿArak	ʿArakin
b.	Babylonian (Talmud)
Barn.	*Epistle of Barnabas*
Ber.	*Berakot*
B. Meṣiʿa	*Baba Meṣiʿa*
Dialogue	Justin Martyr, *Dialogue with Trypho the Jew*
DJG	*Dictionary of Jesus and the Gospels*
DNTB	*Dictionary of New Testament Background*
DSS	Dead Sea Scrolls
ESV	English Standard Version
GNT	Greek New Testament
HB	Hebrew Bible
IDT	Interpreter's Dictionary of the Bible
JPS	Jewish Publication Society
J.W.	Josephus, *Jewish Wars*
KJV	King James Version
LXX	Septuagint
m.	Mishnah
Moses	Philo, *On the Life of Moses*

MS(S)	Manuscript(s)	
MT	Masoretic Text	
NAS	New American Standard	
NEB	New English Bible	
NIDB	*New Interpreter's Dictionary of the Bible*	
NIV	New International Version	
NLT	New Living Translation	
NRSV	New Revised Standard Version	
NT	New Testament	
Num. Rab.	Numbers Rabbah	
OG	Old Greek	
OT	Old Testament	
QE	Philo, *Questions and Answers on Exodus*	
Roš. Haš.	Roš Haššanah	
Šabb.	Šabbat	
Sanh.	Sanhedrin	
Song. Rab.	Song of Solomon Rabbah	
Soṭa	Soṭa	
Str-B	Strack and Billerbeck	
Sukkah	Sukkah	
Ta'an.	Ta'anit	
TDNT	*Theological Dictionary of the New Testament*	
Tg. Isa.	Targum Isaiah	
Tg. Ps.-J.	Targum Pseudo-Jonathan	

INTRODUCTION

THIS STUDY EXAMINES JOHN 2:23—3:21 against the background of God's testing of Israel in the wilderness. John 2:23—3:21 addresses the complex relationship between signs and faith by interacting with the wilderness narrative showing that eyes of faith are necessary to "see" signs. Consider John's logic: The Jerusalemites believe in Jesus because of his σημεῖα (2:23–25); Nicodemus witnesses Jesus' σημεῖα (3:2); Jesus refers him to a faith-testing σημεῖον in the OT wilderness narrative (John 3:14 cf. LXX Num 21:8–9), explains that faith is necessary to see σημεῖα (3:15–16), and that either life or judgment follows depending on one's response (3:18–21). This study applies a "wilderness reading" which proposes intertextual allusions and echoes of LXX Numbers in John 2:23—3:21. Reading John 2:23—3:21 against the background of Israel's wilderness experience illuminates the relationship of signs and faith in John's Gospel as one of divine testing.

According to Kenneth Pomykala, Israel's wilderness experience (Exodus–Deut 34) was a "treasure trove" of stories for reflection and interpretation in later Jewish and Christian traditions.[1] Stories about God, his protection of and provision for his people, their wavering faith, and their eventual entrance into the Promised Land served, in part, to build and strengthen the faith of his people. Both the OT and NT are full of references and allusions to this formative period of the people of God. My focus is on the wilderness as a period of divine testing of faith in John's Gospel. God tested Israel in the wilderness by performing miraculous signs and called them to have faith in his redemptive care. John reflects this testing motif in Jesus' signs as he performs similar redemptive acts that call for belief in his messianic mission.

---

1. Pomykala, ed., *Israel in the Wilderness*, IX.

At first glance, John's Gospel does not seem to have a major wilderness motif. In his book, *Christ in the Wilderness,* Ulrich Mauser states, "In the Gospel of John the wilderness motif plays only a very insignificant role."[2] Similarly, Craig Keener notes that a wilderness motif plays only a "minor" role in John's Gospel.[3] In my view, neither "insignificant" nor "minor" accurately represents John's wilderness motif. I hope to demonstrate that the wilderness motif plays a more significant role in John, especially regarding the relationship of signs and faith. Granted, divine testing is not the only wilderness motif in John but it is significant for Johannine signs and faith. God tested his people in the wilderness with miraculous signs and provisions in order to know which hearts were faithful (Deut 4:34; 8:2, 16; cf. Heb 3:8).[4] This testing theme is an insightful angle from which to view the complex relationship between signs and faith in John.

My belief is that John makes use of the wilderness motif not only in John 3:14, but throughout the pericope (2:23—3:21), and it serves as a window into the larger relationship of seeing signs and believing in John's Gospel. Seeing signs and believing, or not believing, in Christ is analogous to Israel's wilderness experience: the people were continually confronted with God's miraculous signs (Num 14:11, 22) yet many failed to believe in him. Signs ultimately revealed the hard hearts of those who lacked the faith to properly see them. This is also the case in John: many reject Jesus' signs due the hardness of their hearts, while others respond in faith. In the wilderness, the first generation was faithless and died in the desert, while the second generation proved faithful and thus entered the Promised Land. This, too, is the case in John: those who reject Jesus are condemned (John 3:18), while those who believe come into the light (3:21). My overall contribution is to demonstrate that a Johannine wilderness motif illuminates the relationship of signs and faith as one of *divine testing.* Johannine faith, which looks beyond signs themselves to both their source and goal, is analogous to the depth of faith God desired for Israel in the wilderness, and is precisely the point behind John's uplifted serpent reference (3:14–15).

John illustrates this testing theme with his reference to the uplifted serpent (Num 21:8–9) in John 3:14–15. This sign was both a lifesaver and a test of faith for the wilderness community and functions the same way for John. John's uplifted serpent reference becomes not simply a crucifixion/

---

2. Mauser, *Christ in the Wilderness,* 11. Leal, *Wilderness in the Bible,* 51, holds this same view.

3. Keener, *John,* 1:439. However, Keener does acknowledge the importance of the wilderness for John in spite of its seemingly minor role (ibid., 138).

4. This testing went both ways: Deut 8:3 records how God tested the Israelites while Ps 95:7–11 records their testing of God.

exaltation reference but also forms the crucial analogy with the wilderness generation by demonstrating how seeing signs must be accompanied by faith in God. *For John, the uplifted serpent reference points beyond a faith that simply sees signs to one that truly trusts in God, who is their source.* The uplifted serpent is a Johannine reference to Christ's glorification but it is also a perfect, although complex, example of Johannine faith that sees and trusts God's redemptive activity in the glorification of Christ.

I am proposing a fresh reading of John 2:23—3:21 against the background of the wilderness, due, in part, to the reference to the copper serpent. However, by expanding the OT context to include the wider wilderness narratives of Numbers, several additional intertextual connection points exist between John 2:23—3:21 and wilderness narratives of Numbers.[5] The uplifted serpent reference is John's invitation to read Jesus' dialogue with Nicodemus redemptive-historically and defines ideally what "seeing" signs means in John: the recognition and belief that God is the ultimate source and goal of Jesus' signs.

---

5. Keener, *John*, 1:563–64, essentially makes the same point regarding the wider OT context as he comments on John's use of the uplifted serpent story.

Chapter 1

HISTORY OF RESEARCH

ALTHOUGH THE GOSPEL OF John[1] clearly contains wilderness imagery and terminology, only a few studies discuss it as a pervasive motif. More often studies tend to focus on John's exodus typology, which include the events of the wilderness wandering, but lean toward listing typological occurrences rather than delving into the complexity of the imagery itself. Studies on John's wilderness imagery often focus on a specific aspect such as the manna, tabernacle, uplifted serpent, living water, etc., rather than on the wilderness experience as a whole. Put differently, rather than tracing the wilderness motif as a large complex of ideas permeating the

---

1. Specific authorship of John's Gospel does not significantly impact the thesis of this dissertation. I refer to the author as "John" for convenience; however, I believe the apostle to be a strong candidate, and have not found sufficient evidence to completely overturn the position articulated by Westcott in his 1882 commentary. While I believe this author is an eyewitness of the events narrated, as well as the one who is responsible for the Fourth Gospel's traditions, this does not exclude the role of later editors who finalized the Gospel. It is sufficient for this study to note the author's pervasive knowledge and use of the OT. Further, the dating of the Gospel's final form, provenance, and the exact recipients are not critical to the thesis of this study. However, due to prevalent OT symbolism in the Fourth Gospel, the recipients likely had a close familiarity with the Scriptures of Israel. I concur with Menken, *Old Testament Quotations*, 208, who states regarding the Gospel's author and recipients: "The treatment of OT quotations in the Fourth Gospel suggests that this gospel has been written by a Jewish Christian within and for a group that was able to understand his use of Scripture." For apostolic authorship, see Blomberg, *Historical Reliability*, 22–41; Carson, *John*, 68–81; Keener, *John*, 1:81–115; Köstenberger, *Theology*, 72–79; Michaels, *John*, 5–24; Tenney, *John*, 297–303; Westcott, *John*, V–XXV. Against apostolic authorship, see Bauckham, *Eyewitnesses*, 358–411; Culpepper, *Son of Zebedee*, 56–88; O'Day and Hylen, *John*, 3–4.

Gospel, scholars tend to break it into smaller, more manageable pieces. This is also the case in this study, where John's wilderness motif illustrates how miraculous signs[2] function as tests of faith. Where recent research merges the exodus and wilderness into one redemptive-historical event, interpreting them through the lens of exodus typology, this study aims to isolate the wilderness primarily by highlighting intertextual connections to the book of Numbers in John 2:23—3:21, and then to view signs through the interpretive lens of Deut 8 as tests of faith. I will examine John's wilderness typology in more detail in chapter 2 within the context of his overall approach to the Scriptures of Israel.[3] The following history of recent research flows not chronologically, but topically regarding relevance to this study. This chapter will be divided into two sections: the first section interacts with studies of John's exodus/wilderness typology; the second section engages studies on Johannine signs.

JOHANNINE EXODUS/WILDERNESS TYPOLOGY

Ulrich Mauser: Christ in the Wilderness

While Ulrich Mauser's *Christ in the Wilderness* explores the role of wilderness traditions in Mark's Gospel, it addresses them in John's as well, albeit briefly. Mark's Gospel is not replete with wilderness imagery per se; however, Mauser proposes that Mark's references to "wilderness" (ἔρημος) are theologically motivated and recall ancient Israel's wilderness experience.[4] Jesus frequently moved about in desert areas throughout his life and ministry. Therefore, Markan references to "wilderness" could theoretically pass for simple natural, geographical indicators throughout his narrative. However, that still could be the case were it not for the redemptive action of

---

2. Signs need not be miraculous events. Symbolic events, and even words, can be signs in John; this study affirms this fact. Nevertheless, I am more interested in Jesus' miraculous signs as tests of faithfulness as compared with those of Moses in the exodus/wilderness tradition. This study affirms that Johannine miracles *always* function as signs. Simply stated, Jesus' miracles are signs, yet signs are not always miracles. I will address this in more detail later in this chapter, as well as in chapter 2, where I will define signs more specifically for this study.

3. By "Scripture" I mean the sacred writings of Jews and Christians including the Hebrew, Catholic, Orthodox, and Protestant canons as recognized today. When referring to the use of Scripture by the author of John's Gospel, I will use "Israel's Scriptures," or "OT" by which I mean what he and his readers likely regarded as Holy Writ in its Hebrew, Aramaic, and Greek versions.

4. Mauser, *Christ in the Wilderness*, 13–14.

God which took place in the wilderness in the course of Israel's history.[5] Simply stated, the wilderness is frequently a place of divine action in the NT (e.g., 1 Cor 10; Heb 3–4; Rev 12), and Mark's Gospel is consistent with this redemptive-historical usage. "Wilderness" is used throughout the NT in a geographic sense to be sure, but functions more as an absolute noun recalling God's mighty acts of the exodus and requires no further explanation along these lines.[6] Mauser highlights this dual use of ἔρημος but emphasizes its prevalent theological use throughout Mark's Gospel.

Mauser aptly notes that by the eighth century BCE the exodus and wilderness had been fused into one redemptive event.[7] Therefore, the NT makes no systematic distinction between the two OT events. As a result, Johannine scholars also focus on John's exodus typology and include therein the wilderness sojourn.[8] Put differently, scholars often fuse both the exodus proper and the wilderness wanderings into one redemptive-historical event in Johannine studies.

As I referenced in the Introduction, Mauser downplays the wilderness motif in John to a "very insignificant role."[9] This study takes issue with this observation and hopes to illustrate a more pervasive use of the wilderness traditions than Mauser grants. For Mauser, not even the reference to ἐν τῇ ἐρήμῳ ("in the wilderness") in John 3:14 is to be stressed and is more or less accidental.[10] This is puzzling, given his concern in Mark to illustrate the wilderness as *the* location of God's redemptive acts during Israel's exodus. In John, however, Mauser dismisses the geographical location of the mighty deed of God (i.e., the uplifted copper serpent of Num 21:8–9) while focusing instead only on the deed itself.[11] While the uplifting of the serpent is indeed a primary point of comparison in John 3:14, this study will demonstrate that the phrase "in the wilderness" is not insignificant. Mauser sees John's only other reference to a wilderness incident in chapter 6 where Jesus duplicates the manna miracle of Israel's exodus experience, albeit in a superior quality.[12] In spite of Mauser's minimization of the wilderness in John's Gospel,

---

5. Ibid., 14.

6. Ibid.

7. Ibid., 17, 20. I will discuss this in chapter 2 where I will define "wilderness" more precisely.

8. I will discuss John's typological use of the OT in chapter 2.

9. Ibid., 75. See also, Leal, *Wilderness in the Bible*, 51.

10. Mauser, *Christ in the Wilderness*, 76.

11. Ibid.

12. Ibid.

his study is nonetheless a welcomed invitation to view the wilderness as a redemptive-historical motif in the NT.

Robert H. Smith: "Exodus Typology in the Fourth Gospel"

Robert H. Smith's "Exodus Typology in the Fourth Gospel" attempts to lay out a methodology for identifying exodus typology in John. He questions previous attempts at Johannine typology, some of which I will examine in this study, finding them to be methodologically weak. For Smith, typology must be structural rather than in isolated details. Major OT events have typological significance for John and these events contribute to the structure of his Gospel. For example, Smith compares seven plagues from Exodus with seven signs in John's Gospel that he believes have typological significance. Some of the typological proposals are quite far-fetched. One example will suffice. Smith believes the eighth plague in Exodus, the attack by locusts on the foliage and fruit of Egypt, has an "obvious parallel" in the Johannine account of Jesus' feeding of the multitude with bread (John 6:1–15).[13] Not only are some of Smith's typological connections fanciful, his structural proposal does not reflect the parallelism he deems so important.[14] Nonetheless, his thesis that typology be structural and focused on whole events rather than scattered details provides a healthy evaluation of typological theories.

Jacob Enz: "The Book of Exodus as a Literary Type for the Gospel of John"

If Smith isolates a structural quality behind Johannine typology, emphasizing larger events in the OT as types (e.g., exodus plagues paralleling Johannine signs), Jacob Enz sees the structural typology at work literarily in his article "The Book of Exodus as a Literary Type for the Gospel of John."[15] Specifically, the book of Exodus, rather than the exodus event itself, stands

---

13. Smith, "Exodus Typology," 336. To be fair, Smith argues for an inversion of messianic signs; that is, Jesus' signs not only outdo those of Moses, but they often have the opposite effect (i.e., inversion). For example, where the locusts leave the people without sustenance, Jesus leaves them full. However, it is best to view Jesus' feeding against the background of the manna narrative in the wilderness per John's own descriptive elements, rather than the eighth plague. There is no clear indication in the text that John intended the inverted typological connection Smith proposes. For a similar critique of Smith's typological proposal, see Brunson, *Psalm 118*, 160–61.

14. For Smith's inconsistent structural proposal, see "Exodus Typology," 338.

15. For a similar work, see Piper, "Unchanging Promises," 3–22.

as a structural type for the Gospel of John. Enz sees typological occurrences in isolated instances, as well as in the general sequence of events.[16] For Enz, the "I am" (ἐγώ εἰμι) of Exod 3:14 and its repeated occurrences in John are but one instance of Exodus typology.[17] Not all of Enz's typological occurrences prove persuasive however. For example, to suggest that the construction of the tabernacle (Exod 25–31; 35–40) is reflected in John 19:30 (cf. 2:18–21) at the death of Jesus strains the evidence.[18] Granted, John's Gospel does associate Jesus with the tabernacle (1:14), but the Johannine passages Enz refers to as evidence speak unambiguously about the *temple* (2:18–21; 19:30). As for structural parallels, a similar concentration of the term "sign" occurs in the early portions of both documents.[19] This is a brilliant observation that illustrates how both Exodus and John culminate in unbelief or "hardening of heart" (Exod 14:8; John 12:37–40), as well as belief (Exod 14:31; John 20:30–31).[20] Again, not all structural parallels are so obvious. For example, Enz illustrates the early reference to the serpent in both books (Exod 4:4ff; John 3:14) as a structural parallel.[21] However, my study, in concert with the vast majority of Johannine commentators, maintains that John's uplifted serpent analogy in 3:14 refers to Num 21:8–9, not Exod 4:3–4. This is an instance where Enz pushes too hard for structural parallels in Exodus to fit his thesis. Other examples could be multiplied, but these serve to show that a structural parallel between Exodus and John results only when the evidence is stretched and the details ignored. While structural parallels are not necessarily indicators of typological occurrences, Enz finds numerous parallels between the book of Exodus and the Gospel of John that deserve detailed inspection. Nevertheless, his insistence on typological occurrences between whole books of the Bible, rather than scattered pericopes, helps bring some methodological control to a limitless pursuit of finding OT imagery and parallels in John's Gospel.[22]

---

16. Enz, "Literary Type," 209.
17. Ibid.
18. Ibid., 210. Smith, "Exodus Typology," 331n4, makes this same observation.
19. Enz, "Literary Type," 210.
20. Ibid.
21. Ibid., 210n7.
22. Günter Reim's *Jochanan*, 266–68, stands in opposition to typological studies like those of Smith and Enz by finding very little typology in the Fourth Gospel. I will interact with Reim's influential work in more detail below.

Anthony Hanson: The Prophetic Gospel

Anthony Hanson's *The Prophetic Gospel* illustrates the pervasive and prophetic use of the OT in John's Gospel. Hanson's thesis is that John's Gospel is full of OT prophecy fulfilled in the life of Jesus.[23] His presupposition hinges on an understanding of the words "prophet" and "prophetic"; namely, that during the first two centuries of the Christian era, these words could refer to a wide range of Scripture and scriptural activity.[24] Both terms are concerned with much more than foretelling the future. Specifically, forthtelling, which involves both interpreting and declaring the truths of Scripture, was also encompassed by the terms "prophet" and "prophetic." John's Gospel is primarily an example of forthtelling prophecy. Further, a prophet was one who claimed to interpret the Scriptures in terms of contemporary events.[25] Therefore, the author of the Gospel, as well as other characters in the narrative, should be regarded as a prophet.

Hanson begins by illustrating how the revelation of the Logos is an example of the Fourth Gospel's prophetic perspective. He sees the description of the Logos in John 1:18 (πλήρης χάριτος καὶ ἀληθείας, "full of grace and truth") as a prophetic use of Exod 34:6b where Yahweh describes himself to Moses as ורב־חסד ואמת ("abounding in steadfast love and truth").[26] Put differently, the Logos was Yahweh revealed on Sinai to Moses.[27] Hanson attributes John 1:15–18 to John the Baptist and sees his function in the Gospel, given that he interprets contemporary events (e.g., the revelation of the Logos) in the light of Scripture, as a representative of inspired prophecy who is able to witness to the continuity of revelation.[28] John the Baptist interprets Exod 34:6b prophetically in his own time by equating the Logos with the OT theophany. The Fourth Gospel is prophetic in that it is full of these kinds of prophetic interpretations and applications.

While Hanson's concern is with the OT as a whole as it prophetically points to Christ (John 5:39, 46), and as the Johannine author prophetically interprets it, exodus typology comprises much of the evidence. Images such as the uplifted serpent, the well in the wilderness, manna, the Jews who grumble against Jesus, water from the rock, and Jesus as the paschal lamb

---

23. Hanson, *Prophetic Gospel*, 19.
24. Ibid.
25. Ibid.
26. Ibid., 21–25.
27. Ibid., 30.
28. Ibid., 27, 32. See also, ibid., 24, 28, 34, 36, and 40, for John the Baptist as an inspired prophet in line with Judaism's prophets in the OT.

form the backdrop of John's Christology.²⁹ For Hanson, Jesus does not simply fulfill these (among others) OT images, but rather supersedes them in his own person.³⁰ While Hanson's analysis of John's use of the OT goes well beyond exodus typology, also taking into account elements from Genesis, Wisdom of Solomon, Psalms, and the Prophets, it nonetheless includes it. His study is an indispensable contribution to the role of the OT in John's Gospel.

Wayne Meeks: The Prophet-King

John's exodus typology not only includes events but also persons, especially Moses. These are two sides of the same coin. Exodus/wilderness typology and Moses typology naturally overlap in that most of Moses' life in the OT takes place within the wilderness experience of Israel. It is difficult to speak of the wilderness sojourn of Israel without also speaking of Moses as the divinely appointed guide. Though not centered on exodus typology per se, Wayne Meeks's *The Prophet-King*³¹ nonetheless centers on the prominent figure of Moses in John's Gospel. His thesis is that the prophetic and royal elements in the Johannine Christology are not to be understood separately, but exactly in their combination and mutual interpretation.³² For Meeks, various extrabiblical interpretations of Moses' role in Israel serve as the paradigm for the Johannine usage of prophet and king. Meeks states, "Certain traditions about Moses provided for the Fourth Gospel not only the figure of the eschatological prophet, but the figure who combines in one person both royal and prophetic honor and functions."³³ Put differently, Moses serves as a type of prophet-king for John's purpose of presenting Jesus as the Prophet-King. Meeks illustrates how the terms ὁ προφήτης and βασιλεύς occur together only in John 6:14–15:³⁴

οἱ οὖν ἄνθρωποι
 ἰδόντες ὃ ἐποίησεν σημεῖον

---

29. Ibid., 238–39, 241. Scholars debate the last of these, that Jesus is the paschal lamb. See, Brunson, *Psalm 118*, 156n58.

30. Ibid., 148–51.

31. Meeks's discussion of the "signs" of Moses and Jesus, which will be discussed later this chapter, is more relevant to the current study than Moses typology.

32. Meeks, *Prophet-King*, 25.

33. Ibid., 29. Meeks mentions Philo's description of Moses as simultaneously being the ideal king, the most perfect of prophets, and the prototypical high priest.

34. Ibid., 89. According to Meeks, this is unparalleled in the Gospel tradition (ibid., 88).

> ἔλεγον ὅτι οὗτός ἐστιν ἀληθῶς ὁ προφήτης
> ὁ ἐρχόμενος εἰς τὸν κόσμον
> Ἰησοῦς οὖν
> γνοὺς ὅτι μέλλουσιν ἔρχεσθαι καὶ ἁρπάζειν αὐτὸν
> ἵνα ποιήσωσιν βασιλέα,

After Jesus has performed the "sign" (σημεῖον),[35] the crowd takes for granted the juxtaposition of "the Prophet" (ὁ προφήτης) and "King" (βασιλέα) as if the identification needs no further clarification.[36] Meeks traces this mutually interpretive relationship within John's Gospel first before extending it to other background sources for supporting evidence. Meeks's scope of study includes sources like Philo and Josephus, Rabbinic Haggada, Samaritan sources, and Mandaean sources. This takes him well beyond specific OT materials but nonetheless includes them at least indirectly as these sources interpret OT images. While his concern is not to explore exodus typology in the Fourth Gospel, Moses traditions overlap and therefore play a dominant role in contributing to the study of John's use of the OT.

T. F. Glasson: Moses in the Fourth Gospel

That John's exodus typology not only includes events but also persons, such as Moses, is demonstrated pointedly in T. F. Glasson's *Moses in the Fourth Gospel*.[37] Glasson highlights a prominent Mosaic motif that runs throughout John's Gospel. His thesis is that the messianic hope in Second Temple Judaism was in part expressed in terms of the Messiah as a second Moses, and this is one of the keys to understanding the Fourth Gospel.[38] John illustrates this mainly through a series of comparisons and contrasts between Moses and Christ.[39] Again, John's narrative of the feeding of the 5,000 illustrates this well. In John 6:14, after Jesus has duplicated a Moses-like miracle, the crowd identifies him as "the Prophet," presumably of whom Moses prophesied in Deut 18:15: οἱ οὖν ἄνθρωποι ἰδόντες ὃ ἐποίησεν σημεῖον ἔλεγον

---

35. Meeks, *Prophet-King*, 88, notes the singular σημεῖον has strong support in the MS tradition (א, D, W) over the plural σημεῖα.

36. Ibid., 88–89.

37. While Glasson himself does not use the terminology of "typology," his work has been characterized as such by Norquist (Review of *Moses*, 72). See also, Martyn, *History and Theology*, 100–30.

38. Glasson, *Moses*, 10, 19. However, Glasson correctly notes the fluidity of messianic expectations in antiquity and warns against expecting a consistent scheme running throughout the various expressions of Judaism (ibid., 9).

39. Ibid., 20–26.

ὅτι οὗτός ἐστιν ἀληθῶς ὁ προφήτης ὁ ἐρχόμενος εἰς τὸν κόσμον ("Therefore, the people, after seeing which sign he did, said that, 'This is truly the Prophet who comes into the world'"). Although the various sects of first-century Judaism do not quote Deut 18:15 in messianic contexts, it would be a mistake to infer from this that they had no doctrine of a second Moses.[40] This kind of parallelism between Moses and the Messiah runs all the way through Glasson's book. He also notes how Second Temple Judaism saw the likes of the Qumran community, Theudas (*Ant.* 20.97), the anonymous Egyptian of Acts 21:38, and others (*J. W.* 2.259) who led movements "in the desert" in efforts to fulfill Isa 40:3: "In the wilderness prepare the way of the LORD" (ESV).[41] John's Gospel captures in detail how the messianic time was in part modeled on the exodus, not only by adopting similar imagery but also by presenting Moses as a deliverer who foreshadowed the Messiah.[42]

It is important to note Glasson's emphasis on the wilderness.[43] Whereas the previous works surveyed use the language of the "exodus" to express John's redemptive motifs, Glasson prefers to speak more often of the "wilderness." To be sure, as in the previous works, Glasson places the wilderness within the context of a second exodus eschatological expectation.[44] Nonetheless, where the imagery of exodus and wilderness are shared in the previous works, Glasson emphasizes specific wilderness imagery to a higher degree. Put differently, he isolates wilderness imagery. Even so, this wilderness motif is subsumed under the personality of Moses as one aspect of the Gospel's wider wilderness imagery.[45] Therefore, while Glasson demonstrates the importance of the wilderness as a type of the Christian life,[46] his emphasis is more on Moses than on the wilderness per se. The title,

---

40. Ibid., 20. On John's use of the Prophet motif, see Martyn, *History and Theology*, 103–23; Meeks, *Prophet-King*, 87–99; Pryor, *Covenant People*, 132–33. Against the view that John views Jesus as the eschatological Prophet of Deut 18:15, see Teeple, *Mosaic Eschatological Prophet*, 94–97; Schnackenburg, *John*, 2:18–20.

41. Glasson, *Moses*, 18. See also, Brunson, *Psalm 118*, 168–69.

42. Glasson, *Moses*, 18.

43. Ibid., 15–19.

44. Brunson, *Psalm 118*, 153–79, esp. 154n51, works out a detailed portrait of John's exodus eschatology. However, his emphasis lies more on the Isaianic New Exodus eschatological expectation than on Mosaic traditions. Brunson prefers the phrase "new exodus" to "second exodus" because it also encompasses the exile and restoration, and is a more comprehensive portrait of Israel's eschatological expectation than merely the exodus. In short, his emphasis, while including Glasson's second exodus eschatology, goes well beyond it by emphasizing the Isaianic exile and restoration. Brunson focuses more on the Prophets than on the Pentateuch.

45. Glasson, *Moses*, 22.

46. Ibid., 10.

Moses in the Fourth Gospel, is therefore an accurate reflection of the book's contents. Glasson's study is foundational for the present study as both seek to delve deeper than previous works into John's wilderness imagery. A focus on the wilderness more so than on Moses is a distinguishing feature of the present study. Further, where Glasson is concerned with the wilderness in John's Gospel as a whole, this study is limited to its role in John 2:23—3:21.

It is remarkable that Glasson, who is committed to demonstrating the comparison between Moses and Christ, omits any sustained reference to "signs" from his discussion. Both Moses and Christ performed miraculous signs in the midst of the people. Both were met with a mixture of unbelief (Num 14:11; John 12:37) and belief (Exod 4:31; John 2:23 and par.). Certainly, performing miraculous signs is one of the most compared and contrasted aspects of the ministries of Moses and Christ. The Johannine terminology of "signs and wonders" (σημεῖα καὶ τέρατα) has as its background the exodus and wilderness events of the LXX.[47] Granted, a detailed comparison of each miraculous sign would take Glasson well beyond the scope of his book; nonetheless, a discussion of miraculous signs is indispensable for a comparison between Moses and the Messiah, especially if the Messiah is a second Moses. This study aims to make up for Glasson's omission by presenting the function of miraculous signs as tests of faith in both the wilderness and in John's Gospel. Where Glasson focuses on Moses in John's Gospel, this study focuses on miraculous signs as tests of faithfulness in the wilderness and in John's Gospel.

---

47. Brown, *John*, 1:529. While LXX can be used in a narrow sense denoting the first Greek translation of the Pentateuch (ca. third century BCE), I use it in a broader sense referring to any and all ancient Greek translations of Jewish Scripture. Further, because the text forms of John's OT sources are not known with precision, the term LXX refers to our best possibility of access to the Greek texts available to John and his audience in the first century. Because the Septuagint did not exist in the first century CE as a homogenous text (nor does it exist so today), and because John's use of Israel's Scripture is eclectic in its own right (see below), this general usage makes the most sense for the present study. Wagner, *Heralds of the Good News*, 16n60, notes the complicated, eclectic, and ultimately "untraceable" textual history of LXX MSS. For more on the varying referents of the term "Septuagint," see Jobes and Silva, *Invitation to the Septuagint*, 29–33; Tov, "The Septuagint," 161–88; Schuchard, *Scripture Within Scripture*, 154–55, argues that the Old Greek (OG) is the OT of the Johannine Community rather than the LXX. While I appreciate Schuchard's desire to identify the precise text form of OT quotations in John's Gospel, his thesis has little impact on the present intertextual study of allusions and echoes. Schuchard does not mention the role of OT allusions (e.g., 3:14) and/or OT imagery in John; instead, he focuses solely on formal citations, none of which occurs in John 3:1–21.

T. David Gordon: "John 1–12: Israel's Final Wilderness"

T. David Gordon's "John 1–12: Israel's Final Wilderness" presents the wilderness as a more pervasive Johannine motif than the previous studies mentioned. This work is both illuminating as it collates Johannine wilderness imagery into one thematic study, and insightful as it illustrates the many wilderness motifs that run through John's Gospel.

Gordon's thesis is that the fundamental narrative that drives John's portrayal of Jesus in the first 12 chapters, or, the Book of Signs, is "He came to his own home, and his own people received him not" (1:11).[48] Further, the primary source of allusion and illustration for this narrative is provided by the wilderness wanderings of Israel under Moses.[49] Gordon then traces wilderness themes throughout the Book of Signs that include Moses, legal witness, signs, discourses, feasts, Jewish reaction ("grumbling"), and judgment. His emphasis is on the public ministry of Jesus in John's Gospel, but it is unclear as to why wilderness motifs should be limited to this material. While he curiously overlooks some wilderness motifs like the "tabernacling" of the Logos (1:14) and the "voice in the wilderness" (1:23), Gordon nonetheless perceives the prevalent connections of the Johannine narrative to the wilderness narratives in the OT. Gordon's study, at its root, demonstrates that John's Gospel presents the experience of the rejection of Christ by the Jews as analogous to that of Moses in the wilderness by the first, hard-hearted generation. By way of example, Gordon presents the grumbling of the people against Moses as having a strong parallel in John's Gospel where the people grumble against Christ.[50] Exodus 16:2 states: διεγόγγυζεν πᾶσα συναγωγὴ υἱῶν Ἰσραηλ ἐπὶ Μωυσῆν καὶ Ααρων ("All the assembly of the children of Israel grumbled against Moses and Aaron"). Not only were the Israelites grumbling against Moses, but also against God: καὶ ἦν ὁ λαὸς γογγύζων πονηρὰ ἔναντι κυρίου ("And the people grumbled sinfully against the Lord," Num 11:1). Jesus receives the same response from many people during his ministry. The response of the Jews to his "Bread of Life" discourse, which immediately follows the feeding of the 5,000, itself a wilderness-like miracle, is notable: ἐγόγγυζον οὖν οἱ Ἰουδαῖοι περὶ αὐτοῦ ὅτι εἶπεν· ἐγώ εἰμι ὁ ἄρτος ὁ καταβὰς ἐκ τοῦ οὐρανοῦ ("Therefore, the Jews were grumbling concerning him because he said, 'I am the bread that descended from heaven,'" John 6:41; cf. 6:43; 7:12, 32). Gordon summarizes John's use of the OT motif: "This employment of γογγύζω by John reflects

---

48. Gordon, "Final Wilderness," 2. Gordon's translation.
49. Ibid.
50. Ibid., 52.

a conscious attempt to demonstrate that the Jews of Jesus' generation were committing the same offense against God that the wilderness generation had committed. They rejected God's spokesman."[51]

Gordon's thesis is a sustained attempt to demonstrate the importance of Israel's wilderness sojourn under Moses for understanding John's Gospel. His study stands apart from previous ones by focusing specifically on the wilderness wanderings rather than on Moses or the exodus proper. The present study follows Gordon's lead in this respect, and his thesis lays a solid foundation on which this study builds. However, there are certain aspects that clearly differentiate the two studies. The first involves the scope of the two projects. Where Gordon's thesis looks at the wilderness as a pervasive structural motif running through the Book of Signs (John 1–12), this study is narrower and centers mainly on John 2:23—3:21. I hope to isolate wilderness references and probe them further within the context of a smaller pericope. Similarly, where Gordon's study is structural, mine is intertextual. He illustrates wilderness imagery and themes with little detailed interaction with the OT text itself. Conversely, this intertextual study probes the depths of John's wilderness allusions through a detailed interaction with the OT text.

Several other differences can be noted as well. Gordon's thesis examines the rejection motif as John presents the people's reaction to Jesus as analogous to the Israelites' reaction to Moses in the wilderness. The ministries of both Moses and Jesus were met with rejection and grumbling. While Gordon is not alone in pointing this out his study nonetheless gives it more sustained treatment than others do.[52] The present study is focused on the role of signs as tests of faithfulness rather than on the rejection of Jesus. Put simply, the two studies have very different emphases in spite of sharing a broad contour.[53]

The two studies also have differing amounts of attention to second exodus eschatology in John's Gospel. In spite of an eschatologically loaded title such as "Israel's Final Wilderness," second exodus eschatology plays little role in Gordon's discussion. Gordon's primary eschatological discussions revolve around judgment as both a present and future reality,[54] and millennial views.[55] As the first generation of Israelites were judged by God

---

51. Ibid.

52. Barrett, *John*, 295; Beasley-Murray, *John*, 93; Brown, *John*, 1:270; Keener, *John*, 1:684; Köstenberger, *John*, 213; Moloney, *John*, 217; Moloney, *Signs and Shadows*, 51.

53. Gordon, "Final Wilderness," 21–32, discusses the role of signs as a wilderness motif in John's Gospel. I will interact with his helpful presentation later in this chapter.

54. Ibid., 56–60.

55. Ibid., 68–69.

and not allowed to enter the Promised Land, the Jews[56] are judged for their unbelief in John's Gospel. I would argue that the concept of a second exodus undergirds his study; nevertheless, he makes no mention of the redemption of Christ being modeled after the redemption brought through Moses during the exodus and wilderness experience. In contrast, this study takes 1:23 where the Gospel portrays John the Baptist as the "voice in the wilderness" as a significant eschatological entry point for understanding the Fourth Gospel.[57]

Interestingly, there are two obvious references to wilderness narratives that Gordon leaves largely unexplored: the uplifted serpent and the "Bread of Life" discourse. Regarding the former, he deals very little with the uplifted serpent reference in 3:14. His only substantial interaction involves the mediatorial roles occupied by Moses and Christ in the healing of the people.[58] This is astonishing given that the punishment of venomous serpents in Num 21:6 is a result of the complaining of the Israelites against Moses in the wilderness (21:4–5). Granted, John does not make obvious use of this aspect of the narrative, but it nonetheless would serve to strengthen Gordon's thesis in that it is an obvious OT example of complaining in the wilderness. Stated simply, it is not insignificant to connect the rejection motif in both narratives. Rejection is Gordon's major theme that he highlights throughout his thesis, so it is surprising that it plays no role in his uplifted serpent reference. Gordon also lacks sustained interaction with the feeding of 5,000 (John 6:1–15), as well as with the "Bread of Life" discourse (6:22–59). While, as I noted earlier, he does connect the "grumbling" response of the crowds to Jesus with that of the Israelites in the wilderness to Moses (Exod 16:2; Num 11:1), he does not probe the wilderness motif in this context. I wonder if deeper interaction between the OT and NT narratives would have helped underscore the importance of the wilderness for John in

---

56. Gordon correctly illustrates John's ambivalent use of οἱ Ἰουδαῖοι in John's Gospel (ibid., 53–55). He ultimately identifies them as hostile Jewish leaders, including those who followed them in their unbelief and ultimate rejection of Jesus (ibid., 54). Gordon highlights this under his thesis which illustrates Jesus' rejection by "his own," and this is the reason their hostility is recorded (ibid., 55). Gordon clarifies the severe note of judgment in the Fourth Gospel: "John's implication is not that *only* the Jews rejected Christ, but that *even* the Jews rejected Him." For more on John's use of "the Jews," see Brown, *Introduction*, 157–88; Carter, *Storyteller*, 67–73; Culpepper, *Anatomy*, 125–32; Esler and Piper, *Lazarus*, 159–64; Johnson, "Salvation," 83–99; Keener, *John*, 1:214–27; Köstenberger, *Encountering John*, 248–49; Kysar, *Maverick Gospel*, 67–70; Kysar, *Voyages with John*, 147–59; O'Day and Hylen, *John*, 69–70; Pryor, *Covenant People*, 181–84; Smith, *Theology*, 169–73; von Wahlde, "The Johannine 'Jews,'" 33–60.

57. I will discuss John's second exodus theology in chapter 2.

58. Gordon, "Final Wilderness," 8.

Gordon's fine thesis. Other minor examples can be noted but these suffice to demonstrate the differences between the two studies. Nonetheless, Gordon's study is a fine-tuned addition to works dealing with the exodus/wilderness in John's Gospel. The present study seeks to build on his solid foundation.

JOHANNINE SIGNS

Johannine signs typically receive more attention in scholarly writings than Johannine wilderness concerns.[59] Nevertheless, I am proposing in this study that the two are not mutually exclusive. Both have roots in the OT wilderness narratives, and John recalls these narratives throughout his Gospel. While I will define "signs" more precisely in the next chapter, it is sufficient to note here that a "sign" (σημεῖον) is essentially John's way of referring to a miracle performed by Jesus. Put differently, "sign" is the term most closely associated with the Fourth Gospel's portrayal of Jesus' miracles.[60] As I will show below, this miraculous dimension does not exhaust John's use of the term, for he describes Jesus' entire earthly ministry, of which miracles played only a part, as the doing of signs: πολλὰ μὲν οὖν καὶ ἄλλα σημεῖα ἐποίησεν ὁ Ἰησοῦς ("Now, Jesus also did many other signs," John 20:30).[61] That John uses the term σημεῖον seventeen times in his Gospel illustrates the importance he attaches to Jesus' signs.[62] Commenting on the Johannine terminology that Jesus "did many signs," Marianne Meye Thomson suggests, "Clearly the phrase is significant for the Gospel, and because it is used to summarize Jesus' earthly ministry it provides a clue to the Johannine perception of Jesus as one who 'dwelt among us'" (1:14).[63] Further, this dwelling of Jesus among humanity provides a glimpse of his "glory" (δόξα, 1:14), which he reveals through his signs: ταύτην ἐποίησεν ἀρχὴν τῶν σημείων ὁ Ἰησοῦς ἐν Κανὰ τῆς Γαλιλαίος καὶ ἐφανέρωσεν τὴν δόξαν αὐτοῦ ("This, the first of his

---

59. On Johannine signs generally, see Bernard, *John,* 1:CLXXVI–VI; de Jonge, *Stranger from Heaven,* 117–40; Ladd, *Theology,* 308–12; Lohse, "Miracles in the Fourth Gospel," 64–75; Morris, *Theology,* 242–43; Morris, *John,* 607–13; Remus, "Miracle," 4:845–69, esp. 4:865–67; Rengstorf, "shmei/on, su,sshmon," 7:200–69; Schnackenburg, *John,* 1:515–28; Selvaggio, *Seven Signs*; Smith, *Theology,* 106–09, 164–65; Thielman, *Theology,* 162–70; Thompson, "John, Gospel of," 368–83, esp. 379–80.

60. Von Wahlde, *Earliest Version,* 11.

61. Köstenberger, "The Seventh Johannine Sign," 87–103. I agree that other symbolic events (even words) can be signs, but I also affirm that Johannine miracles *always* function as such. Simply stated, Jesus' miracles are signs, yet signs are not always miracles.

62. Morris, *Theology,* 242.

63. Thompson, *Humanity of Jesus,* 53.

signs, Jesus did in Cana of Galilee, and thus revealed his glory," 2:11). John, therefore, draws a close connection between Jesus' signs and his glory.

Because signs are such an important component of Johannine Christology, the literature about them is vast and daunting. For this reason, I will organize the literature on Johannine signs into three broad categories which canvass the most salient parts of the subject: 1) a signs-source, 2) the relationship of signs to faith, and 3) the OT background to signs.

Sēmeia-Quelle

The Gospel of John has been the object of vigorous literary source criticism, similar to that done on the Pentateuch.[64] Implicit in source-critical analysis is the presupposition that the Gospel in its present form is not the production of a single individual but rather the end product of a series of editions.[65] The text of the Gospel is said to exhibit "difficulties," called *aporias*, which disrupt the flow of the narrative and point to literary sources that have been woven into the fabric of John's text.[66] Robert Fortna notes that while these phenomena are not unique to John, they are more numerous and prominent in his Gospel.[67]

The most relevant aporia to this study involves the enumeration of Jesus' first and second signs (2:11; 4:54). John clearly states that the turning of water into wine at the wedding in Cana was the "first" (ἀρχήν) of Jesus' signs (2:11).[68] He then goes on to mention that Jesus did multiple signs (σημεῖα) in Jerusalem (2:23; cf. 3:2). Then he specifically states in 4:54 that the healing of the official's son was the "second" (δεύτερον) of Jesus' signs. How can John say that the healing of the official's son is the second of Jesus' signs when he has previously recorded not only the first sign at Cana, but also additional signs in Jerusalem? Perhaps more is made of this "difficulty" than is necessary, for John does not simply state that the healing of the official's son was the second of Jesus' signs, but that it was the second sign that Jesus performed "after coming from Judea into Galilee" (ἐλθὼν ἐκ τῆς Ἰουδαίας

---

64. Von Wahlde, *Earliest Version*, 12. For a concise discussion of source criticism of John from a sympathetic perspective, see Burge, *Interpreting the Gospel of John*, 57–83. On the difficulty of source-critical success in John, see Beasley-Murray, *John*, XXXVIII–XLIII; Carson, *John*, 41–49; Keener, *John*, 1:37–39; Streeter, *Four Gospels*, 377–82; Witherington, *John's Wisdom*, 5–11.

65. Von Wahlde, *Earliest Version*, 11.

66. Burge, *Interpreting the Gospel of John*, 63–66; Fortna, *Gospel of Signs*, 2–8.

67. Fortna, *Gospel of Signs*, 8n1.

68. However, Köstenberger, *John*, 99, notes that ἀρχή may also be translated as "primary."

εἰς τὴν Γαλιλαίαν, 4:54). Therefore, the point is not simply to enumerate Jesus' signs in general, but rather to highlight the geographical setting of Galilee as opposed to Judea. One possible reason why these two signs are singled out is that John wanted to connect the signs in Galilee, which led to true faith in contradistinction to the signs in Jerusalem which led to fickle faith (2:23–25).[69] Nevertheless, other aporias are not so easily solved, and for this reason some scholars hold that it is unlikely that a single author would leave so many similar gaps in what would otherwise be a smooth and seamless story. The solution for some is to propose literary sources that the Evangelist incorporated into his own narrative.

Rudolf Bultmann theorizes in his commentary on John that one such source behind the Gospel is a σημεῖα-source—a collection of miracle stories.[70] Based on the enumeration of Jesus' first two signs, as well as the signs summaries in 12:37 and 20:30–31, Bultmann proposes that the miracles in the signs source were originally numbered, and that John excised them, edited them, and fitted them into his own Gospel.[71] Fortna has worked out Bultmann's theory in minute detail in *The Gospel of Signs*. Although admitting the signs source to be a hypothetical document, he has nonetheless proposed a Greek reconstruction of it.[72] Fortna no longer holds to the details of his reconstructed document, but nevertheless remains "fairly convinced" of a signs source's existence in antiquity.[73] Of course, the signs source theory is not universally accepted, and scholars question it on a variety of fronts, including 1) the interrelationship of the signs to the interpretive discourses, 2) a lack of literary parallels in pre-Christian antiquity, and 3) the stylistic unity of the Fourth Gospel.[74] This latter criticism seems to be the most threatening to Bultmann's initial thesis. The Gospel, as we have it, is a stylistic unity.[75] Of course, this does not de facto rule out John's use of sources;

---

69. De Jonge, *Stranger from Heaven*, 122–23; Painter, "The Signs of the Messiah," 233–56, esp. 245.

70. Bultmann, *John*, 113. In support of Bultmann's signs source (*Sēmeia-Quelle*) theory, see Ashton, *Understanding*, 178–94; Becker, "Wunder und Christologie," 130–48; Fortna, "Signs Gospel," 149–58; Fortna, *Gospel of Signs*; Martyn, *History and Theology*, 150–51; Nicol, *The Semeia in the Fourth Gospel*; Von Wahlde, *Earliest Version*.

71. Bultmann, *John*, 113.

72. Fortna, *Gospel of Signs*, 5, 235–45. See also Fortna, *The Fourth Gospel and its Predecessor*.

73. Fortna, "Signs Gospel," 150.

74. Brown, *Introduction*, 50–52. See also Barrett, *John*, 18–19; de Jonge, *Stranger from Heaven*, 117–18; Keener, *John*, 1:252; Lincoln, *John*, 29–30; Painter, "Signs of the Messiah," 243–45; Schweizer, *Ego eimi*; Smith, *Composition*; Thielman, *Theology*, 165–68; Witherington, *John's Wisdom*, 9–10.

75. Keener, *John*, 1:252.

source critics maintain that he (or a later redactor) carefully edited those sources, thus giving them his own stylistic stamp upon weaving them into his own work.[76] Nevertheless, are we to suppose that the author/redactor was so sloppy in his craft, that although he left a clear Johannine stamp throughout the entire work, we are able to excise and reconstruct his original source material based on the gaps left behind?[77] D. A. Carson's comment is instructive regarding Johannine source criticism:

> There is no need to doubt that John used sources: his fellow-Evangelist Luke certainly did (Luke 1:1–4), and there is no need to think that the fourth Evangelist followed some different course . . . the presumption that the Evangelist used written sources is quite different from the assumption that we can retrieve them.[78]

In summary, the composition history of John is admittedly complex, but the text as it now stands receives more attention in recent scholarship.[79] While this study is not a source-critical one, it is noteworthy to mention source criticism's influence on biblical intertextuality.[80] Source criticism's goal of recovering literary sources is not altogether irrelevant to the intertextual method of this study. Both share the concern of textual influence where a primary text utilizes a source text. Not that source criticism and intertextuality can be equated, but both share similar textual concerns regarding the influence of prior texts on later ones.

Relationship Between Signs and Faith

As the composition history of John's Gospel is complex, so also is the relationship between signs and faith. Signs are ambiguous in John and need to be interpreted by those who see them.[81] Some characters interpret rightly (e.g., the royal official in John 4:43–53), while others do not (e.g., the lame

---

76. Fortna, *Gospel of Signs*, 14; Fortna, "Signs Gospel," 152.

77. De Jonge, *Stranger from Heaven*, 117–18; Carson, *John*, 45; Painter, "Signs of the Messiah," 245.

78. Carson, *John*, 41.

79. Burge, *Interpreting the Gospel of John*, 74–82.

80. Hatina, "Intertextuality and Historical Criticism," 28–43. I do not want to overstate the similarities between source criticism and intertextuality, especially since the latter does not reconstruct hypothetical written sources as does the former. The primary overlap between the two involves the influence of earlier texts on later ones.

81. Thielman, *Theology*, 168.

man at the pool of Bethesda in 5:1–15).⁸² The former man's faith influences his entire household so that they, too, come to believe in Jesus (4:53), while the latter man, when given an opportunity to testify before the Jews in Jesus' defense, commits treason instead (5:15). Simply put, at times signs lead to faith, while at other times they do not.

The Gospel is full of characters that respond to Jesus' signs in one way or another. Some characters, like the crowds, exhibit utter unbelief: τοσαῦτα δὲ αὐτοῦ σημεῖα πεποιηκότος ἔμπροσθεν αὐτῶν οὐκ ἐπίστευον εἰς αὐτόν ("Though he had done so many signs before them, they still did not believe in him," 12:37); while others, such as the man blind from birth, display full-fledged belief as the result of Jesus' signs: πιστεύω, κύριε ("Lord, I believe," 9:38). It is obvious from these two examples that there is no simplistic correlation between signs and belief. Further, it is unclear what role signs play in coming to faith in John. On one hand, Jesus seems to disparage signs-based faith: ἐὰν μὴ σημεῖα καὶ τέρατα ἴδητε, οὐ μὴ πιστεύσητε ("Unless you all see signs and wonders, you will not believe," 4:48; cf. 2:23–25). Bultmann believes signs to be concessions to human weakness; i.e., faith should not depend on them, but Jesus graciously obliges when necessary.⁸³ On the other hand, in her article, "Signs and Faith in the Fourth Gospel," Thompson shows that the Evangelist's purpose statement indicates that specific signs have been written *so that* readers may believe: πολλὰ μὲν οὖν καὶ ἄλλα σημεῖα ἐποίησεν ὁ Ἰησοῦς ἐνώπιον τῶν μαθητῶν [αὐτοῦ], ἃ οὐκ ἔστιν γεγραμμένα ἐν τῷ βιβλίῳ τούτῳ· ταῦτα δὲ γέγραπται ἵνα πιστεύ[σ]ητε ὅτι Ἰησοῦς ἐστιν ὁ χριστὸς ὁ υἱὸς τοῦ θεοῦ ("Now Jesus did many other signs before his disciples, which are not written in this book; but these have been written so that you may believe that Jesus is the Christ, the Son of God," 20:30–31).⁸⁴ Still others, such as Craig Koester in "Hearing, Seeing and Believing in the Gospel of John," hold that signs are irrelevant for initializing faith; instead, hearing Jesus' words leads to faith while signs simply reaffirm and deepen existing faith.⁸⁵ This is especially true with regard to later readers of the Gospel who do not have the luxury of seeing the signs of

---

82. For an insightful comparison of these two contrasting characters, see Koester, "Hearing, Seeing, and Believing," 327–48, esp. 336–38.

83. Bultmann, *John*, 209.

84. Thompson, "Signs and Faith," 89–108. Whether πιστεύω is aorist subjunctive (πιστεύσητε) or progressive subjunctive (πιστεύητε) is irrelevant for the current discussion. Either way, the signs that are recorded are intended to increase faith.

85. Koester, "Hearing, Seeing, and Believing," 327–48; Koester, *Word of Life*, 163–70. Koester notes the royal official who "believed the word that Jesus spoke" (John 4:50a). Thus, "Readers learn that *to believe is to return home without visible proof that the boy is alive*" (ibid., 166).

Jesus' public ministry.⁸⁶ In short, there is no shortage of scholarly opinions regarding the relationship between Johannine signs and faith.⁸⁷ Thompson's view, that faith should result from signs, is most in line with the Gospel's own purpose statement. Nevertheless, the Gospel does not present a consistent correlation between signs and belief, for they often result in unbelief as well.⁸⁸

Much of the complexity of the relationship between Johannine signs and faith has to do with the Gospel's ambiguous portrayal of faith.⁸⁹ As the relationship between signs and faith is complex, so also is faith itself in John's Gospel. The ninety-eight times that faith is referenced, it is a verb (πιστεύω) not a noun (πίστις).⁹⁰ This statistic alone illustrates its importance for the Fourth Gospel's theology. For John, faith is not a momentary act but a continual, habitual relation between Jesus and the believer.⁹¹ Another reason that further exacerbates the interpretive crux regarding the relationship of signs to faith is the lack of precision with which John refers to the process of coming to believe in (πιστεύειν εἰς)⁹² Christ. This is often a long journey where the transition from unbelief to belief is blurry. For example, John implies that the faith of the Jerusalemites, after seeing the signs which Jesus performed, is fickle, especially given that in the next verse Jesus lacks faith in them (2:23–25). Similarly, what are we to make of Thomas's journey from sheer skepticism (ἐὰν μὴ ἴδω ... οὐ μὴ πιστεύσω, "Unless I see ... I will surely not believe") in 20:25 to confession and commitment (ὁ κύριός μου καὶ ὁ θεός μου, "My Lord and my God") in 20:28? Further, the growing

86. Koester, *Word of Life*, 163.

87. Anderson, "Authentic Faith," 257–60; Carter, *Storyteller*, 96–99; Gordon, "Final Wilderness," 28–29; Guthrie, "Importance," 72–83; Keener, *John*, 1:276–79; Koester, "Hearing, Seeing and Believing," 327–48; Koester, *Word of Life*, 163–70; Ladd, *Theology*, 306–08; Olbricht, "Theology of the Signs," 171–81; Rengstorf, 7:250–52; Thielman, *Theology*, 162–70; Thompson, *Humanity of Jesus*, 53–86; Thompson, "Signs and Faith," 89–108.

88. De Jonge, *Stranger from Heaven*, 132; Painter, "Signs of the Messiah," 244.

89. I appreciate Thompson's definition of faith: *faithfulness in trusting the God who is made known in Jesus Christ* in "Signs and Faith," 95. For additional discussions of faith in John's Gospel, see Bultmann "πιστεύω, ὀλιγοπιστία," 6:174–228, esp. 222–28; Carter, *Storyteller*, 93–96; Dodd, *Interpretation*, 179–86; Keener, *John*, 1:325–28; Köstenberger, *Encountering John*, 56; Köstenberger, *Theology*, 470–79; James Gaffney, "Believing and Knowing," 215–41; Kysar, *Maverick Gospel*, 78–96; Ladd, *Theology*, 306–11; Morris, *Theology*, 274–76; Morris, *John*, 296–98; Thompson, "Signs and Faith," 95–96; Schnackenburg, *John*, 1:558–75; Vos, *Biblical Theology*, 390–92.

90. Morris, *Theology*, 274.

91. Vos, *Biblical Theology*, 391.

92. For more on this Johannine faith formula, see Bultmann, 6:222–23; Morris, *Theology*, 274–75; Reim, *Jochanan*, 138.

faith of the man born blind is arguably the greatest example of character development in the Gospel:[93] ὁ λεγόμενος Ἰησοῦς ("The man called Jesus," 9:11); προφήτης ἐστίν ("He is a prophet," 9:17); εἰ μὴ ἦν οὗτος παρὰ θεοῦ, οὐκ ἠδύνατο ποιεῖν οὐδέν ("If this man were not from God, he could do nothing," 9:33); πιστεύω, κύριε· καὶ προσεκύνησεν αὐτῷ ("'Lord, I believe,' and he worshiped him," 9:38). Johannine character sketches reveal similar trends in several characters, but the blind man is the most pronounced. Such character sketches can prove frustrating when trying to understand what John means by πιστεύειν.

Robert Kysar's *John, the Maverick Gospel* proposes a particularly nuanced way of analyzing Johannine faith by segmenting it into three "stages": 1) openness to faith or embryonic faith, 2) signs-faith, and 3) mature faith.[94] Kysar correctly emphasizes that John does not depreciate any of these stages in the maturation of faith, but urges it to grow beyond the first two stages.[95] Put differently, signs-faith is inadequate in John's Gospel, but it is a valid step on the way to full discipleship.[96] No matter how one defines faith in the Gospel of John, signs certainly play a role in its development, at least to some degree. Granted, faith cannot solely be based on signs (2:23–25; 6:2, 30), but signs are meaningful tools for building faith.

OT Background to Signs

The third major area of investigation of Johannine signs involves their OT contexts. The two most significant contexts for signs are prophetic symbolism and the exodus. Both of these will be addressed here with the bulk of the emphasis on the latter. I share the assumption of M. J. J. Menken that due to the pervasive use of the OT in John's Gospel, John's audience likely had significant grounding in the OT itself, particularly the LXX,[97] and John's use of σημεῖον strikingly reflects that scriptural tradition.[98] Craig Keener captures the current state of affairs: "Whereas early Judaism did not always associate the Messiah with miracles, the exodus narrative made it impossible not to

---

93. Lincoln, *John*, 280; Culpepper, *Anatomy*, 139–40.
94. Kysar, *Maverick Gospel*, 85.
95. Ibid.
96. Keener, *John*, 1:276.
97. Menken, *Textual Form*, 208. I will address John's methodological use of the OT in chapter 2.
98. Brown, *John*, 1:529. I will address John's use of the LXX's terminology of σημεῖα in chapter 2.

associate 'signs' with Moses."[99] Therefore, the OT, specifically the exodus and wilderness narratives, likely forms the background imagery and use of Johannine σημεῖον. This excludes neither Greco-Roman nor Palestinian contexts, but simply maintains that the OT forms the primary background for Johannine signs.[100]

While miracles in the Fourth Gospel are spectacular indeed, often to the point where John expresses their "level of difficulty,"[101] their primary function seems to be symbolic.[102] The prophetic symbolism of the OT comes into play here as an OT background to Johannine signs.[103] While σημεῖον is normally John's word for "miracle," there are several non-miraculous signs in the Gospel. Andreas Köstenberger's article "The Seventh Johannine Sign," traces the prophetic symbolism of signs. The point is that as several OT prophets performed non-miraculous signs or symbolic actions, so also does Jesus in John's Gospel. Köstenberger's initial assumption is that the use of the term "sign" underwent a transformation in the OT, changing from referring to the miracles of the exodus to referring to the non-miraculous symbolic actions of the prophets.[104] He argues that Jesus' temple cleansing (2:12-22) should be interpreted as a sign in spite of its non-miraculous nature. Köstenberger notes, "When Jesus, immediately after cleansing the temple, is asked to perform a sign, he explains the significance of what he has just done, thus apparently implying that the temple cleaning itself already constituted the sign people were asking for."[105] It functions as a sign because it is a non-miraculous symbolic action similar to those of OT prophets. Certain prophets performed similar, non-miraculous symbolic actions (Isa 20:3; Jer 13:1–11; Ezek 4:3; 12:1–16). For three years Isaiah walked stripped and barefoot as signs (σημεῖα) against Egypt who would be led stripped and barefoot as captives by the king of Assyria (Isa 20:2-4). Such signs are revelatory motifs; i.e., they convey the word of God to the recipients. They are

---

99. Keener, *John*, 1:276.

100. For both Greco-Roman and Palestinian backgrounds to Johannine signs, see Keener, *John*, 1:254–70. Similarly, on Bultmann's θεῖος ἀνήρ ("divine man") proposal, see Bultmann, *Theology*, 1:130; Keener, *John*, 1:268–70.

101. The invalid was afflicted for thirty eight years (5:5); the blind man was blind from birth (9:1); Lazarus was in the tomb for four days (11:39); etc. For more on this, see Köstenberger, *John*, 98.

102. Brown, *John*, 1:526.

103. Barrett, *John*, 76; Brown, *John*, 1:527–30; Köstenberger, "Seventh Johannine Sign," 87–103; Schnackenburg, *John*, 1:527.

104. Köstenberger, "Seventh Johannine Sign," 91.

105. Ibid., 97.

not merely sermonic illustrations or visual aids, as Köstenberger proposes,[106] but rather divinely inspired images that declare in visible form a message from God. It is in this context that Rudolf Schnackenburg writes about the "revelatory character" of the symbol that is shared by the Johannine and the prophetic "signs."[107] Köstenberger's observation is a welcome corrective to an oversimplification that equates signs with miracles apart from their symbolic function. Nevertheless, it is only partly accurate, for prophets such as Elijah and Elisha also performed miraculous signs.[108] As Jesus feeds a crowd with "barley loaves" (John 6:1–15), so did Elisha (2 Kgs 4:42). As Jesus raises the dead (John 11:1–44), so did both Elijah (1 Kgs 17:17–24) and Elisha (2 Kgs 4:32–37). Whether non-miraculous or miraculous, symbolic prophet-like actions are prevalent throughout Jesus' ministry, and as such are firmly rooted in the soil of the OT.

The second major area of research on Johannine signs in relation to the OT, and the one that will receive priority in this study, involves their connection to the exodus and wilderness narratives of the Pentateuch.[109] While contrasting John with the Synoptic use of σημεῖα, D. Moody Smith states succinctly the connection of Jesus' signs to the exodus tradition: "But such miracle working, particularly the working of signs (σημεῖα), the specifically Johannine term, also belongs to the Mosaic Exodus tradition."[110] Similarly, Andrew Brunson's observation captures the driving assumption of this study: "The signs in the Fourth Gospel find their most natural background in the events of the exodus, and are most often associated by scholars with the signs of Moses."[111] Therefore, I argue here that John's signs terminology is best situated in the exodus and wilderness narratives of the OT. In John, although Jesus is one greater than Moses, he is nevertheless also one through whom God multiplies miraculous signs, as God did through Moses (Exod 10:1; Num 14:22; Deut 7:19).[112] As J.-P. Charlier notes, these verbal associations were already common in the OT, particularly in the stories of the exodus (which in most cases are in the books of Exodus and Numbers),

---

106. Ibid., 91.

107. Schnackenburg, *John*, 1:527. See also, Barrett, *John*, 76.

108. Smith, *Theology*, 126–27. See also, Keener, *John*, 1:278.

109. Barrett, *John*, 75; Brown, *John*, 1:528–29; Brunson, *Psalm 118*, 159–62; Cerfaux, "Les miracles," 41–50; Charlier, "La notion de signe," 434–48; Gordon, "Final Wilderness," 30–31; Hunt, *Johannine Problems*, 57–64; Keener, *John*, 1:276, 278–79; Reim, *Jochanan*, 137–38; Rengstorf, 7:255–57; *John*, 113; Riga, "Signs of Glory," 402–24; Schnackenburg, *John*, 1:521–26; Smith, "Exodus Typology," 333–42.

110. Smith, *Theology*, 108, 126.

111. Brunson, *Psalm 118*, 161.

112. Brown, *John*, 1:529.

whereby God performs many signs by the hand of Moses.¹¹³ Specifically, Glasson has already noted the connection between Jesus and Moses above. However, as stated before, Glasson gives little attention to the doing of signs by both Moses and Jesus. This emphasis on miraculous signs comprises a major component of the comparison between these two agents of God and will be highlighted in this study. My concern is not with a comparison between Moses and Jesus as agents of God, but rather how their signs function in the context of the wilderness. The parallels between Moses' signs and those of Jesus run deep and go beyond the mere doing of specific signs. For example, both men, despite being agents of God, are rejected by their people, even while performing signs among them. Consider the similarity between John's summary account of Jesus' signs, and those of God done through Moses in the wilderness:¹¹⁴

> τοσαῦτα δὲ αὐτοῦ σημεῖα πεποιηκότος ἔμπροσθεν αὐτῶν οὐκ ἐπίστευον εἰς αὐτόν. (John 12:37)

> Although he performed so many signs in their presence, they did not believe in him.

> ἕως τίνος οὐ πιστεύουσίν μοι ἐν πᾶσιν τοῖς σημείοις οἷς ἐποίησα ἐν αὐτοῖς; (Num 14:11)

> How long will they not believe in me, in spite of all the signs I have performed among them?

A second example involves the summary statements of the ministries of both Moses and Jesus which also emphasize their doing of signs:¹¹⁵

> πολλὰ μὲν οὖν καὶ ἄλλα σημεῖα ἐποίησεν ὁ Ἰησοῦς ἐνώπιον τῶν μαθητῶν αὐτοῦ. (John 20:30)

> Now Jesus performed many other signs before his disciples.

> ἐν πᾶσι τοῖς σημείοις καὶ τέρασιν ὃν ἀπέστειλεν αὐτὸν κύριος ποιῆσαι αὐτὰ ἐν γῇ Αἰγύπτῳ. (Deut 34:11)

> For all the signs and wonders that the Lord sent him to perform them in the land of Egypt.

---

113. Charlier, "La notion de signe," 435–36. Reim, *Jochanan*, 137, makes a similar remark but also emphasizes the gap between Moses and Jesus: Moses was a fallen human being through whom God did signs; Jesus was one with the Father, so his works were one with God's (John 4:34; 9:4; 14:10).

114. Brown, *John*, 1:529; Gordon, "Final Wilderness," 30–31.

115. Brown, *John*, 1:529.

As Gordon aptly notes, "Both ministries could be characterized as σημεῖα ποῖειν."[116] Connections such as these could be multiplied, and they suggest that John alludes to the LXX wilderness narratives for his portrayal of Jesus' signs.

In addition to the rejection motif and the summary statements previously mentioned, the exodus/wilderness background to Johannine signs has been approached from two general angles: 1) the revelation of glory (δόξα),[117] and 2) the external form of wilderness signs.[118] The signs that witness to Jesus also reveal the divine δόξα—the glory of God.[119] In the OT, the people of Israel saw God's glory in the wilderness in signs such as the manna and the cloud (Exod 16:7, 10). God revealed his presence to Israel through visible acts, or miraculous signs.[120] Similarly, with his first miraculous sign at the wedding feast in Cana, Jesus "revealed his glory" (ἐφανέρωσεν δόξαν αὐτοῦ, John 2:11) to his disciples. Before raising Lazarus from the dead, Jesus told Martha that if she believed she would "see the glory of God" (ὄψῃ τὴν δόξαν, 11:40). It is noteworthy that these two signs, the first and last of Jesus' public ministry in John, reveal his glory, forming an *inclusio* for his entire public ministry demonstrating that signs are pointers to his glory.[121] Therefore, signs in John, as in the wilderness, reveal the glory of God. Peter Riga's insightful article, "Signs of Glory" traces the connection between God's glory as revealed in the signs of Moses, and the glory of Jesus that was similarly manifested through signs.[122] He writes, "In the Book of Exodus, especially, God reveals his glory by performing wonders; he marvelously demonstrates his power to save the world, and especially Israel."[123] Riga then illustrates that miraculous events, such as the crossing of the Red Sea, the manna in the wilderness, and the water from the rock, revealed the presence and power of God and that John places Jesus' miraculous signs in the

---

116. Gordon, "Final Wilderness," 30.

117. Brown, *John*, 1:529; Brunson, *Psalm 118*, 162; Cerfaux, "Les miracles," 43; Charlier, "La notion de signe," 441–44; Keener, *John*, 1:276, 278–79; Rengstorf, 7:253–54; Riga, "Signs of Glory," 402–24; Schnackenburg, *John*, 1:524.

118. Gordon, "Final Wilderness," 29–30; Smith, "Exodus Typology," 333–42; Hunt, *Johannine Problems*, 57–64.

119. Ladd, *Theology*, 311.

120. Ibid.

121. Keener, *John*, 1:276.

122. Riga, "Signs of Glory," 402–24.

123. Ibid., 411. However, Cerfaux, "Les miracles," 43, observes that the formula ποιεῖν σημεῖα has a special connection to the book of Numbers as well: "All of the men who saw my glory and the signs that I did in Egypt and in this wilderness" (Num 14:22).

History of Research 25

same context.[124] In John, the signs function as divine self-revelation[125] and illustrate a clear connection between signs and glory.

The second major angle from which scholars approach Johannine signs in relation to the OT wilderness narratives involves the external forms of the signs themselves. Put differently, if the revelation of glory accentuates the function of signs, the signs themselves resemble in form those of Moses in the OT. They are similar in appearance to the signs of Moses.[126] I have already noted Robert H. Smith's typological proposal in his article "Exodus Typology in the Fourth Gospel" where he parallels specific Johannine signs with Mosaic plagues done in Egypt in the book of Exodus. The plagues which God brought through Moses are often called "signs" in Exodus (Exod 3:12; 4:8–9; 7:3; 8:23; 10:1–2) thus allowing Smith to seek Johannine parallels. His primary assumption is as follows: "Johannine signs individually, which are so similar to the Mosaic signs that it seems that the fourth evangelist has deliberately arranged them as parallels."[127] My conclusion earlier in this chapter was that many of Smith's proposed parallels were gratuitous, and in the end strained the limits of typology proper. After all, Jesus' signs are not plagues in John and "inversion" is not the same as typology.[128] I believe Smith would be more accurate to look also to the book of Numbers in order to find parallels between Moses' signs and those of Jesus. Nonetheless, Smith's article serves as a stimulus for seeking more accurate parallels between the signs of Moses in the Pentateuch and Jesus in John. B. P. W. Stather Hunt's *Some Johannine Problems* proposes a similar, although less gratuitous, comparison between Moses' signs in the wilderness and those of Jesus in John.[129] Hunt's driving assumption is that John presents Jesus as the Prophet of Deut 18:18–19. He theorizes, "There was a Jewish tradition that when the Messiah came, he would duplicate on a higher plane the miracles that Moses did in the wilderness."[130] Chief among these messianic

---

124. Riga, "Signs of Glory," 411. Charlier, "La notion de signe," 441–44, also illustrates the connection between Jesus' glory as revealed in the signs and that of God revealed through Moses' signs. Charlier traces John's glory theme illustrating that it ultimately climaxes at the sign of the cross.

125. Keener, *John*, 1:279.

126. Gordon, "Final Wilderness," 30.

127. Smith, "Exodus Typology," 334.

128. Ibid., 335.

129. Hunt, *Johannine Problems*, 57–64. See also, Brunson, *Psalm 118*, 160n77.

130. Hunt, *Johannine Problems*, 57. See also, Rengstorf, 7:245–46. Hunt's thesis is only half-true; he overlooks the well-known tradition of a Davidic Messiah who was not expected to perform miraculous signs. This has been probed by Martyn, *History and Theology*, 90–98. I will interact with Second Temple Judaism's messianic expectations in chapter 3 when discussing Jesus' kingship in John. Suffice it to say here that

miracles would be those that duplicate four specific wilderness miracles: 1) the sweetening of the brackish waters of Marah (Exod 15:23–26); 2) the provision of food (Exod 16:11–36); 3) the provision of water from the rock (Num 20:7–13); and 4) the healing by means of the brazen serpent (Num 21:8–9).[131] Hunt then demonstrates how Jesus performs these messianic miracles in John's Gospel. All of this is well and good until Hunt runs into a dilemma: not all Jesus' signs fit this wilderness pattern. Hunt lists four, but what of Jesus' other signs?[132] From a strictly miraculous standpoint, which Hunt insists reflects Jewish tradition, there are only two clear candidates in John that definitely reflect the *form* of Mosaic signs: water turned into wine and the feeding of the 5,000.[133] While I appreciate Hunt's emphasis on wilderness signs more than Smith's emphasis on exodus plagues, his typological system suffers the same methodological fate as Smith's in seeking parallelism in superficial appearances. Instead of seeing Johannine signs as formal parallels to Mosaic signs, that is, seeking Johannine signs that are visible duplicates of those worked by God through Moses, it is best to look at them as *functional* parallels. This is the primary contribution of the current study.

CURRENT CONTRIBUTION: SIGNS AS TESTS OF FAITHFULNESS

Instead of analyzing the specific form of Johannine signs, and how they reflect the external forms of Moses' signs in the wilderness, I want to propose another angle from which to look at their function—divine testing. Put differently, this is a study about the function of signs in John, not their form. Deuteronomy 8 explicitly states the testing function of signs. On one hand, the wilderness experience itself was a test. God tested (ἐκπειράσῃ) his people in the wilderness in order to know whose hearts were faithful:

> καὶ μνησθήσῃ πᾶσαν τὴν ὁδόν ἣν ἤγαγέν σε κύριος ὁ θεός σου ἐν τῇ ἐρήμῳ ὅπως ἄν κακώσῃ σε καὶ ἐκπειράσῃ σε καὶ διαγνωσθῇ τὰ ἐν τῇ καρδίᾳ σου εἰ φυλάξῃ τὰς ἐντολὰς αὐτοῦ ἢ οὔ. (Deut 8:2)

John presents Jesus as both the Prophet like Moses and the Davidic Messiah.

131. Hunt, *Johannine Problems*, 57.

132. Smith, "Exodus Typology," 332, makes a similar observation.

133. Jesus' water walk (John 6:16–21) may reflect the parting of the Red Sea by Moses. For more on this, see Burge, *John*, 195–96; Culpepper, *Anatomy*, 194.

> And you shall remember all the way that the Lord your God led you in the wilderness so that he may humble you and may test you and that the things in your heart may be known if you will keep his commands or not.

On the other hand, while this verse illustrates that the wilderness experience as a whole is viewed in Deuteronomy as a divine test, the portrayal of miraculous signs as tests is explicit in Deut 8:16 where God's miraculous provision of manna becomes an explicit example of divine testing:

> τοῦ ψωμίσαντός σε τὸ μαννα ἐν τῇ ἐρήμῳ ὃ οὐκ εἴδησαν οἱ πατέρες σου ἵνα κακώσῃ σε καὶ ἐκπειράσῃ σε καὶ εὖ σε ποιήσῃ ἐπ'ἐσχάτων τῶν ἡμερῶν σου.

> Who fed you the manna in the wilderness which your fathers knew not, so that he might humble you and test you and do you good until your last days.

Similarly, Deut 8:4 remembers the fact that the Israelites' clothing did not wear out along the journey, and while the text does not mention "signs" per se, the context suggests that this providential act of God was nonetheless miraculous, and tested the faith of the people. Although not an exhaustive list of wilderness signs, Deut 8 portrays signs as divine tests of faithfulness. Deuteronomy 4:34 provides additional evidence that signs functioned as tests of faithfulness in the wilderness, because no other god has taken a people for himself as the LORD has done "by tests, and by signs, and by wonders" (πειρασμῷ καὶ ἐν σημείοις καὶ τέρασιν, 4:34). In summary, the Deuteronomic evidence illustrates that the wilderness sojourn itself was a test, as were the miraculous signs worked by God on Israel's behalf. Simply stated, God tested the hearts of the Israelites in the wilderness with his signs performed through Moses. However, the first wilderness generation proved their hardness of heart when they repeatedly saw God's signs worked through Moses, but persisted in their rebellion and rejection.

John notices this testing motif as it relates to miraculous signs. Signs test the hearts of various characters and crowds to see whether they believe Jesus' claims about himself and his relationship to the Father. Jesus' statement to Philip prior to the feeding of 5,000 in John 6:6 is notable: τοῦτο δὲ ἔλεγεν πειράζων αὐτόν ("But he said this testing him"). As God tested (ἐκπειράζω) Israel with miraculous signs such as the manna in the wilderness, Jesus tests (πειράζω) Philip with reference to a similar miraculous sign. The crowd later recognizes the miraculous feeding as a σημεῖον (6:14). Given the connection here between manna as a sign and the testing of Philip, John echoes Deut 8:16 rather resoundingly: τοῦ ψωμίσαντός σε τὸ μαννα ἐν τῇ ἐρήμῳ ὃ οὐκ εἴδησαν οἱ πατέρες σου ἵνα κακώσῃ σε καὶ ἐκπειράσῃ ("He fed you manna in the wilderness which your fathers had not known so that he might humble you and test you"). God tests (ἐκπειράζω) his people with the miraculous provision of manna, as well as with other miraculous signs in the wilderness. While the term πειράζω only occurs twice in John's Gospel (John 6:6; 8:6), the connection with the manna sign helps frame the other signs as tests of faith as in Deut 8 (cf. Exod 16:4). Further, by taking into account the testing of Philip in John 6:6, this testing motif, while not often repeated verbally in John's Gospel, undergirds each of Jesus' signs so that they become tests of faith.[134]

Paul Anderson also summarizes the wilderness experience as one of testing: "The crisis in the wilderness was not only a time of God's provision for Israel, but it was also their 'testing,' designed to teach them humility and covenant faithfulness."[135] In his book, *The Christology of the Fourth Gospel*, Anderson also comments on the relationship between signs and testing in John 6, but he leaves this relationship unexplored elsewhere in the Gospel.[136] He illustrates the connection between the testing of Philip in the context of the feeding of the 5,000 in John 6 and the testing of Israel with the manna miracle under Moses. Anderson's comment is instructive and applicable to this study:

> Likewise, in John 6 the 'testing' of the actants in the narrative is designed to test the Johannine audience regarding whether or not they will be responsive to God's saving and providing activity in Jesus. The provision of the loaves and fishes in the desert and the sea-crossing narrative are clearly reminiscent of God's mighty acts of deliverance of Israel in the wilderness.[137]

Therefore, this study will focus on the wilderness as a period of divine testing where miraculous signs specifically served as tests of faithfulness. I want to build on Anderson's perception by developing further the relationship between signs and testing. My overall contribution is to demonstrate that a Johannine wilderness motif illuminates the relationship of signs and faith as one of divine testing by using Jesus' dialogue with Nicodemus (John 3:1–21) as a test case.

---

134. Anderson, *Christology of the Fourth Gospel*, 16.
135. Ibid., 204.
136. Ibid., 86, 106–07, 138, 173, 185, 193, 202, 204.
137. Ibid., 202.

Nicodemus as Test Case

This study presents Nicodemus as a wilderness traveler who is on a faith journey toward the Promised Land (Johannine eternal life), and who is tested by Jesus' signs. Miraculous signs test his faith much like signs tested that of the wilderness generations. The first generation saw the miraculous signs of God yet refused to believe, thus forfeiting its right to enter the Promised Land. So also in John, many people see Jesus' miraculous signs but refuse to believe, thus forfeiting eternal life. Nicodemus, like other characters in John, becomes a test case in that his own wilderness experience is one of divine testing in the presence of signs. Will he have a heart of flesh, believe, and enter eternal life, or will he have a hard heart, refuse to believe, and die in the wilderness? John notices the testing function of signs, applying it to Nicodemus.

I will demonstrate that John illustrates this testing theme with his reference to the uplifted serpent (Num 21:8–9) in John 3:14–15. This sign[138] was both a lifesaver and a test of faith for the wilderness community and functions the same way for John. John's uplifted serpent reference becomes not only a crucifixion/exaltation reference, but also forms the crucial analogy with the wilderness generation by demonstrating how seeing signs must be accompanied by faith in God. *For John, the uplifted serpent reference points beyond a faith that simply sees signs to one that truly trusts in God as their source.* The uplifted serpent is a Johannine reference to Christ's glorification, but it is also a perfect, although complex, example of Johannine faith that sees and trusts God's redemptive activity in the crucifixion/exaltation of Christ. The driving methodology for this study is an intertextual analysis of John 2:23—3:21 and the wilderness narratives of Numbers, as well as interpretive comments of Deuteronomy (Deut 4:34; 8:2, 16) which sees signs as tests of faith. I will now turn to defining this methodology in detail.

---

138. Charlier, "La notion de signe," 444–45, insightfully sees the uplifted serpent as a sign in that it ultimately points to the greatest sign in the Gospel—the cross. While John's reference to the uplifted serpent is not narrated as a miraculous sign per se, it is certainly one in its original context in Numbers. What is more, John assumes his audience knows this and is able to see this reference as pointing to the cross as the most miraculous sign in his Gospel. I will demonstrate this in greater detail while interacting with John 3:14 in chapter 4. See also, Brown, *John,* 1:528.

Chapter 2

METHODOLOGICAL APPROACH

Having investigated the history of research on the roles of both the wilderness and signs in John's Gospel, I now turn to an explanation of the methodology that drives this study. The methodology for the present study is a "wilderness reading" of John 2:23—3:21, primarily by way of intertextual allusions and echoes to the wilderness narratives in the book of Numbers, while also interacting with Deuteronomy's understanding of signs as tests of faith. John alludes most clearly to the wilderness experience by way of the uplifted copper serpent (3:14–15; cf. Num 21:8–9) but also exhibits numerous additional "connection points" by echoing specific thematic and structural elements from the wilderness narratives of Numbers. Once I have established intertextual connections between the two texts, I will then interpret the function of Johannine signs against the background of signs in the wilderness recount of Deut 8 as tests of faithfulness. Not every instance of wilderness imagery that I propose will be directly related to the issue of signs as tests of faith in the wilderness; however, the cumulative effect of the evidence will, I hope, weigh in favor of this thesis. In an effort at precision, I will now propose working definitions for "wilderness" and "signs" as I am using them in this study.

DEFINING WILDERNESS

Due to the complexity and diversity of both "wilderness" and "signs" in Scripture, and given the wide semantic range of their Hebrew and Greek terms, it is important to lay out working definitions for this study. The definitions suggested here are not so much meant to be definitive as they are functional for the present study. In the HB, the English term "wilderness" is subsumed under a variety of Hebrew words, the most prevalent being מדבר. "Wilderness" refers broadly to "unsettled and uncultivated land, the natural habitation of wild animals but not of humans, a place through which shepherds and Bedouin pass following pasturage and travelers hasten to safer havens."[1] As an experiential place, it can take a decidedly negative tone in Scripture, and does not necessarily describe the place of Yahweh's care and cultivation of the Israelite people through a formative period in their history. Even so, it is sometimes referred to as a time of God's care and cultivation: "He knows your going through this great wilderness. These forty years the LORD your God has been with you. You have lacked nothing" (Deut 2:7 ESV; cf. Ps 78:14–16). It is at other times a "great and terrifying wilderness, with its fiery serpents and scorpions and thirsty ground where there was no water." (Deut 8:15; cf. 1:19). Further, the first generation of Israelites died in the wilderness, underscoring the fact that the wilderness is not always described as a positive place under God's protection. However, this negative association stems from Israel's own incessant complaining and rebelliousness.[2] Further, the wilderness experience, as dreadful as it was, had a divine purpose as well, and was not solely the result of human sin and rebellion.[3] Deuteronomy 8:2 reminds Israel that God's intent behind the wilderness wanderings was so that he might "humble you, testing you to know what was in your heart." Again, the first generation died, clearly illustrating the principle of divine punishment. But such was not the goal of the wilderness journey itself; rather, the biblical account, according to Deut 8, reflects divine discipline and training, as in a classroom.[4] In spite of periodic negative associations in Scripture, the wilderness period was Israel's formative years where God raised up a people for himself. The experience was not easy for Israel or God. Both "tested" each other in different ways and for different reasons. More narrowly, the HB uses מדבר most frequently to refer to the wilderness through which the Israelites sojourned on their journey

---

1. Brian Jones, "Wilderness," 5:848–52. For a list of the Hebrew terms translated as "wilderness," see ibid., 5:848–49. I am indebted to Jones for my summary treatment of the biblical references to "wilderness" and refer the reader to his entry for more details. See also, Leal, *Wilderness in the Bible*, 51; Mauser, *Christ in the Wilderness*, 15–52; Talmon, "Desert Motif," 31–63; Talmon, "Wilderness," 946–48.

2. Jones, "Wilderness," 5:849. For even more negative associations, see ibid.

3. Wright, *Deuteronomy*, 122. Wright adds that Yahweh wanted to know if the people really would do what they had promised (cf. Exod 24:3, 7).

4. Ibid.

to Canaan or to some other definite, but unnamed, wilderness.[5] Even more pointedly for this study, מדבר designates the period between Israel's exodus from Egypt and the conquest of Canaan.[6] As will become evident, it is significant for this study to note that the LXX uses ἔρημος primarily to translate מדבר, as well as many of the other Hebrew words.[7] Just as God brought the Israelites "to the wilderness" (אל-מדבר, ἐν τῇ ἐρήμῳ) of Shur after crossing the Red Sea (Exod 15:22), he continued to lead them "in the wilderness" (במדבר, ἐν τῇ ἐρήμῳ) of Sinai (Num 1:1). It should not be overlooked that the Hebrew title of the book of Numbers is במדבר (lit. "In the wilderness"), and more accurately describes the geographical location of the journey, as well the narrative contents of the book, than the Greek ΑΡΙΘΜΟΙ, the Latin *Numeri*, or the English Numbers.

The LXX consistently uses ἔρημος to refer to Israel's forty-year sojourn in the wilderness. In fact, it does so ninety seven times in the Pentateuch and nearly always with reference to the wilderness of the sojourn.[8] The OT also speaks of wilderness in the prophetic traditions as referring to an eschatological second exodus made lush as a garden, safe from danger, where a new covenant will be with God's people (Jer 31:31–34; 32:36–41), and where Judah and Jerusalem will be transformed from a wilderness into an edenic garden (Isa 35; 40–55; Ezek 36:8–12, 33–36).[9] Gerhard von Rad em-

---

5. Jones, "Wilderness," 5:848–49. Although, Jones notes that ישימן is used as a synonym for "the wilderness" of the sojourn (Deut 32:12; Pss 68:8; 78:40; 106:14; Isa 43:19, 20), additionally he points out that מדבר can also refer broadly to semi-arid, unsettled, and uncultivated land with pasturage sufficient to support migratory flocks and herds (Gen 36:24; Ps 65:12). So, מדבר need not be limited to Israel's forty-year sojourn from Egypt to Canaan.

6. Burden, *Wilderness Traditions*, 5.

7. Jones, "Wilderness," 5:849.

8. Funk, "Wilderness," 205–14. Funk discusses the much debated geographical locale of Israel's wilderness journey, as well as the mythological aspects of the wilderness in the ANE; both are beyond the scope of this study.

9. Jones, "Wilderness," 5:850; Childs, *Isaiah*, 299. Barstad, *Way in the Wilderness*, questions the presence of "exodus texts" (also "second exodus") in Deutero-Isaiah. He argues for a non-literal (i.e., metaphorical) reading of Deutero-Isaiah's (Isa 40–55) supposed "second exodus" texts (Isa 40:3–5; 41:17–20; 42:14–16; 49:8–12; 50:1–3; 55:12–13) where he rejects the proposed historical reconstruction of a literal return of Judeans through the desert from Babylon to Jerusalem as the background to Deutero-Isaiah (ibid., 5–6, 107–08). His argument is that metaphorical texts do not reflect actual historical circumstances; therefore, "exodus texts" cannot be taken at face value to reflect actual historical circumstances. Nevertheless, whether or not "exodus texts" literally reflect the historical reconstruction that Barstad rejects (i.e., return of the exiles to Judah) is secondary to their eschatological emphases. Barstad even acknowledges a "restoration" not only of exiles, but of the Judean nation as a whole (ibid., 109). Even more to the point, he acknowledges that "exodus texts" (esp. those with desert motifs)

phasizes the same eschatological journey which recalls the wilderness narratives of the Pentateuch: "Jahweh would do a new thing—he would once more redeem Israel in the same way as he had done at the beginning and lead her again through the wilderness" (Isa 43:16–21).[10] As Isa 48:21 states, καὶ ἐὰν διψήσωσεν δι' ἐρήμου ἄξει αὐτούς ὕδωρ ἐκ πέτρας ἐξάξει αὐτοῖς σχισθήσεται πέτρα καὶ ῥυήσεται ὕδωρ καὶ πίεται ὁ λάος μου ("And if they should thirst, he will lead them through the wilderness; he will bring forth water to them from the rock: the rock will be split, and the water will flow forth, and my people will drink").

The NT consistently uses ἔρημος for "wilderness," which can simply refer to an arid and solitary place, Israel's forty-year sojourn in the Pentateuch narratives, or the ministry of John the Baptist who is the "voice in the wilderness" (John 1:23).[11] The usage varies throughout the NT, but the Pentateuch's wilderness imagery is often paramount for the NT writers. There are, of course, interpretative decisions involved in deciding which instances of ἔρημος in the NT may allude in some way to Israel's sojourn in the Pentateuch; clearly some do not: Jesus drives out demons and sends them into the wilderness (εἰς τὰς ἐρήμους, Luke 8:29); Philip travels from Jerusalem to Gaza, a desert place (αὕτη ἐστὶν ἔρημος, Acts 8:26); Paul describes Sarah as the desolate woman (τῆς ἐρήμου) in Gal 4:27. Others are less clear: Jesus withdraws to desolate places (ἐν ταῖς ἐρήμοις) to pray (Luke 5:16) and exits Jerusalem to the region near the wilderness (ἐγγὺς τῆς ἐρήμου), the city of Ephraim (John 11:54). A careful analysis is needed to decide in each case and is beyond the scope of this study. With that said, I have categorized the ἔρημος passages in Appendix 1 based on three common uses in the NT: 1) an arid, solitary, or desolate place, 2) Israel's sojourn, and 3) John the Baptist/second exodus eschatology.[12] My point is simply that like the

---

do in fact reflect the scriptural exodus tradition (ibid., 108). So a literal vs. metaphorical reading of "exodus texts" does not negate their allusive use of the exodus tradition in the Pentateuch, or their eschatological use in the NT. For the purpose of this study I will accept "exodus texts" (esp. Isa 40:3) as reflective of exodus-wilderness imagery in the Pentateuch. Marsh, *Fulness of Time*, sets forth a Reformed biblical-theological study of time by noting the Bible's second exodus terminology. Marsh goes so far as to suggest that Israel's identity rested more in the exodus event than in Abraham as their father (ibid., 52). While Marsh's work is focused more on a biblical philosophy of time than on second exodus eschatology per se, it nonetheless comprises much of the biblical portrait (esp. ibid., 53–107). Exodus eschatology is important for understanding John's Gospel as well, but Marsh leaves this largely unexplored. For the most recent acceptance of a Johannine second exodus motif, see Brunson, *Psalm 118*.

10. Von Rad, *Theology*, 1:284.

11. Jones, "Wilderness," 5:849.

12. A case can be made for interpreting passages about John the Baptist as the "voice in the wilderness" as at least indirectly referring to Israel's sojourn based on

OT, the NT is diverse in its use of "wilderness," but alludes in some way to the narratives of Israel's sojourn on many occasions. While acknowledging the prevalence of the terms for wilderness used in Scripture, the imagery is equally as important. Wilderness imagery is also prevalent in Scripture, even where the terminology is lacking. John's Gospel is a good case in point as it uses the term ἔρημος fairly infrequently. Nevertheless, this study will demonstrate how John's wilderness imagery outweighs his infrequent use of the term ἔρημος.

For the present study, a working definition of "wilderness" is in order in an effort to understand its appropriation in John's Gospel. Before moving to John's usage, I will combine a few previously proposed definitions into one working definition that will then illuminate his use of wilderness images in the Gospel. Because none of the proposed definitions alone completely addresses what I believe John does with his wilderness imagery, I will combine the most salient aspects of each into one working definition for the present work. Kenneth Pomykala defines "wilderness" broadly as the narrative material concerning Israel's sojourn through the wilderness in Exod 16–Deut 34.[13] At first glance, this may seem too broad for an intertextual study such as the one attempted here, but the scriptural references for the narrative accounts are accurate, and therefore a good starting point. More specific is Terry Burden's definition: "The wilderness traditions are those narratives found in the books of Exodus and Numbers that refer to the wanderings of the Israelites in the wilderness under the leadership of Moses following the exodus from Egypt."[14] Highlighting the person of Moses is helpful here due to the prominence given to Mosaic traditions in John's Gospel.[15] Alison Schofield describes "wilderness" as a literary motif.[16]

---

second exodus eschatology (see below). I argue here that the passages that link Isa 40:3 with John the Baptist recall Israel's wilderness sojourn. Therefore, my chart (Appendix 1) could easily have merged those two columns, but I want to isolate the passages that make probable allusions to the Pentateuch's wilderness narratives. The chart is based not only on the use of ἔρημος in the NT but also its cognates.

13. Pomykala, *Israel in the Wilderness*, IX.

14. Burden, *Wilderness Traditions*, 1. As indicated in his definition, Burden makes no distinction between "traditions" and "narratives."

15. Boismard, *Moses or Jesus*; Brunson, *Psalm 118*, 161–62; Day, *Moses Connection*; Glasson, *Moses*; Harstine, *Moses as a Character*; Martyn, *History and Theology*, 100–30; Meeks, *The Prophet-King*; Pryor, *Covenant People*, 117–22.

16. Schofield, "Wilderness Motif," 37–53. Schofield defines literary motif as a recurring thematic element (word, phrase, image, metaphor, actions, situation), appearing in the course of one or more texts (ibid., 38). To this should be added Talmon's conviction that a motif is historical in nature and gives expression in a secondary text to ideas and experiences inherent in the primary text (Talmon, "The Desert Motif," 39). Schofield helpfully illustrates that the wilderness traditions of Exodus, Leviticus, and Numbers

However, this is too broad in and of itself for this study because the literary motif she identifies is embedded even earlier into the patriarchal narratives of Genesis (esp. Gen 12–25).[17] This is unsuitable for our present purposes because John 3:14 alludes to a specific event in the forty-year wilderness sojourn recorded in the Pentateuch in Numbers; the patriarchal narratives of Genesis are not in view when John uses wilderness imagery.[18] Therefore, the narratives of Israel's forty-year sojourn in the wilderness as recorded in Exod 16–Deut 34 (à la Pomykala) remain the primary sources for "wilderness" in Scripture. As Brian Jones notes, "The wilderness is preeminently the place of the forty-year sojourn, and the most frequent and significant references to wilderness in the OT pertain to Israel's experience there."[19] T. David Gordon's more specific definition should be added to the previous ones: "Events associated with the wilderness as well as the journeying itself. Thus, the Exodus is an element of the wilderness, insofar as it precipitates the wilderness wanderings. Also included in 'wilderness' are the central themes, characters, and miracles associated with it."[20] To Gordon's definition should also be added the feast traditions of the Pentateuch wilderness traditions given the prevalence of OT festal symbolism in John's Gospel (esp. Passover and Tabernacles). All elements are now in place for a working definition of "wilderness" for this study: Wilderness is a literary motif reflected in the Pentateuch's wilderness narratives (Exod 16–Deut 34) where the Israelites journeyed under the leadership of Moses following the exodus from Egypt, including its imagery, events, themes, central characters, miracles, and feast traditions.

Divine Testing as a Wilderness Motif

Divine testing is one of many themes of the wilderness tradition. The wilderness was a time of testing and discipline, of instruction and teaching.[21]

---

are recorded in three distinct sections in the Pentateuch: the exodus from Egypt (Exod 1–18), the Sinai narratives (Exod 19–Num 10:10), and the journey from Sinai to the Promised Land (Num 10:11–36:12) (Schofield, "Wilderness Motif," 39).

17. Schofield, "Wilderness Motif," 39n5.

18. Although, note the mention of "our father Jacob" in Jesus' discussion with the Samaritan woman at the well (John 4:12). John's Gospel does contain allusions to Genesis, some of which are to the patriarchal narratives; however, these are not within wilderness contexts per se. For John's allusions to Genesis, see Reim, *Jochanan*, 98–105.

19. Jones, "Wilderness," 5:849.

20. Gordon, "Final Wilderness," 4.

21. Miller, *Deuteronomy*, 115. Schofield, "Wilderness Motif," 38, Mauser, *Christ in the Wilderness*, 34, Jones, "Wilderness," 5:850, Wright, *Deuteronomy*, 121–22, and

As mentioned previously, Deuteronomy boasts how no other god has taken a people for himself as the LORD has done πειρασμῷ καὶ ἐν σημείοις καὶ τέρασιν ("by trials, and by signs, and by wonders" Deut 4:34). These trials, or "testings" (NIV), were the miraculous means by which God revealed himself to the Israelites as he brought them out of Egypt. His people were to know that the LORD was the true God once they witnessed and experienced his mighty acts of deliverance (Deut 4:35).

Because John 3:14 clearly alludes to the uplifted serpent narrative of Num 21:8–9, this study will be primarily concerned with the wilderness narratives of Numbers while interacting with Deuteronomy when discussing signs as tests of faith. It is important to note that John does not limit his wilderness references to Numbers; Exodus also plays a crucial role. Nonetheless, because John 3:14 alludes to the uplifted serpent of Num 21:8–9, Numbers will be the source text for the current intertextual study of John 2:23—3:21. It will then take into account the divine testing motif of Deut 8, via signs, and how John's Gospel appropriates that motif in its own presentation of miraculous signs.

Wilderness in John's Gospel

Wilderness themes, characters, miracles, and theology saturate John's Gospel.[22] As stated before, the Pentateuch's wilderness narratives are John's primary referents for "wilderness" (John 3:14; 6:31, 49).[23] Although John

---

Craigie, *Deuteronomy*, 185, 189, illustrate the wilderness as a time of testing. This testing went both ways: Deut 8:3 records how God tested the Israelites (cf. Wis 11:9–10) while Ps 95:7–11 records their testing God (cf. Heb 3:8–9). Wilderness testing in the DSS and in the NT is taken as eschatological refinement by Stegner, "Wilderness and Testing," 18–27.

22. Gordon, "Final Wilderness," 2.

23. Two exceptions are John 1:23 and 11:54. According to Keener, *John*, 1:439, the latter verse is "unclear" in its wilderness reference. However, the presentation of John the Baptist as the "voice of one crying out ἐν τῇ ἐρήμῳ" in the former is not insignificant for my purpose. John places his own ministry within the eschatological expectation of Isa 40:3. Keener, *Bible Background*, 266, observes how John presents himself as the herald of a second exodus, announcing that God is about to redeem his people from captivity as he had in the days of Moses. Burge, *John*, 72, illustrates that John is not the prophet of Deut 18:15–19 (cf. John 1:21) but simply the "voice" (φωνή) of LXX Isa 40:3. Although this passage in John does not speak directly of the wilderness event of the Pentateuch, it recalls it and speaks of it indirectly as the new exodus of Isa 40:3. For more on this, see Köstenberger, *Theology*, 407–08; Köstenberger, "John," 425–30. Brown, *John*, 1:50, points out that Qumran's use of Isa 40:3 explains why they chose to live out in the desert: they were preparing the way for the Lord by studying and

only uses ἔρημος five times, most of which refer to the wilderness sojourn, this fact does not exhaust his use of wilderness imagery and themes. He is interested in the exodus as well and merges both into one grand image of redemption.[24] It is in an exodus context that John's Gospel most frequently mentions the wilderness.[25] However, for the purposes of this study, I will use "wilderness" according to the previous working definition, reflecting the narratives of the forty-year sojourn of Israel; this is John's primary use of the term.

My claim in this study is that John's Gospel connects Jesus to the Pentateuch's wilderness traditions more explicitly than do the Synoptics.[26] As the wilderness was central in Israel's history,[27] so it is also in John's Gospel. Images such as the tabernacle (1:14),[28] the uplifted serpent (3:14), manna (6:35, 48–51), living water (4:7–15; 7:37–39), and others are all rooted in the Pentateuch's wilderness narratives. These wilderness events are significant in John's Gospel, first, because they recall God's redemptive activity in the first exodus, and second, they bring the messianic community through analogous experiences in the second exodus. As T. F. Glasson observes, "For the people of Israel, the exodus was not only the outstanding deliverance of the past and the beginning of the national history, but it became a symbol and pledge of the expected deliverance of the future. The messianic time was thus in part modeled upon the exodus and its sequel."[29] Andrew Brunson summarizes, "John invites his readers to interpret Jesus' ministry and works in the light of the first exodus by weaving exodus allusions and symbols

---

observing the Law (1QS 8:13–16).

24. Brunson, *Psalm 118*, 156–63; Enz, "Literary Type," 208–15; Reim, *Jochanan*, 106–07; Smith, "Exodus Typology," 329–42. On the exodus motif in all four Gospels, see Kline, *Biblical Authority*, 181–95. On exodus typology in the NT generally, see Daniélou, "La Typologie," 131–43.

25. Keener, *John*, 1:439.

26. Jones, "Wilderness," 5:852. Although, see Mauser, *Christ in the Wilderness*; Moessner, "Good News," 1–34; Stegner, "Wilderness and Testing," 18–27.

27. Keener, *John*, 1:438.

28. Carson, *John*, 127, argues that the "tabernacling" (ἐσκήνωσιν) of the Word (1:14) alludes to the tabernacle (Exod 25:8–9) but also reserves the option of it alluding to the "tent of meeting" (Exod 33:7). The LXX uses σκηνή for both. The result is the same as Carson notes, "God has chosen to dwell amongst his people in a yet more personal way, in the Word-become-flesh" (ibid., 127). It is important here to recognize that John 1:14 is an allusion to the wilderness in John's Gospel although the term ἔρημος is absent.

29. Glasson, *Moses*, 15–16.

throughout the Gospel."[30] John's Gospel announces via the φωνή βοῶντος ἐν τῇ ἐρήμῳ (1:23) that the second exodus has begun.

DEFINING SIGNS

At its core, a sign (אות, σημεῖον) stands for something else or points to something other than itself. In the OT it may be an action, event, ritual, or object.[31] In the Pentateuch, Exodus gives prominence to signs that is unmatched elsewhere in the OT. Signs, or "signs and wonders" (אותת ומפתים, Exod 7:3), play a significant role in the narrative of God's deliverance of Israel from Egyptian slavery.[32] Although Moses is the mediator through whom God performed "signs," they ultimately point to God himself. While the exodus context emphasizes what the NIV translates as "miraculous signs" (Exod 4:8, 17, 28; 7:3; 10:1; Deut 4:34; 6:22; 7:19; 26:8; 29:3; 34:11), this by no means exhausts the use of אותת in the OT.[33] Symbolic, non-miraculous actions of certain prophets are also signs.[34] It is significant for the present study that the LXX uses σημεῖον to translate אות in most cases.[35] Even more to the point is the fact that this occurs consistently in the exodus narratives. Raymond E. Brown notes that God multiplied signs through Moses (Exod 10:1; Num 14:22; Deut 7:19); he also illustrates that Deuteronomy ends on a note of the "signs and wonders" (σημείοις καὶ τέρασιν) that Moses performed before Israel (Deut 34:10–11).[36] The exodus narratives of the LXX, especially the interpretive comments of Deut 8, emphasize the "signs" (σημεῖα) through which God delivered his people from Egyptian slavery. While Moses performed signs and wonders in the sight of the people, these signs and wonders ultimately pointed to God as their source (Exod 4:5; 8:19; 10:1–2; Num 14:11, 22; Deut 4:34; 6:22; 7:19; 11:3; 26:8).[37] In summary,

---

30. Brunson, *Psalm 118*, 157.
31. Tull, "Signs in the Old Testament," 5:254.
32. Ibid.
33. Tull provides a nice summary of the OT uses of "sign" providing examples of its diversity (ibid).
34. Köstenberger, "Seventh Johannine Sign," 87–103, esp. 90–91. For specific examples, see 1 Sam 2:34; 2 Kgs 19:29; 20:8, 9; 2 Chron 32:24; Ps 74:9; Isa 7:11, 14; 20:3; 38:7, 22; 44:24–25; 66:18–19; Ezek 4:3; 9:4, 6; 20:12; Sir 36:6.
35. Ibid., 90n6.
36. Brown, *John*, 1:529.
37. Reim, *Jochanan*, 139.

signs are theological (i.e., about God) more than they are anthropological (i.e., about Moses).[38]

Like the wilderness itself, one function of signs in the wilderness narratives is to test the faith of the people of God, to see whether or not they would have believing hearts that trust his power and presence through the forty-year sojourn in the wilderness (Deut 4:34; 8:2, 16). As mentioned earlier, God tested his people in the wilderness with miraculous signs and provisions in order to know whether their hearts were faithful. Granted, this is only one function among many of signs in the OT, but it is the one that will receive the most attention in this study.

The use of σημεῖον in the NT is as diverse as in the OT. Philppa Carter notes, "With some exceptions, where it means simply 'symbol' or 'mark,' a sign is an apparent indication of supernatural or divine presence and activity."[39] Thus, when applying to miracles, the NIV properly translates σημεῖα as "miraculous signs." Most notable is the virtual absence of the term in reference to Jesus' miracles in the Synoptics where the authors typically render them by δυνάμεις (NIV "miracles"). When the Synoptic authors speak of Jesus' "signs and wonders" (σημεῖα καὶ τέρατα), they often place them in the eschatological context of the close of the age when false messiahs and false prophets will perform σημεῖα μεγάλα καὶ τέρατα (Matt 24:24; cf. Mark 13:22).[40]

ΣΗΜΕΙΑ in John's Gospel

John's use of σημεῖον is in stark contrast to that of the Synoptics, and bears greater theological and christological weight in his Gospel.[41] This is John's favorite and most characteristic designation for a miracle.[42] Further, he

38. That signs ultimately point beyond Moses to God has been aptly stressed by Brunson, *Psalm 118*, 161–62.

39. Carter, "Signs in the New Testament," 5:252–54. Carter's entry is a good survey of the NT use of σημεῖον.

40. Ibid., 5:253. Carter however, does note Luke 23:8 when reporting Herod Antipas's desire to see Jesus perform a "sign" (σημεῖον) where one might expect to read δύναμις. Further, Carter mentions the σημεῖα καὶ τέρατα throughout Acts 1–15 (Acts 2:19–22, 43; 4:30; 5:12; 6:8; 7:36; 8:6, 13; 14:3; 15:12).

41. Ibid., 5:252. There will be more on the theological and christological implications of signs throughout this study.

42. Brown, *John*, 1:528. For a survey, see Morris, *Theology*, 242–43. Morris mentions that John's Gospel uses "signs" seventeen times, highlighting its importance (ibid., 242). Brown notes another word, ἔργα ("works"), is also used in reference to miracles in John. The term is used in a much wider context and even stands for the whole ministry of Jesus (Brown, *John*, 1:528). Carter, "Signs in the New Testament," 5:253, notes that

tends not to use σημεῖα καὶ τέρατα except in John 4:48, which may reflect his distrust of the marvelous element in the miracle at the expense of its christological significance.[43] John does not view Jesus as a miracle worker, but rather as the unique Son who performs signs as object lessons pointing to the Father. However, for John, σημεῖον is not limited to miracles for even statements can "signify" (σημαίνων) certain realities such as the manner in which both Jesus and Peter would die (12:33; 18:32; 21:19).[44] Further, symbolic events such as Jesus' cleaning of the temple (2:13–22) are also signs in conjunction with OT prophets.[45] Granted, σημεῖα does not always mean "miracles"; however, in John's Gospel it refers to the various miracles that Jesus performed.[46] Nevertheless, as Brown notes, every specific use of σημεῖον refers to a miraculous deed[47] and this is the primary use of the term in this study. However, it is not *simply* a miraculous deed as the term "sign" itself implies. Rudolf Bultmann's insight is helpful as he describes signs as pictures or symbols.[48] But of what are they pictures or symbols? It is imperative for this study to recognize that Johannine signs, which Jesus the Son performs, ultimately point to God the Father. As in the exodus narratives, so also in John: miraculous signs point beyond the deeds themselves to God who ultimately stands behind them. George Eldon Ladd states, "In John miracles are mighty works that authenticate the person and mission of Jesus and demonstrate the miracle-working presence of God in his words and deeds."[49] This is precisely what John means by "signs." As in the exodus, they signify not primarily marvelous deeds, but rather the power and presence of God on behalf of his people. As mentioned in chapter 1, the exodus context of σνμεῖα in the LXX is the foremost background to Johannine

---

the term is never used directly for a miracle of Jesus in the Synoptics. The phrase "signs and wonders" is used often in eschatological contexts. For more on John's use of σημεῖα and ἔργα, see de Jonge, *Stranger from Heaven*, 117–40.

43. Brown, *John*, 1:528.

44. Ibid.

45. Köstenberger, "Seventh Johannine Sign," 87–103. For more on the OT prophetic background to Johannine signs, see Barrett, *John*, 76; Schnackenburg, *John*, 1:527–28.

46. Thompson, "John," 182–200.

47. Brown, *John*, 1:528. Brown indicates that the uplifted serpent reference might be a candidate for a non-miraculous sign in John's Gospel (ibid., 528). The reference in John 3:14 is to LXX Num 21:9 where Moses sets the serpent on a σημεῖον. This study will argue that this is indeed a miraculous event, and John likely intended it to be understood that way by his readers who knew the wording of the LXX.

48. Bultmann, *Theology*, 2:44. However, Ridderbos, *John*, 113, argues that signs are not simply symbolic actions or parabolic stories, but actual miraculous events (i.e., grounded in history).

49. Ladd, *Theology*, 309.

signs.⁵⁰ So when the reader of John's Gospel reads about Jesus' σημεῖα, he is to think of God's σημεῖα in the exodus narratives of the Pentateuch. There is a christological function to Johannine miracles,⁵¹ but they also function theologically by pointing to God who ultimately stands behind them. When commenting on Jesus' ἔργα, which include his σημεῖα, C. K. Barrett illustrates the unmistakable connection between Jesus' works and those of God: "The miracles of Jesus are described as his works (ἔργα). As such, they are also the works of God himself; there is a complete continuity between the activity of Jesus and the activity of the Father (5:36; 9:3; 10:32, 37; 14:10)."⁵² In summary, the OT background to Johannine σημεῖα is that of the exodus narratives, which of course includes the wilderness narratives.

The close connection between signs in the exodus narratives and those in John's Gospel is evident in their testing function. As signs tested the faith of the wilderness generations (Deut 4:34; 8:2, 16), so also they test those who witness them in John's Gospel. John 6:6, Jesus' testing (πειράζων) of Philip, specifically draws this out while recalling the manna miracle of Israel's wilderness sojourn.⁵³ Therefore, considering this brief description of Johannine signs, a working definition for "sign" in this study is *a miraculous revelatory event performed by Jesus that tests people's faith by pointing beyond itself to God, who is its source.*

CONTEXTUAL FOCUS

Johannine scholars generally agree that John 3:14–15 alludes to the uplifted serpent narrative of Num 21:4–9.⁵⁴ At first glance, this seems to be the only

---

50. Brown, *John*, 1:529; Brunson, *Psalm 118*, 161. Ridderbos, *John*, 113, references the OT background for σημεῖα as well.

51. Barrett, *John*, 75.

52. Ibid. Barrett also points out the Stoic association of σημεῖα (ibid., 76). However true this may be, I hold the OT background to be primary in John's thought as well as that of his readers.

53. Anderson, *Christology*, 202. Anderson argues that this "testing" motif is prevalent throughout John 6 (pp. 107, 203). He also points out that the testing theme runs throughout the entire Gospel as well (ibid., 193).

54. Although Enz, "Literary Type," 210n7, maintains that John alludes to Exod 4:4 when Moses' staff becomes a serpent, he bases his view on the chronological difficulty of John placing the feeding of the 5,000 after the serpent incident, thus switching the OT chronology. However, that John's allusions to the exodus (or to Exodus, as Enz argues) are chronological is far from demonstrable (Hanson, *Prophetic Gospel*, 241–42). Further, Enz's view is difficult to reconcile given the numerous additional parallels between John's text and the narrative in Numbers. It should be noted there is no quotation here of the Numbers text, but rather an allusion to it. For this reason, John 3:14–15

obvious reference to a wilderness narrative in the entire pericope. However, John alludes to several other wilderness elements, especially from the wider wilderness context of Numbers, throughout the pericope that allow for certain parallels between Nicodemus and the wilderness generations. Of particular importance are Jesus' signs (σημεῖα), which Nicodemus readily recognizes. I will give special reference to the role of miraculous signs as tests of faith in the wilderness, thereby illuminating their function in John's Gospel. Signs in the OT wilderness narratives are either rejected or accepted as signifiers of God's protection and presence. This same phenomenon occurs throughout John where characters and crowds respond with either hard or soft hearts. My purpose, therefore, is to demonstrate that miraculous signs function in part as divine tests of faith in John's Gospel as in ancient Israel's wilderness experience (Deut 4:34; 8:2, 16).

OT Contextual Awareness of NT Authors

C. H. Dodd states that the Scripture that an author has in mind is not necessarily limited to the amount that he quotes.[55] Further, commenting on the NT's methodology of quoting the OT, he illustrates that the authors understood that particular verses or sentences served as "pointers" to the whole [OT] context rather than as isolated testimonies in and of themselves.[56] According to Dodd, the "governing intent" of an OT reference was to exploit the whole context, or "unit of reference," from which it was drawn.[57] Put differently, an OT quotation (and I would argue an allusion by analogy) serves as a window into the wider OT context rather than serving as an isolated proof text, detached from the wider context. While I do not believe every OT quotation or allusion in the NT can be exhaustively explained by an appeal to its wider OT context, I do believe it is valid for this study because, as I intend to show, there are several connection points (i.e., allusions and echoes) to Numbers in John 2:23—3:21. Simply put, a wilderness reading is warranted here because wilderness imagery pervades the entire pericope.

With that said, scholars do not universally accept Dodd's contention that biblical quotations in the NT often appeal to the wider OT context.

---

is omitted from books such as Dodd's *According to the Scriptures*, Freed's *Old Testament Quotations*, Schuchard's *Scripture Within Scripture,* and Menken's *Old Testament Quotations*.

55. Dodd, *According to the Scriptures,* 47n1.

56. Ibid., 126.

57. Ibid., 61, 132. Brunson, *Psalm 118,* 19–20 takes a similar approach in his intertextual study of Ps 118 in John. In essence, he demonstrates that although John formally quotes Ps 118 only once, the larger context of the psalm permeates the Gospel.

They hotly debate the degree to which NT authors appeal to the OT context of a quotation.[58] While the discussion of the OT context is tied most closely to formal citations, its application to allusions and echoes is not irrelevant. Because both deal with the use of an older source text by a newer primary text, I must address contextual concerns. Albert Sundberg argues against Dodd in favor of an atomistic use of the OT by the NT writers where the larger OT context was irrelevant to its use in the NT.[59] Similarly, Donald Juel states, "Christian interpreters were capable of abstracting a verse or a sentence from its literary context to make a point or to discover a new truth in it."[60] The implication is that the context of the OT verse is not connected to its appropriation in the NT. Sundberg illustrates the use of Isa 40:3 in John 1:23 as one example. Here, John the Baptist identifies himself as φωνή βοῶντος ἐν τῇ ἐρήμῳ. While ignoring the precise text form of the quotation,[61] Sundberg suggests that John's use of Isaiah serves *only* to highlight that John the Baptist preached in the wilderness, calling for repentance.[62] Further, its purpose is a rejection of the suspicion that John the Baptist was the Christ or Elijah.[63] I take no issue with the latter observation. The quotation is meant in part to distinguish between John the Baptist and Christ where the former points away from himself to the latter.[64] However, Sundberg's former observation is difficult to reconcile given John's second exodus emphasis that depends on the larger eschatological context of Isa 40. Therefore, the eschatological expectation of Isa 40 indicates that John's quotation of Isa 40:3 is inextricably connected to the OT context, and contrary to Sundberg, context matters in this case.[65] I choose to address John 1:23 mostly because Sundberg mentions it as an example in contrast to Dodd's thesis; it also happens to be extremely relevant for this study of the wilderness in John. However, this need not be the only instance where John is faithful to the OT context of his citations. As Bruce Schuchard notes after

---

58. Beale, *Revelation*, 81–86; Berding and Lunde, eds., *Three Views*; Marshall, "An Assessment," 1–21; Moyise, *Old Testament in Revelation*, 139–42.

59. Sundberg, "Response," 182–94. Sundberg, ibid., 189n34, does acknowledge that there are certain instances where the larger OT context may be in view for the NT authors (Ps 22:22 cited in Heb 2:12; Isa 53:7 cited in Rev 5:6, 12; 13:8; Isa 53:4–5 cited in 1 Pet 2:21–25).

60. Juel, *Messianic Exegesis*, 21.

61. For good discussions of the textual matters related to this verse, see Schuchard, *Scripture Within Scripture*, 1–15; Menken, *Textual Form*, 21–35.

62. Sundberg, "Response," 189. Italics added.

63. Ibid.

64. Reim, *Jochanan*, 5.

65. Reim expresses this same view (ibid.).

an exhaustive analysis of John's OT citations: "The Gospel of John evinces a consistently high regard for such [OT] contexts."[66]

Barnabas Lindars, in contrast to Dodd, argues for a lesser degree of contextual awareness on the part of the NT writers. He illustrates an apologetic use of the OT where the NT authors compile and adapt OT proof texts when it suits the purpose of proving that Christ is the fulfillment of the promises of God.[67] For Lindars, the NT writers do not take an OT book or passage and ask, "What does this mean?" Instead, they use the OT texts in an ad hoc way as it suits their apologetic purposes.[68] Dodd sees these proof texts, along with their OT contexts, as testimonies or collections of texts, standing behind the NT authors' uses of the Old. The first Christians, in their attempts to work out the meaning of the redemptive work of Christ, thought through the OT proof texts in light of their contexts.[69] However, for Lindars, this is much less about an appeal to the larger OT context as a foundation for meaning, and more about the prophetic nature of Scripture itself. Since the NT writers believed that Christ was the fulfillment of all of Israel's Scriptures, they appealed to OT texts with less concern for contextual meaning and more from a christological conviction regarding the nature of Scripture (John 5:39).[70] Because of the prophetic nature of Scripture itself, they tended to place more concern on contemporary application than on original context. Put differently, a text's ultimate meaning is found in its christological application, which is the natural result of its prophetic nature as sacred Scripture. Therefore, when a NT writer, like John, shows Jesus to be the fulfiller of events in the wilderness, it means that he treats the Pentateuch *as a whole* as prophecy.[71] The OT prophetically points to the New; therefore, this prophetic property of the OT allows the NT authors to use whatever portion for their purposes. Such proof-texting, according to Lindars, is not altogether arbitrary, and the OT contexts are not irrelevant to a verse's appropriation in the New.[72] Nonetheless, according to Lindars, appeal to the larger context is secondary to contemporary application. Steve Moyise furthers this discussion in his book, *Evoking Scripture*, noting that at times NT authors "evoke" the surrounding context of a quotation while at

---

66. Schuchard, *Scripture Within Scripture*, 152.
67. Lindars, "Place of the Old Testament," 59–66.
68. Ibid., 64.
69. Lindars, *Apologetic*, 14.
70. McCartney, "New Testament's Use of the Old Testament," 101–16.
71. Lindars, *Apologetic*, 274–75. Italics added. As Lindars notes, "The entire record of God's dealings with Israel is a *Heilsgeschichte*" (ibid., 275).
72. Ibid., 19.

other times they do not. Mark 1:2–3 evidences the former when citing Isa 40:3 ("The voice of one crying in the wilderness"), which introduces Mark's new exodus theme. Mark's placement of the citation at the beginning of his Gospel suggests a pervasive and ongoing emphasis throughout the remainder of his Gospel.[73] Conversely, according to Moyise, Paul evidences the latter in Rom 2:24 when quoting Isa 52:5 ("The name of God is blasphemed among the Gentiles because of you"), where the verse was part of a salvation oracle in Isaiah; whereas, Paul uses it as a judgment oracle in Romans.[74] All in all, the extent to which a NT citation of the OT evokes the larger context is best studied on a case-by-case basis. This very brief discussion of contextuality in NT references to the OT is enough to illustrate that the debate will continue. In the final analysis, it may be best to confess with Greg Beale that the NT writers have varying degrees of contextual awareness when they refer to an OT passage.[75]

John's uplifted serpent allusion, then, serves as an invitation to read the whole Nicodemus pericope (3:1–21)[76] against the wider OT background of Israel's wilderness experience. There is a clear clue in the text that the wider wilderness context is in view, for not only does John mention that Moses lifted up the serpent, but also that this event occurred ἐν τῇ ἐρήμῳ (3:14). Although Ulrich Mauser, as stated previously, does not see this phrase as significant and argues that it should not be stressed,[77] others have under-

---

73. Moyise, *Evoking Scripture*, 6–20.

74. Ibid., 33–48.

75. Beale, *What We Worship*, 31.

76. For more on the literary arrangement of John 3, see Moloney, *Text and Context*, 43–44. Based on how scholars tend to organize their commentaries, they generally illustrate that Jesus' encounter with Nicodemus runs from 3:1–21, and that a new, although not unrelated, thought appears at 3:22–36. For example, Ashton, *Understanding*, 277, notes that the section beginning at v. 22 is clearly marked. Thus, the Nicodemus pericope, which includes 3:1–21 (although 2:23–25 thematically leads into it) and 3:22–36, encompasses a new section with a different emphasis—the baptizing ministries of John the Baptist and Jesus. John's "after these things" (μετὰ ταῦτα, 3:22) is here taken not only as a chronological marker, but also as a shift away from the Nicodemus pericope. As Barrett, *John*, 220, comments on μετὰ ταῦτα: "The previous incident is now closed." Mendner, "Nikodemus," 293–323, argues that the authentic setting for the Nicodemus dialogue is ch. 7, where Nicodemus takes a front and center role at the Sanhedrin meeting. The section composed of vv. 22–36 is also fraught with rearrangement theories. See Brown, *John*, 1:153–55, for a discussion of these and others. Nevertheless, as Keener notes, these fail to reach consensus (*John*, 1:575n384). On rearrangement theories in John's Gospel, it is difficult to do better than Bryant and Krause, *John*, 102: "Possible displacement in John's texts have been discussed all through this century, but the discussion never advanced beyond imaginative guesswork, and the new arrangements never seem to improve the meaning of the texts."

77. Mauser, *Christ in the Wilderness*, 76.

stood the reference to the contrary. For example, Craig Keener notes that John probably mined the wider OT wilderness context for information other than the uplifted serpent: the account of the well in the wilderness that follows in Num 21:16–18 may inform the story about the Samaritan woman at the well (John 4:1–26).[78] Where Jesus fulfilled the serpent's role from Num 21:8–9, he now fulfills the role of the well from 21:16–18.[79] This may be an instance where John shows knowledge of the Hebrew text. For example, the "living water" (John 4:10) that Jesus claims to provide will become a well of water ἅλλομαι ("welling up" ESV) to eternal life (4:14). While Num 21:16–18 LXX makes no mention of the well welling or springing up, the MT has the Israelites singing, עלי באר ("Spring up, O well!"). An intertextual relationship between these two texts cannot be ruled out; however, well imagery is abundant throughout the OT and an explicit connection to the well of Num 21:16–18 remains uncertain.[80]

What is most important to note here is that the wider wilderness context of Numbers illuminates John's repeated references to its narratives throughout his Gospel. As indicated previously, the appeal to the wider OT context has become commonplace in NT studies, especially when dealing with OT quotations and allusions. As Moyise observes, many scholars now realize that a text cannot be studied in isolation because it belongs to a web of texts that are present whenever a text is read or studied.[81] Thus, NT quotations and allusions often (but not always) "evoke" the larger scriptural framework of their original literary context. Richard Hays makes this point when describing OT allusions in the writings of Paul. When text B (NT text or "primary text") alludes to text A (OT text or "precursor text"), there is a broad interplay that encompasses aspects of text A beyond those explicitly echoed.[82] The singular quote or allusion is not all there is in either context. Rather, both literary contexts reverberate off each other, illuminating them as wholes rather than isolated proof texts.

To mention one instance beyond our current text of what Hays calls *metalepsis*, the resonance of echoes within whole contexts, the wider wilderness context is in view in John 6:31: οἱ πατέρες ἡμῶν τὸ μάννα ἔφαγον ἐν τῇ ἐρήμῳ, καθώς ἐστιν γεγραμμένον· ἄρτον ἐκ τοῦ οὐρανοῦ ἔδωκεν

78. Keener, *John*, 1:563–64.
79. Ibid., 1:590–91.
80. Ibid. Glasson, *Moses*, 55–56, is more certain of the connection.
81. Moyise, "Intertextuality," 14–41
82. Hays, *Echoes of Scripture*, 20. Hays follows Hollander in describing this phenomenon as *metalepsis*—when a literary echo links the text in which it occurs to an earlier text, the figurative effect of the echo can lie in the unstated or suppressed points of resonance between the two texts. For Hollander's use, see Hollander, *Figure of Echo*.

αὐτοῖς φαγεῖν ("Our ancestors ate the manna in the wilderness, just as it has been written: 'He gave to them bread from heaven to eat'"). The specific source of the quotation, governed by a typical Johannine quotation formula (γεγραμμένον, 2:17; 6:31, 45; 10:34; 12:14), is unclear (Ps 77:24 LXX is the likeliest candidate). However, John 6 as a whole draws on the traditions found in Exod 16, Num 14, and Ps 78.[83] Therefore, OT quotations and allusions in the NT exist not in isolation, and may be examined in light of their wider original contexts in an effort to illuminate their uses in the NT. Granted, scholars may judge the results consistent or inconsistent with the OT context, but this does not change the fact that text A (OT text) does not exist in isolation any more than text B (NT text). Therefore, John's uplifted serpent reference is an invitation to read the Nicodemus pericope against the wider wilderness background of its original context in Numbers.

Wilderness Typology

Perhaps it is not an "either/or" regarding the contextual use of the OT in the New, but a question of how the two contexts relate.[84] This is especially true with John's Gospel given its allusive nature. Old Testament imagery and symbols saturate the Gospel more than quotations. I have already noted many of these images and symbols. Scholars often characterize many of John's OT symbols as typological.[85] I will discuss typology further when I analyze the uplifted serpent of John 3:14. For now, it is necessary to lay out the way John employs the OT wilderness motif in his Gospel; that is, typologically. While his use of Israel's Scriptures cannot be forced into one interpretive scheme, whether it be allegory, typology, midrash, etc., his use of typology is particularly noteworthy. His typological emphases include, among others, Jesus as the true Temple (2:21), the antitype of the bronze serpent (3:14-15), the true manna (6:35, 50-51), the true water-giving rock (7:37-39), the true fiery pillar (8:12), the eschatological Moses (6:14), the new Torah (5:39; 13:34), and the true paschal sacrifice (1:29).[86] John employs each of these typological occurrences in service to his Christology where Christ stands as their final fulfillment in the messianic era. Scholars

83. Lieu, "Narrative Analysis," 144–63.

84. Moyise, "Out of Context?" 133–43.

85. Enz, "Literary Type," 208–15; Hanson, *Prophetic Gospel*, 238–39. Smith, "Exodus Typology," 329–42; Daniélou, "La Typologie," 138–39. However, Reim, *Jochanan*, 266–68, finds typology clearly at work only in John 3:14, 6:35–59, and 7:37–39.

86. Longenecker, *Biblical Exegesis*, 136. Additional examples are proposed in Brunson, *Psalm 118*, 156–59; Enz, "Literary Type," 208–15; Hanson, *Prophetic Gospel*, 238–39; Smith, "Exodus Typology," 329–42.

have proposed various definitions for typology. "Typology is the interpretation of earlier events, persons, and institutions in biblical history which become proleptic entities, or 'types,' anticipating later events, persons, and institutions, which are the antitypes."[87] I. Howard Marshall is more detailed:

> Typology may be defined as the study which traces parallels or correspondences between incidents recorded in the OT and their counterparts in the NT, such that the latter can be seen to resemble the former in notable respects and yet to go beyond them. Redemption in Christ shows an analogy to the deliverance of Israel from Egypt but goes beyond it. Thus, we see that God works on the same principles in both eras. The OT incident can thus be said to point forward to the NT one, but it does not lose its own significance in and for its own time.[88]

Typology is redemptive-historical throughout Scripture and involves the unfolding of God's redemptive purposes linearly through history. History in the Bible is important for typology precisely because it has a goal and is not circular.[89] Foundational for typology is the prophetic view of history.[90] The biblical assumption regarding history is that God is taking it somewhere; he has a goal for history. Thus, persons, places, institutions, and events become redemptive-historical as God employs them in his plan of salvation. Events such as the exodus (which includes the wilderness sojourn) not only serve God's immediate purpose (i.e., to redeem Israel from Egyptian bondage), but also anticipate his future purpose in a fuller salvific sense. This fuller salvific sense is essential for typology because the antitype (NT fulfillment) must be greater than the type (OT person, place, event, or institution).[91] Typology is not about the repetition of earlier events in later times, but instead points to the superlative character of the later event. Günter Reim notes that typology in John is not the return of the same thing that happened in an earlier time in a later time, but that what happened in the earlier time points to the real event in Christ's time.[92] There is a strong sense of "lesser to greater"

---

87. McCartney and Clayton, *Reader*, 162–63. Typological discussions can be quite complex. McCartney and Clayton are helpful both in their clarity and in concision (ibid., 163–74). The classic text on typology is Goppelt, *Typos*. See also, Ellis, "Biblical Interpretation," 691–725; Evans, "Typology," 862–66; Elliott, "Typology," 5:692.

88. Marshall, "An Assessment," 16.

89. McCartney and Clayton, *Reader*, 163.

90. Lindars, *Apologetic*, 274.

91. McCartney and Clayton, *Reader*, 167.

92. Reim, *Jochanan*, 268. Typology is profoundly christological for Reim. He holds that specifically in John's Gospel, typological interpretation is not about comparing two equal events, persons, or institutions, but rather typology highlights the "completely

fulfillment in John's use of typology. What God had done in the past was an indication of his greater deeds in the future.[93] As Dan McCartney and Charles Clayton explain, "When Israel faced exile, the hope of deliverance from exile was cast in the language of the exodus. And the hope for a final redemptive work of God was also cast in this language."[94] For exilic Israel, the exodus served not only as a reminder of God's redemption in the past, but also anticipated a greater and more complete redemption in the future messianic age by employing similar language. Even more to the point, God's future redemption was not only cast in similar language as the exodus, but there was also an expectation of similar deeds as those of the exodus. Exilic Israel not only believed that deliverance was certain but that it would also take a similar form of exodus deliverance.[95] Jean Daniélou observes that Judaism in the time of Christ held the same eschatological expectation as the prophetic tradition, and represents the time of salvation with terms borrowed from the exodus: Moses represents the Messiah; Israel will be nourished as at the time of exodus with manna and living water; salvation will take place in the spring, like the Passover.[96] The second exodus gives fuller expression to the persons, events, and institutions of the first. Therefore, the messianic age follows a similar pattern as the redemptive events of the past.[97] Simply stated, the language and imagery are consistent because there is a certain expectation that God will do similar, although greater, things in the future.

John is deeply familiar with typological expressions of redemptive-history, especially those of the Pentateuch.[98] Redemptive-historical events of the OT are like the backcloth in a play for John's Gospel.[99] His second exodus imagery is a clear indication of his typological interpretation of redemptive motifs in Israel's Scriptures. The wilderness serves as a type of a redemptive-

---

different kind" (*die vollkomene Andersartigkeit*) of the antitype, Christ. Daniélou, "La Typologie," 131, 135, 143, expresses this same sentiment.

93. McCartney and Clayton, *Reader*, 163. Daniélou, "La Typologie," 132, suggests that the OT is both memorial and prophecy.

94. McCartney and Clayton, *Reader*, 163.

95. Marsh, *Fulness of Time*, 62.

96. Daniélou, "La Typologie," 134–35.

97. Hanson, *Prophetic Gospel*, 240.

98. Lindars, *Apologetic*, 274.

99. Hanson, *Prophetic Gospel*, 240. Hanson helpfully clarifies that OT redemptive-historical events in John do not follow the chronological order of the OT (ibid., 241). He writes, "There is, then, no *scheme* of salvation history lying behind the Gospel, but it is impossible to deny that salvation history is in the background throughout" (ibid., 242).

historical event in John as he shows Jesus to be the fulfiller of events in the wilderness.[100] Not only John, but other writers of the NT also repeatedly reference the wilderness wanderings as a type of the Christian life.[101] For example, Paul expresses a typological correspondence between the church and Israel's wilderness generation.[102] He exhorts the church in Corinth to heed the warning of Israel's history in the wilderness where they were tempted by idolatry, sexual immorality, and grumbling (1 Cor 10:1–13). Israel's history in the wilderness serves, ultimately, as "types" or "examples" (τύποι, τυπικῶς vv. 6, 11 respectively) for the later church. Again, he encourages the Corinthians to spread their wealth to the believers in Jerusalem, using the manna in the wilderness as his illustration (2 Cor 8:8–15). Paul quotes Exod 16:18 in 2 Cor 8:15: "As it is written, 'Whoever gathered much had nothing left over, and whoever gathered little had no lack'" (ESV). The writer of Hebrews warns the church against unbelief and hardness of heart by the use of Israel's wanderings in the wilderness (Heb 3:7–19). Revelation, too, has its own wilderness motif placed within a redemptive-historical paradigm (Rev 12:5–6, 14). The woman flees into the wilderness where God has prepared for her a place of safety from the dragon.[103] There is abundant evidence that early Christians saw themselves as experiencing a second exodus and for whom Jesus fulfilled multiple typological roles, including, but not limited to, leading them through the wilderness.[104] Therefore, the messianic community saw itself as a wilderness community. The Gospel of John is thus consistent with other NT works by viewing Israel's wilderness experience typologically through the lens of redemptive-history. This methodological approach encapsulates much, though not all, of the Fourth Gospel's use of Israel's Scriptures.

---

100. Lindars, *Apologetic*, 274–75.

101. Glasson, *Moses*, 10.

102. Hays, *Echoes of Scripture*, 87–94.

103. For a good discussion of Revelation's wilderness motif, see Beale, *Revelation*, 639–46.

104. Marsh, *Fulness of Time*, 137–38 describes the church as a wilderness community where the sacraments of baptism and communion served as reenactments of the exodus. As Israel was baptized into Moses in the Red Sea during the exodus, Christians are baptized into Christ during the second exodus. As the Israelites ate the Passover, so Christians eat their own Passover-type meal. Daniélou, "La Typologie," 131–43, sees a similar sacramental angle.

INTERTEXTUALITY

That OT symbolism, themes, and motifs saturate John's Gospel is without question. Scholars debate *how* John uses the Scriptures of Israel, not *that* he uses them. While this dissertation is not solely focused on the complexity of John's methodological use(s) of Israel's Scriptures, the fact that John's Gospel is "richly allusive"[105] to them is a springboard for an intertextual study such as this one. The profundity with which John uses the Scriptures has not gone unnoticed. Whether the discussion centers on quotation formulas, typology, the replacement motif, or allusions,[106] John's Gospel is fruitful territory for an intertextual dialogue with the OT. B. F. Westcott goes so far as to say, "The writer of the Fourth Gospel is penetrated throughout—more penetrated perhaps than any other writer of the New Testament—with the spirit of the Old."[107] Similarly, C. K. Barrett draws attention to the fact that whereas John's Gospel contains fewer direct quotations of the OT than the Synoptics, it is more concerned with the sense and the whole of the OT more than with isolated proof texts.[108] Brevard Childs mounts a similar case when he states that John "used Old Testament themes to structure his Gospel which functions, as it were, below the surface of the text."[109] However, it is not as if John is unconcerned with proof texts. To the contrary, he retains the practice while illustrating that what happened to Jesus—his rejection and eventual crucifixion—was in accordance with the divine will as expressed in Israel's Scriptures.[110] The idea here is that John's Gospel is in a broad intertextual dialogue with the OT by utilizing symbols and motifs more than precise quotations. The reader of John's Gospel is struck not by a large number of proof texts or massive quantities of quotation formulas,

---

105. Moyise, *Old Testament in the New*, 71.

106. Carson discusses each of these as different ways John uses the OT in "John and the Johannine Epistles," 245–64.

107. Westcott, *John*, LXIX.

108. Barrett, "Old Testament," 155–69. For John's use of the OT, see, Beasley-Murray, *John*, LIX–LX; Bernard, *John*, 1:CXLVII–CLVI; Beutler, "The Use of Scripture," 147–62; Brown, *Introduction*, 132–38; Brown, *John*, 1:LIX–XI; Brunson, *Psalm 118*, 141–53; Carson, "John and the Johannine Epistles," 245–64; Carter, *Storyteller*, 131–40; Childs, *Biblical Theology*, 284–86; Hanson, *Prophetic Gospel*; Keener, *John*, 1:172–74; Köstenberger, *Theology*, 299–310; Moyise, *Jesus and Scripture*, 67–78; Reim, *Jochanan*; Smith, *Theology*, 76–77. The Synoptics are not simply concerned with proof texts and quotations, but also contain many allusions to Israel's Scriptures. Hays, "Canonical Matrix," 53–75, illustrates that all four canonical Gospels developed within the "matrix" of Israel's Scriptures.

109. Childs, *Biblical Theology*, 285.

110. Lincoln, *John*, 79.

but by the constant and colorful OT threads that have been woven into the fabric of the text.

In Hays's view, John understands Israel's Scriptures as a vast matrix of symbols; a web of signifiers pointing to Jesus.[111] Because of the penetrating spirit of the OT in the Gospel, its Jewishness has become a fruitful area of investigation in Johannine studies.[112] Gary Burge records Israel Abrahams's (1858–1925) comment in 1924 that to Jews (himself an orthodox Jew and Rabbinics scholar), John's Gospel is the "most Jewish of the four!"[113] Burge goes on to note the Gospel's "numerous allusions" to the OT and its "Semitic hints."[114] Motifs such as ἐν ἀρχῇ, wisdom, tabernacle, voice in the wilderness, Jacob's ladder, Son of Man, temple, Holy Spirit, serpent in the wilderness, Jacob's well, living water, manna, Moses, Jewish feasts, Sabbath, Abraham, shepherd and his sheep, vine and the branches, the law, ἐγώ εἰμί, and others have biblical roots. These images inform John's Christology as Jesus is the fulfillment of Israel's Scriptures, cultic institutions, and symbols. Such OT allusions and echoes are fertile ground for intertextual studies. Hays gives readers of the four Gospels a task: to trace the lines of intertextual linkage between the gospel stories and their OT precursors.[115] The task I undertake in this study is tracing the lines of intertextual linkage between John 2:23—3:21 and the wilderness narratives in the book of Numbers. John's allusion to the uplifted serpent (3:14) of Num 21:8–9 is the window through which to look at the wider wilderness context of Numbers for an illuminating intertextual interaction with the Johannine text, portraying

---

111. Hays, "Canonical Matrix," 72. Moyise, "Intertextuality," 15–16, echoes Hays's thought on the "matrix" of Scripture. Basically, a text cannot be read in isolation because it belongs to a web of texts (i.e., a canon of Scripture) which are present whenever it is read or studied.

112. For an overview of some of the more salient issues, see Scholtissek, "Johannine Gospel," 462–65. For a more penetrating discussion, see Pryor, *Covenant People*, 117–42.

113. Burge, *Interpreting the Gospel of John*, 20.

114. Ibid.

115. Hays, "Canonical Matrix," 72. The book of Revelation is ideal for an intertextual analysis as well. Not to draw too close a connection between it and John's Gospel, but an analogy exists in their allusive use(s) of the OT. As Hanson, *Prophetic Gospel*, 247, notes, "John the Divine never openly quotes Scripture, but his work is soaked in Scripture." Further, Moyise, "Intertextuality and Historical Approaches," 25–32, writes, "The Apocalypse was an ideal text to explore notions of intertextuality because it does not quote Scripture but utilizes its language and imagery for a variety of rhetorical purposes." This can almost equally be said of John's Gospel. The analogy is not exact, of course, because Revelation does not quote Scripture, whereas John does. Nonetheless, allusions and imagery are far more prevalent than quotations, which I believe allows the analogy to stand.

miraculous signs as tests of faith. As I continue defining terms, I now turn to the "art" of intertextuality.[116]

Julia Kristeva first introduced *intertextualité*, the interconnections among "texts," in 1969 while interacting with the work of Russian theorist Mikhail Bakhtin.[117] Kristeva's work is rooted in semiotics—systems of signs or codes that make up texts.[118] For Kristeva, "text" is the name for any sign complex.[119] This is not primarily a written piece of communication, but rather what makes up culture, the "general text." Hays summarizes Kristeva's effect on literary criticism with the following: "Kristeva's approach broadened the notion of 'text' to include all aspects of cultural significance—indeed, the distinction between 'text' and 'culture' was dissolved altogether."[120]

While acknowledging Kristeva's insights, I use the term "text" in this study in a narrower literary manner as a written piece of communication. However, I also see text in a broader phenomenological way as a living and lasting communicative act. The text is not simply the physical document written in the past; it continues to be living and active in the present (and presumably in future). The text has lasting effects because it is intended to reach beyond the author to an audience. That is, the text as a communicative act extends beyond the past of the author and reaches into the present of the reader. Therefore, in contrast to Kristeva, the text cannot be dismissed as an endless network of arbitrary signs (semiotics) but instead *is* and *preserves* a communicative act.[121]

Due in part to the influence of Childs's "canonical approach," which stresses the intertextual connection of canonical texts, it has become commonplace to read every biblical writing in light of every other biblical writing

---

116. Beale recognizes that intertextuality, specifically the weighing of allusions and echoes, is not an exact science. See Beale, *What We Worship*, 25. Hays also makes this same point in *Conversion of the Imagination*, 30. Similarly, Beetham, *Echoes of Scripture in Colossians*, 35.

117. Moyise, "Intertextuality and Historical Approaches," 23. See also, Bakhtin, *Dialogic Imagination*.

118. Moyise, "Intertextuality and Historical Approaches," 23. For a detailed presentation of structural semiotics according to Kristeva, see Kristeva, "System," 24–33; Kristeva, "Word," 34–61; Kristeva, "Symbol," 62–73; Kristeva, "Semiotics," 74–88; Patte, "Structural Criticism," 183–200.

119. Alkier, "Semiotics," 3–21. Alkier's article is an excellent historical overview of intertextuality as stemming from semiotics. For a shorter, but similar treatment, see O'Day, "Intertextuality," 155–57. For intertextuality in biblical studies as opposed to that of structuralism semiotics, see Wall, "Intertextuality, Biblical," 541–51.

120. Hays, forward to the English edition of *Reading the Bible Intertextually*, XIII.

121. For more on text as communicative act, see Vanhoozer, *Is There a Meaning in This Text?*

as the texts dialogue with each other.[122] Intertextuality, then, stresses the inherent dialogical communication present among *written* texts. Bakhtin's dialogism, therefore, is applied at the diachronic literary level where written texts dialogue with each other. They are not isolated, but rather are parts of larger wholes composed of other texts. As Moyise notes, "Because no text is an island . . . it cannot be understood in isolation. It can only be understood as part of a web or matrix of other texts, themselves only to be understood in the light of other texts."[123] Therefore, all communication, whether written or oral, is understood as a communicative act because it builds on presuppositions and prior learning.

Intertextuality has come a long way since Kristeva introduced the concept to literary criticism in 1969. The term is used so broadly, especially in today's biblical studies climate, it is difficult to know what one means when she says it. Intertextuality is both descriptive as a property of texts (i.e., their interconnectedness) and prescriptive as a "method" of exegesis. In biblical studies, the term covers anything from direct citations of the OT in the NT to faint "echoes," barely audible to anyone except the practitioner. It has become an umbrella term referring to various types of textual linkage and even branches into different categories of itself. Moyise proposes three such categories to help clarify what scholars mean by the term: (1) intertextual echo, (2) dialogical intertextuality, and (3) postmodern intertextuality.[124] The first category, intertextual echo, is the preferred method of this study.

The present intertextual analysis will interact with the method most closely associated with Richard Hays. Although Hays, with his *Echoes of Scripture in the Letters of Paul* (1989), brought intertextuality to the fore in biblical studies, many have undertaken similar pursuits and built on his work.[125] Hays's work is somewhat related to Bakhtin's dialogism although Hays is more concerned with the intertextual matrix of Scripture than with culture:

---

122. Alkier, "Semiotics," 12. For Childs's "canonical approach," see Barton, *Reading the Old Testament*, 77–103; Callaway, "Canonical Criticism," 142–55; Childs, *Introduction to the Old Testament*; Childs, *Biblical Theology*; Childs, *New Testament as Canon*; Yarchin, *Biblical Interpretation*, 307–19.

123. Moyise, "Intertextuality and Historical Approaches," 23.

124. Moyise, "The Study of the OT in the NT," 14–41.

125. Beale, *What We Worship*, 22–35; Beetham, *Echoes of Scripture in Colossians*; Wagner, *Heralds of the Good News*; Watson, *Hermeneutics of Faith*. For works on intertextuality similar to, but independent of Hays, see Boyarin, *Intertextuality and the Reading of Midrash*; Fishbane, *Biblical Interpretation in Ancient Israel*; Fishbane, "Inner-Biblical Exegesis," 3–21; For interactions with and critiques of Hays's methodology in *Echoes of Scripture*, see Evans and Sanders, eds., *Paul and the Scriptures of Israel*, 42–96.

In Hays's usage, "intertextuality" refers to the *diachronic* influence of specific precursor texts on an author's work, not as in the work of R. Barthes, J. Kristeva, and their followers, to the *synchronic* semiotic matrix within which a text "converses" with all other "texts," written and unwritten, available in a culture."[126]

Hays's work is scripturally focused for he finds Paul "wrestling" with the same great precursor text—Israel's Scriptures.[127] Portions of the earlier Scriptures appear in Paul's letters, not only in the form of quotations but also in more subtle allusions and echoes. As Francis Watson notes, "Intertextuality becomes explicit in scriptural citation but is not to be reduced to it."[128] This is where intertextuality in John's Gospel is fertile ground for research: its allusive use of the OT. Although there are some differences between Paul's and John's use of Scripture, there is nonetheless a similarity in their pervasive use of scriptural allusions and echoes. As Paul's letters are soaked in Scripture and ideal for intertextual analyses, so too is John's Gospel. Granted, Paul makes more frequent use of formal citations than John, but they both are richly allusive in their uses of Israel's Scriptures.

Hays's method is perhaps best known for its seven criteria used to identify intertextual allusions and echoes.[129] They are not meant to be scientific, but instead pointers to help evaluate the plausibility of an allusion or echo. In Hays's own words, they are "modestly useful rules of thumb."[130] Admittedly, Hays's research focuses on intertextuality within the Pauline corpus, not the Johannine; nevertheless, scholars frequently apply his criteria to Johannine studies as well.[131] In an effort to avoid applying each of Hays's seven criteria in a mechanical fashion so as to validate every proposed allusion and echo, something not even Hays himself does,[132] I, too, will not treat them as a checklist. Instead, as with Hays, the criteria serve as a base

---

126. Wagner, *Heralds of the Good News*, 9n35.

127. Hays, *Echoes of Scripture*, 14.

128. Watson, *Hermeneutics of Faith*, 40n23.

129. Hays, *Echoes of Scripture*, 29–32. Hays's seven tests for identifying allusions and echoes are 1) Availability, 2) Volume, 3) Recurrence, 4) Thematic Coherence, 5) Historical Plausibility, 6) History of Interpretation, and 7) Satisfaction. For a recent refinement of Haysian criteria, see Beetham, *Echoes of Scripture in Colossians*, 27–35.

130. Hays, *Conversion of the Imagination*, 34.

131. Brawley, "Absent Complement," 427–43; Brunson, *Psalm 118*, 14–16; Daly-Denton, *David in the Fourth Gospel*, 11; Hägerland, "Power of Prophecy," 84–103; Köstenberger, "John," 420–21; Manning, *Echoes of a Prophet*, 8–14; Moyise, "Study of the OT in the NT," 26–37; Moyise, *Revelation*, 20–21, 108–38; Thomas, "Healing," 23–39.

132. Hays, *Echoes of Scripture*, 29. I will, however, subject each allusion and echo I propose to Hays's criteria in an effort to be as objective as possible.

for my own intertextual exegesis by providing a foundation for the proposed reading. By an intertextual method similar to that of Hays, this study will highlight allusions and echoes of the wilderness narratives of Numbers in John 2:23—3:21. I now turn to defining "allusions" and "echoes" for this study.

Allusions and Echoes

John, when compared with the Synoptics, has relatively few direct quotations of the OT. In contrast, allusions are the main type of reference to the OT in his Gospel.[133] Identifying allusions and echoes is less certain than identifying quotations. There may be a word or phrase from the precursor text (OT text) embedded in the primary text (NT text), or there may simply be a thematic link without any explicit verbal connections. One of the more popular aspects of Hays's intertextual method involves identifying allusions and echoes of the precursor text in the primary text. His seven criteria allow for a modest evaluation of the weight of each allusion and echo in a given text. Without Hays's criteria, the result can easily lead to eisegetical madness where scholars identify allusions and echoes to their own fancy with little regard for demonstrable exegesis. The current study aims for more probable demonstration.[134] While Michael Fishbane's research has been on inner-biblical exegesis within the HB, his appeal for an investigative-analytical approach applies across the spectrum of intertextual studies.[135] Similarly, Samuel Sandmel's caution in 1962 against "parallelomania" still rings loudly and clearly today.[136] Hays's criteria, as helpful as they are in minimizing rampant, personal readings, are only rules of thumb and not entirely objective[137]; therefore, identifying allusions and echoes remains primarily a personal affair reflecting the exegetical integrity of the practitioner.

---

133. Labahn, "Deuteronomy," 82–98.

134. This is essentially the terminology and concern of Brunson, *Psalm 118*, 15.

135. Fishbane, *Biblical Interpretation*, 12.

136. Sandmel, "Parallelomania," 1–13. I want to make a concerted effort to avoid the rampant, personal readings Sandmel and others have cautioned against. Although I hope Hays's criteria will help solidify the textual connections I make, I have no doubt that some readers will not see every allusion or hear every echo that I propose.

137. Moyise, "Study of the OT in the NT," 18n13. Daly-Denton, *David in the Fourth Gospel*, 11, adds, "Yet, while such controls have their place, we must acknowledge, in the end, that the nature of echo is such that it resists schematization."

Allusions

Biblical scholars often discuss allusions and echoes in terms of "volume," Hays's second criterion.[138] How loud is the resonant effect of the allusion or echo? As Moyise illustrates, "The embedded text might be a faint echo, which barely disturbs the primary text, or a clanging cymbal which demands attention."[139] Although there are no clear boundaries between the two, an allusion normally reflects the conscious intentions of the author as he makes reference to a precursor text, while an echo is a subtler, almost subconscious reference, resulting from a mind saturated with Scripture.[140] Margaret Daly-Denton is worth quoting at length:

> The three modes of reference to an existing text—quotation, allusion, and echo—function on a "sliding scale" of diminishing intentionality on the part of the author and decreasing visibility on the surface of the text, requiring a correspondingly increasing competence on the part of the reader. Authors quote intentionally, their allusions may plausibly be presumed to be intentional, but they can echo an earlier work quite inadvertently. Quotations, because they are "sign-posted" in the text by a formula of quotation, are of their nature obvious. Allusions, although more fragmentary and periphrastic, must still be recognizable if they are to perform their function. Echoes, however, are covert, faint, blurred, subliminal, often as small as a single word or elusive as a particular cadence or turn of phrase.[141]

Therefore, I define "allusion" as an author's conscious reference to a source text, while lacking a quotation formula, exhibiting verbal and/or thematic parallels with its source text.[142] Given that allusions are more subtle than quotations, which in turn leave more room to debate their existence at all, it is important for this study to be as precise as possible regarding the volume of an allusion. In an effort at precision, I will classify allusions to a source text as obvious or probable.[143]

---

138. Hays, *Conversion of the Imagination*, 34–37; Hays, *Echoes of Scripture*, 30.

139. Moyise, "Study of the OT in the NT," 14.

140. While these definitions are my own based on my understanding of Hays, they are similar to Moyise, ibid., 18.

141. Daly-Denton, *David in the Fourth Gospel*, 9. See also, Brunson, *Psalm 118*, 11–13.

142. This is similar to Labahn's definition ("Deuteronomy," 88).

143. "Obvious" and "probable" reflect Reim's categories of *offensichtliche* and *wahrscheilichen* respectively (*Jochanan*, 108).

Verbal repetition is paramount for Hays's "volume" criterion; the more shared words, phrases, and syntactical patterns, the louder the allusion or echo.[144] An allusion to a source text can share substantial verbal parallels with it. For example, John's ἐν ἀρχῇ (1:1) certainly alludes to the creation narrative of LXX Gen 1:1, which also begins with ἐν ἀρχῇ. Such verbal parallels are indicators of an intertextual relationship between texts, and their volume resounds quite loudly. However, verbal sharing may not be present at all, and John's Gospel is a good case in point. Verbal allusion to the OT is quite rare in John; instead, thematic parallels dominate.[145] In such cases, thematic parallels can ring loudly even when there is little or no verbal sharing. Such allusions fall under Hays's "thematic coherence" criterion.[146] Given its placement between the feeding miracle in John 6:1–15 and the Bread of life discourse in 6:22–59, the example of 6:16–21, the account of Jesus walking on the water, recalls the miraculous parting of the sea by Moses during the exodus (Exod 13–15; cf. LXX Ps 76:16, 19–20).[147] While there are no verbal allusions beyond the fact that both miracles involved a sea (θάλασσα), a strong thematic allusion exists as John relates his second exodus motif to the first exodus, although in a greater fashion.[148] Where Moses divided the waters, Jesus walked on them. Such thematic allusions predominate over verbal allusions throughout John's Gospel.

Echoes

Echoes, on the other hand, are less precise and more difficult to define. Because echoes are so subtle and often barely audible, Daly-Denton has classified them as 1) verbal echoes, which may consist of as little as one word, 2) thematic echoes, which may not even have any actual words in common with the precursor text, and 3) structural echoes, which may occur when a more extended OT passage can be perceived as functioning as a framework or as generating the sequence of thought in a NT passage.[149] Unlike allusions that to a greater degree reflect the conscious intention of an author,

---

144. Hays, *Conversion of the Imagination*, 34–35.

145. Daly-Denton, *David in the Fourth Gospel*, 30.

146. Hays, *Conversion of the Imagination*, 38–41.

147. Beasley-Murray, *John*, 89; Brown, *John*, 1:255–56; Burge, *John*, 195; Bryant and Krause, *John*, 162; O'Day and Hylen, *John*, 73; to a lesser degree, Keener, *John*, 1:673; Sloyan, *John*, 66.

148. Brunson, (*Psalm 118*, 161–62) stresses that John portrays Jesus as being greater than Moses. See also, Köstenberger, *Encountering John*, 85.

149. Daly-Denton, *David in the Fourth Gospel*, 9.

echoes may or may not reflect an author's conscious intent. Nonetheless, because echoes are often faint, they result more from the scriptural milieu of the author as he lives, moves, and has his being in the literary world of the scriptural text. In this scriptural sense they are "conscious" as the author subtly alludes to aspects of the precursor text rather than overtly alluding to them. Echoes result from a mind steeped in Scripture. As with allusions, to guard against "parallelomania," it is important to be as precise as possible when dealing with echoes. Each of Daly-Denton's echo classifications plays a major role in the present intertextual study. This study will aim for precision regarding the type of echo in each case based on whether it is verbal, thematic, or structural. Therefore, an "echo" is a faint, subtle, sometimes barely audible allusion resulting from a mind soaked by scriptural influences.

Allusions to the Book of Numbers

Allusions to the book of Numbers in John's Gospel have been the topic of some scholarly exploration. Tobias Hägerland notes the following echoes:[150]

Table 1. Johannine echoes of Numbers.

Numbers	Gospel of John
11:4–9	6:49
12:2	9:29
16:28	5:30
21:8–9	3:14–15
22–24	20:19–23
27:17	10:9

Source: Tobias Hägerland, "Power of Prophecy," 90.

To these I would add those of Reim who is more precise at identifying the specific type of allusion (*Anspielung*):[151]

---

150. While Hägerland describes these references as "echoes," clearly some are allusions (Num 21:8–9; John 3:14–15), and some approximate direct quotations (Num 12:2; John 9:29). Hägerland does not mention "allusions" in his intertextual study but instead opts for the terminology of "echoes." However, given the volume of several of Hägerland's echoes, I would classify them as allusions.

151. Again, I appreciate Reim's classifications of allusions as "obvious" (*offensichtliche*), "probable" (*wahrscheilichen*), and "possible" (*mögliche*) in the Gospel of John. They are essentially the same as Beale's "clear," "probable," and "possible" in his Revelation commentary (*Revelation*, 78). I classify "possible" allusions as echoes.

Table 2. Johannine allusions to Numbers.

	Numbers	Gospel of John
Citation	9:12	19:36
Obvious allusion	21:8ff	3:14; (6:40)
Probable allusion	20:11ff (Exod 17:6)	7:37ff
Possible allusion		
Jewish laws and customs (*Jüdisches*)	27:21 (Exod 28:30)	11:51
Formal parallel	6:26	14:27
	27:17	10:2–4, 9

Source: Günter Reim, *Jochanan*, 108.

I should emphasize that Reim does not believe that John alludes directly to the OT text but rather to "the tradition" which was composed of 1) the tradition related to the Synoptics, 2) the Signs-source, 3) the living Jewish-Christian discussion, and 4) a Christian circle of wisdom with which John must have had contact.[152] However, each of the traditions that Reim has identified is hypothetical and does not outweigh the tangible evidence that John works directly from the OT text. Further, the sheer saturation of John's Gospel with OT imagery, themes, allusions, and echoes weighs against Reim's conclusion.[153] Nonetheless, OT allusions noted by Reim and Hägerland indicate John's deep familiarity with the content of the Pentateuch, whatever the precise form available to him. Although not exhaustive lists, Reim's and Hägerland's examples serve to highlight that there are indeed intertextual connections, most of which center on Israel's forty-year wilderness sojourn. My hope is that the intertextual allusions to Numbers explored in this study may be added to similar lists in the future.

Allusions to the Book of Deuteronomy

Because I will view Johannine signs as tests of faith, a word is in order about John's use of Deuteronomy. While John rarely quotes Deuteronomy, allusions to it disseminate throughout his Gospel. Reim identifies the following references to Deuteronomy:[154]

---

152. Reim, *Jochanan*, 188.

153. This is essentially the point made by Hanson, *Prophetic Gospel*, 250–51. While it is true that John tends to avoid using OT passages as messianic proof texts, he uses it as a whole and as a background to his Gospel (Barrett, "Old Testament," 168).

154. Reim, *Jochanan*, 108. Again, Reim sees these as allusions to the "tradition" rather than the biblical text. Additional allusions to Deuteronomy have been noted by

Table 3. Johannine allusions to Deuteronomy.

	Deuteronomy	John
Citation	19:15	8:17
Obvious allusion	4:12	5:37
	8:3	4:34
	12:5	4:20
	18:15; 18:18 (34:10)	1:21; 1:25; 1:45 5:46; 6:14; 7:40; 7:52
	18:18	12:49; 17:8 (8:26; 15:15) 14:10; 14:24
Probable allusion	15:11	12:8
	32:47	6:63
Possible allusion	31:3	10:4; 10:27
	31:26	5:45
Jewish laws, customs (*Jüdisches*)	1:16	7:51
	21:22ff	19:31
Formal parallel	31:2	10:9
	33:3	11:36

Source: Reim, *Jochanan*, 108–9.

While this is not an exhaustive list, it at least shows that John has a deep familiarity with Deuteronomy's contents. To these should be added John's references to the Prophet (John 6:14 cf. Deut 18:15–22; 34:11–12), the emphasis on the oneness of God (John 10:30; 17:21–23 cf. Deut 6:4), the emphasis on the Fatherhood of God[155] (cf. Deut 1:31; 32:6), and the Farewell discourse (John 14:1–16:33 cf. Deut 33).[156] Both Numbers and Deuteronomy are important for purposes of this study. The bulk of John's intertextual

---

Labahn, "Deuteronomy," 82–98. He does not see John's allusions as referring back to the text of Deuteronomy per se, but rather to the "cultural memory" of Second Temple Judaism which prized the themes and motifs of Deuteronomy as a whole. In this, he is similar to Reim who views John's allusions to the "tradition "(as differentiated from the Deuteronomic text per se). While this is difficult to prove, and it is probably easier to affirm that John works directly from the text of Deuteronomy, Labahn's allusions provide a thought-provoking intertextual study.

155. Morris, *Theology*, 248–55. Morris notes that John uses "Father" for God 122 times (ibid.,248).

156. Keener, *John*, 2:897, and Smith, *John*, 265, note that Jesus' Farewell discourse in the Fourth Gospel alludes to that of Moses in Deuteronomy.

allusions refer to the wilderness narratives of Numbers while the view that signs are tests of faith comes from Deut 8.

Merely identifying allusions to Israel's Scriptures is not the goal of this study but rather understanding them in a new context in John's Gospel. This is what Lindars referred to as "shift of application."[157] A "shift of application" is seen by comparing the *actual* use of the quotation with the *original* usage inferred from the OT context interpreted in relation to the NT kerygma.[158] Intertextuality is not just about finding and "proving" allusions and echoes based on certain criteria. It is also about appropriating those allusions and echoes in new contexts. To guard even more against "parallelomania," practitioners need to explain the results of the allusions and echoes they hear by placing them in their new context. When speaking of the function of echoes and allusions, Daly-Denton notes, "The capacity to invoke other meanings is central to the concept of echo. As allusion, literally word-play, is of its nature an adaptation or accommodation of an earlier work, its revisionary power is easily recognized."[159] A text speaks not only to its original audience, but also to those who are far off, that is, readers in new contexts whenever and wherever they may be. Moyise notes, "The very act of referring to another text automatically puts it in some sort of correspondence or relationship with the new material."[160] Inherent in the concept of intertextuality is that later texts utilize, in some way, previous texts. Scripture is not stagnant; it is living and active and contemporaneous for each new generation.[161] In analyzing John's allusions to the wilderness narratives of Numbers, I will take into account both the original context of the precursor text and the new context of the primary text in an effort to understand John's appropriation.

AUTHORIAL INTENT AND READER RECEPTION: CAUTION AND AFFIRMATION

Allusions and echoes are difficult, if not impossible, to demonstrate objectively in every case. Not only do these notions depend on authorial intent, but also on reader reception.[162] Did the author intend the allusion or echo,

---

157. Lindars, *Apologetic*, 17–24.

158. Ibid., 19–20.

159. Daly-Denton, *David in the Fourth Gospel*, 9. Hays also identifies the new contextualization inherent in intertextuality (*Echoes of Scripture*, 1, 4–5, 19).

160. Moyise, *Revelation*, 111.

161. Moyise makes this same point when analyzing historical approaches to Scripture that solely seek authorial meaning ("Study of the OT in the NT," 32).

162. Hays, *Echoes of Scripture*, 29.

and did the audience hear it? If so, how loud was it? While Hays's criteria help to bring some methodological control to the art of intertextuality, "volume," as a criterion, is largely in the ears of the practitioner. In addition to dissecting the mind of the original author, practitioners risk dissecting the ears of the original audience, an equally speculative task. Moyise warns, "It is better to admit that the 'volume' of a particular echo will depend on the reader (including the possibility that some will not hear it at all) than to try to judge whether the author intended it or not."[163] All of this can be treacherous territory, especially when a practitioner sets out to prove what the author intended or how exactly his audience received the message.[164]

Authorial meaning, which includes both import of information as well as application, results from a complex, dynamic, and multifaceted interaction of author, text, reader, and interpretive community.[165] Meaning is not confined to any one of these in isolation from the others. It is a complex dialogue, dependent upon the author's will to convey a communicative act, the medium through which he communicates, and the reader's comprehension and contribution to the communication process within an interpretive community.[166]

As demonstrated in the earlier discussion of the saturation of John's Gospel with the OT, the assumption in this study is that John wrote with a conscious eye to the scriptural matrix of Israel and that his Gospel reflects the language, symbolism, and motifs of that matrix. His thought is by no means limited to the matrix of Israel's Scriptures; but there is little doubt that the Scriptures play a formative, even if allusive, role in his Gospel. Put differently, his writing naturally engages his scriptural milieu and the way he weaves into his Gospel allusions and echoes to Israel's Scriptures plays a large part in how he uses them for his own purposes. As with any writer steeped in Scripture, John exhibits a mixture of both conscious and subconscious intent behind literary allusions and echoes. To place too much stress solely on conscious authorial intent diverts from the interconnections between scriptural texts. To use a musical analogy, people go to symphonies to hear the music, not to watch the director, but the director keeps the music ordered and structured and from lapsing into cacophony.

163. Moyise, *Revelation*, 20.

164. I believe authorial meaning may be adequately, though not exhaustively, ascertained.

165. Hays, *Echoes of Scripture*, 26–27.

166. On the complex issue of where meaning resides, see Fish, *Is There a Text in This Class?*; Hirsch, *Validity in Interpretation*; McCartney and Clayton, *Reader*, 291–301; Poythress, *God Centered Biblical Interpretation*; Poythress, "Human Authors," 81–99; Vanhoozer, *Is There a Meaning in This Text?*; Westphal, *Whose Community*.

While structuralism presents textual meaning as disconnected from the author's intent (i.e., the "intentional fallacy"), the adoption of intertextuality by biblical studies has changed this, at least to a certain degree.[167] The historical rootedness of Scripture, with its ancient languages, customs, and its plurality of cultural milieus, not to mention the occasional nature of the documents themselves, has restored the author (and/or editor) as a valid participant in textual communication *in addition* to the reader. Merold Westphal asks a pointed question in this regard: "Might not the meaning(s) of a text be coproduced by author and reader, the product of their interaction?"[168] Simply put, meaning is shared within the overall context of a communicative act. Granted, intertextuality is a property of texts, not authors; nevertheless, authors produce texts. Moyise observes that "texts are vehicles of communication and one cannot talk of communication without speaking of both author and reader."[169] The nature of language as a communicative act naturally includes the author, although only partially, in the communication process.[170] While authorial meaning is only one component of meaning, it is still a component. It is illegitimate to *limit* meaning to the author's intention, but it is legitimate to consider his intent while also taking into consideration other factors that contribute to the communication process. This is where Hays's criteria come into play as they help to raise the issue of authorial intent regarding allusions and echoes, thereby restoring the author as a valid contributor to the meaning of the text. Where structuralism and semiotics all but ignore authorial intent, Hays is concerned to demonstrate that it is a valid component of meaning; it is the missing piece of the intertextual puzzle that biblical studies inherited from literary structuralism. Nonetheless, Hays perceives the potential pitfalls of placing too much stress on authorial intent and audience reception. What he says about Paul, I believe, may be said about John:

> Because the question of authorial intentionality is a slippery one, we should not place too much weight upon it; for the present let

---

167. Schofield, "Wilderness," 39n7.
168. Westphal, *Whose Community*, 54.
169. Moyise, *Evoking Scripture*, 3.
170. I understand authorial intent as only one component of meaning. Moyise notes, "Every quotation is a bridge to another text, but what travels across is not limited to the author's intentions" ("Study of the NT in the OT," 32). Any hermeneutical approach that pursues authorial meaning as the sole component of meaning misses the complexity of the text as a communicative act. Conversely, any hermeneutical approach that pursues the reader as the sole contributor to meaning also misunderstands the text as a communicative act. Moyise recognizes that "meaning is not an isolated phenomenon" (ibid., 32).

us simply say that to interpret Paul discerningly, we must recognize the embeddedness of his discourse in scriptural language (or the embeddedness of scriptural language in his discourse) and explore the rhetorical and theological effects created by the intertextual relationships between his letters and their scriptural precursors.[171]

Hays, therefore, is aware of the potentially rampant personal nature of intertextual analysis and ultimately makes no distinction between "allusion" and "echo" regarding the author's conscious or subconscious intent.[172] I will do the same in this study by seeing both as ultimately flowing from the author, both consciously and subconsciously. Again, I will classify allusions as obvious or probable, while echoes are less clear and fainter than allusions. I will attempt to make a "reasonable explanation"[173] for the intertextual allusions and echoes I hear throughout this study based on Hays's criteria, some of which relate directly to the author's intent while others stem from the interplay between texts as well as the interpreter's judgments. Ultimately, my focus is on the text as living and active communication while understanding that text to be the intentional production of an author. As an intertextual practitioner, I will lean toward being what Beale calls a "maximalist"—that is, open to exploring more intertextual connections than others might be.[174] My aim is that Hays's criteria, as well as a healthy dose of self-critical awareness and hermeneutical humility, will prevent the intertextual echoes I hear from lapsing into an orchestra with an audience of one.

TEXT FORM(S)

The exact text form(s) of Israel's Scriptures that John used continues to elude scholars. We do not even know in what form(s) they were available. However, I will discuss textual variants of LXX Numbers that may have influenced John's allusions to particular passages as they occur. This may lead to tentative conclusions regarding specific text forms available to John. Not only are the OT textual traditions used by John uncertain, so also is the

---

171. Hays, *Conversion of the Imagination*, 29.

172. Hays, *Echoes of Scripture*, 29. Wagner opts for the same solution: "I will follow Hays in making no systematic attempt to distinguish 'echo' from 'allusion,' although generally 'echo' will refer to more subtle methods of alluding to a prior text" (*Heralds of the Good News*, 9n35). Conversely, see Beetham, *Echoes of Scripture in Colossians*, 27–36.

173. Beale, *What We Worship*, 24.

174. Ibid. This is in contrast to a "minimalist," who is leery of seeing allusive literary connections.

"canonical" status of different books during his time.[175] Although debated, the Pentateuch was established and stabilized in the Babylonian exile with minor edits following.[176] Even so, the Torah read by Ezra (Neh 8) in the fifth century BCE was clearly the Torah as we know it in the MT and was basically stable for all time to come.[177] While much debate swirls around the contents of the Jewish canon in John's day, the Pentateuch stands apart as a closed list of writings in both its Hebrew and Greek versions.[178] While there are no doubts regarding the availability of the Pentateuch to John, the precise text forms remain uncertain. This is not to mention the various Aramaic traditions in use in the synagogues during the first century with which he would have no doubt been familiar. Regarding the text forms of John's sources, due to the vast number of MS traditions, textual variants, and revisions, we simply cannot be precise in every case. Opinions on John's sources should not be dogmatic.[179]

There is a legion of problems surrounding the precise identification of John's sources. Donald Juel observes that in the early church "we do not know precisely what portions of Israel's Scriptures were read, how they were read, or even what form they were available."[180] John is quite eclectic in his use of Scripture. His "default" version seems to be the LXX because he uses it (or a variant form) for thirteen of his fourteen formal quotations.[181] However, he also betrays knowledge of a Hebrew text (similar to MT, John 19:37; cf. Zech 12:10). In John 19:37, John's use of ἐκκεντέω ("to pierce") goes against the LXX which misreads the Hebrew consonants דקר ("to pierce") as רקד ("to mock").[182] John quotes the LXX verbatim (10:34; cf. Ps 81:6a; 12:13; cf. Ps 117:26a; 12:38; cf. Isa 53:1; 19:24; cf. Ps 21:19) but mostly freely (although not to exclude the possibility of verbatim quotations from a *Vorlage*, John

---

175. By "canonical" I mean a closed list of writings. For discussions of the canonization of Israel's Scriptures, see Beckwith, "Formation," 39–86; Brettler, "Books," 108–12; Sanders, "Stabilization," 225–52.

176. Sanders, "Stabilization," 234.

177. Ibid.

178. Jobes and Silva, *Invitation to the Septuagint*, 31, 34, 45. Charlesworth, "Interpretation," 253–82. See also, Sanders, "Stabilization," 246; Greenspoon, "Hebrew into Greek," 80–113.

179. Hanson, *Prophetic Gospel*, 249.

180. Juel, "Interpreting," 283–303.

181. Köstenberger, "John," 417.

182. Barrett, *John*, 558–59. Reim, *Jochanan*, 96, also sees here evidence of John's knowledge of a Hebrew text. However, Menken, *Textual Form*, 177, and Schuchard, *Scripture Within Scripture*, 149, do not see here an instance of John's use of a Hebrew text, but rather an independent Greek translation (*Vorlage*) of a Hebrew text. In short, the precise text form of John 19:37 is debated.

1:23; cf. Isa 40:3; John 2:17; cf. Ps 68:10; John 6:31; cf. Ps 78:24; John 6:45; cf. Isa 54:13a; John 15:25; cf. Ps 34:19 or 68:5; John 19:36; cf. Exod 12:46 or Num 9:12; Ps 33:21).[183] John also reflects interpretive traditions similar to those found in the Aramaic Targumim. One example involves John's Logos theology in the Prologue (1:1–18). By referring to Christ as "the Word," John may reflect the Targumic practice of referring to the *Memra* ("Word") of God. While John's rationale is quite different from the Targumists who used *Memra* to avoid using God's name, such language would not be lost on his Jewish readers. As Leon Morris notes, "They were familiar with the use of 'the Word' as a designation of the divine."[184]

Krister Stendahl's observation regarding Johannine quotations of the OT is relevant: "On the whole John's way of quoting the OT is consistent in its inconsistency."[185] If this is also essentially Edwin Freed's conclusion after his analysis of John's OT quotations,[186] how much more can we say this about his *allusions* to the OT that are much less precise than quotations? Simply put, John spans the spectrum in his use of diverse text forms of Israel's Scriptures, perhaps reflecting the diversity of those scriptural forms themselves. As A. J. Droge notes, "Israel's 'Scriptures,' both collectively and individually, had a messy and complicated textual history and nowhere is this perhaps more evident than in Johannine usage."[187] As I pointed out earlier, John absorbs Israel's Scriptures as a whole more than as isolated proof texts into his Gospel. Scriptural images, themes, and theology penetrate his Gospel but his exact textual sources have not yet revealed themselves. John's use of the OT is as eclectic as the MS traditions with which he works.

John's allusions to Numbers, some of which I sampled earlier, indicate a deep familiarity with it. Given the sheer number of allusions to Numbers,

183. Köstenberger, "John," 417–18. I have changed the Psalms references from Köstenberger to reflect the LXX numbering.

184. Morris, *John*, 105–06. For more on this, see, McNamara, "*Logos* of the Fourth Gospel," 115–17; McNamara, "Interpretation," 167–97; McNamara, *Targum and Testament*, 101–06, 142–59. For other examples, see Dodd, *Interpretation*, 74–96; Ridderbos, *John*, 111. Most recently, Ronning, *The Jewish Targums and John's Logos Theology*. For additional discussions of the relevance of Second Temple literature and rabbinic materials to the study of the NT generally see, Beale and Carson, *Commentary*, XXIV; Brown, *Introduction*, 138–39; Brown, *John*, 1:LXI–LXII; Chilton, "Aramaic Paraphrase," 23–43; Chilton, "Rabbinic Traditions," 651–60, esp. 657–60; Chilton, "Targums," 800–04, esp. 802–03; Daube, *Rabbinic Judaism*; Evans, ed., *Ancient Texts*, 3–6; Ferguson, *Backgrounds of Early Christianity*, 490–501; Keener, *John*, 1:180–94; Maccoby, "Rabbinic Literature," 897–902, esp. 898–99; Neusner, *Rabbinic Literature*.

185. Stendahl, *School of St. Matthew*, 163.

186. Freed, *Old Testament Quotations*, 126. Menken makes a similar observation (*Textual Form*, 205).

187. Droge, "Revisionary Criticism," 169–84.

it is likely that John knew the entire book.[188] Numbers has a complex compilation history due to its diverse literary genres, not to mention numerous source-critical issues.[189] R. Dennis Cole discusses the compilation history in detail and concludes, "The Book of Numbers has an editorial and textual history that continued for more than a thousand years."[190] The MS tradition is stable with relatively few variants in the Hebrew text.[191] Even so, Numbers exhibits editorial cohesion and is not haphazard in its arrangement and compilation.[192] Even the variants of LXX Numbers are mostly limited to the spelling of names and occasional verse order.[193] Because the LXX is John's default version, this study will primarily be concerned with allusions and echoes to LXX Numbers. However, because John also knows the Hebrew text and betrays an awareness of Aramaic traditions on occasion, I will consult those pertinent to the discussion. Suffice it to say here, John betrays knowledge of certain interpretive traditions to the uplifted serpent narrative of Numbers, especially those traditions reflected in Wisdom of Solomon (hereafter Wisdom), the Mishnah, and *Targum Pseudo-Jonathan*. While John's argument is not dependent upon on any of these per se, he reflects a similar interpretive tradition. Due to the later dating of the Mishnah and *Targum Pseudo-Jonathan*, I do not argue for a genetic influence on John's Gospel, for this is surely anachronistic. However, the written texts, as late as they are, likely reflect much earlier interpretive traditions and are similar to those in antiquity.[194] While the use of later rabbinic materials for the study

188. Hägerland, "Power of Prophecy," 90.

189. Source criticism of Numbers is beyond the scope of this study. For concise discussions, see Ashley, *Numbers*, 3–7; Olson, *Numbers*, 2–3. For more detailed discussions, see Budd, *Numbers*, XXI–XXV; Cole, *Numbers*, 26–36; Levine, *Numbers 1–20*, 48–84, 89–109.

190. Cole, *Numbers*, 36. For more on the composition history of Numbers, see Childs, *Introduction to the Old Testament*, 194–99; Harrison, *Introduction to the Old Testament*, 615–22.

191. Exceptions include the narrative and poetic segments of Num 20–21. However, even these seemingly disconnected chunks of material are not without a cohesive structure, especially when viewed from a distance rather than as disparate parts, as Milgrom suggests in *Numbers*, 463–67; Milgrom, "Numbers" 4:1146–55.

192. For more on the structural integrity of Numbers, see Cole, *Numbers*, 36–40; Gane, *Leviticus, Numbers*, 476–79; Olson, *Numbers*, 3–7; Wenham, *Numbers*, 16–21.

193. Ashley, *Numbers*, 13. See also, Wevers, *Text History of the Greek Numbers*.

194. Similarly, Evans, *Ancient Texts*, 2; Keener, *John*, 1:191, 194. I will address the dating of Wisdom of Solomon, the Mishnah, and *Targum Pseudo-Jonathan* in chapter 4. Some scholars, such as Brown, *Death of the Messiah*, 1447, question the methodological relevance of such material for NT studies. On the other hand, others like Daly-Denton, *David in the Fourth Gospel*, 17–19, have found them helpful for intertextual analysis. This is especially the case when reading John's Gospel intertextually, which evidences

of the NT is controversial, the commonly accepted background to John's Gospel as some kind of "synagogue conflict," which was proposed by Raymond E. Brown and J. Louis Martyn, has made their use in Johannine studies acceptable.[195] In this study, I simply note some "notable commonalities"[196] between the Fourth Gospel and later rabbinic tradition that may shed light on the broader interpretive milieu of first-century Judaism.

John 3 receives a battery of source-critical theories. While such theories are pervasive throughout John's Gospel, scholars particularly debate John 3 regarding its literary structure, development, and origins.[197] An aura of mystery penetrates the entire chapter given its diverse themes, such as signs, the new birth, serpent symbolism, the Son of Man, summary of the gospel (3:16), belief and unbelief, light and darkness, etc.[198] The structure is notoriously difficult to decipher. Verses 1–8 flow without interruption; vv. 16–21 are thematically connected (i.e., people's responses to the Son). What lies between is structurally less certain. Scholars have proposed natural breaks after vv. 8, 9, 10, 12, and 13.[199]

Chronological concerns appear as well. According to 3:2, Nicodemus is clearly interested in Jesus' miracles, some of which have taken place in Jerusalem (2:23). However, that John has narrated none of them to this point raises a chronological concern.[200] This is not insurmountable, however. Simply because John mentions Jesus' miracles in Jerusalem (2:23; 4:45) does not necessitate narrating them in detail. This, too, is John's point regarding the "many other things" that Jesus did which have not been written down (21:25). John's concern to show a sub-par faith in Nicodemus follows naturally the fickle faith of the Jerusalemites (2:24). So there is at least a thematic connection if not a chronological one. Brown's comment summarizes it best: "To seek perfect chronological sequence in John is a vain endeavor."[201]

Speculation swirls around deciphering between the words of Jesus from those of the Evangelist, as well as the thematic unity of the chapter. The words of Jesus are thought to conclude at v. 11, while vv. 12–21 present

---

similarities with Palestinian traditions.

195. Keener, *John*, 1:185–86.

196. Ibid., 1:187.

197. Marrs, "Raised Serpent," 132–47n29. For discussions, see Ashton, *Understanding*, 277–80; Barrett, *John*, 202–18; Brown, *John*, 1:134–36; Bultmann, *John*, 131–75; Dodd, *Interpretation*, 303–11.

198. Bryant and Krause, *John*, 86.

199. Ashton, *Understanding*, 277. I will discuss the structure of John 3 below.

200. Brown, *John*, 1:135.

201. Ibid.

an extended homily of the Evangelist.[202] Certainty is elusive regarding these matters. As D. Moody Smith observes, "Whether Jesus or the evangelist here speaks is probably a matter of indifference, for their voices typically become one."[203] While these and other similar concerns may raise interesting questions about the historicity of the narrative, a solid nucleus of traditional material remains.[204] The present study is not focused on the history of the text but on the text as it now stands.

The intertextual methodology set forth in this chapter will be used to underscore wilderness connections in John 2:23—3:21. While many of these lay beneath the surface of the text, a close reading brings them closer to the surface. I will now turn my attention to illustrating allusions to, as well as verbal and thematic echoes of, LXX Numbers in John 2:23—3:21 with the purpose of viewing Johannine signs as divine tests of faith as reflected in Deut 8.

---

202. Ashton, *Understanding*, 277–80; Brown, *John*, 1:136; Moloney, *Text and Context*, 45. For a discussion of the historical reliability of John 3:1–21, see Blomberg, *Historical Reliability*, 91–95.

203. Smith, *Theology*, 27.

204. Brown, *John*, 1:136. Hanson, *Prophetic Gospel*, 243, questions the historicity of the uplifted serpent account.

Chapter 3

SEEING IS NOT ALWAYS BELIEVING

My assumptions in this study are twofold: 1) wilderness symbolism permeates John 2:23—3:21 and 2) John presents signs as divine tests of faithfulness. I will underscore these with an intertextual reading of John 2:23—3:21 and Numbers.[1] Further, signs should be understood through the lens of Deut 8:2, 16 (cf. Deut 4:34), which interprets God's signs worked through Moses in the wilderness as tests of faithfulness. Specifically, John 3:14, the uplifting of the Son of Man, addresses the complex Johannine relationship between signs and faith by alluding to the uplifted serpent of Num 21:8–9, showing that eyes of faith are necessary to "see" signs.[2] Put differently, seeing signs is a matter of the heart: the softhearted are open to seeing the theological significance of Jesus' signs while the hardhearted see only their miraculous qualities. John's logic is as follows: Nicodemus is confronted by Jesus'

---

1. As previously stated, I will also probe allusions and echoes to LXX Exodus and Deuteronomy when necessary; nevertheless, the bulk of the intertextual relationship will be between John 2:23—3:21 and LXX Numbers.

2. Throughout this study, I will refer to the visible act of seeing signs. This brings up the complex nature of *vision* in John's Gospel. While I will discuss this in more detail when dealing with the role of vision in John 3:14 (cf. Num 21:8–9), it is sufficient at this stage to point out that John illustrates that there are different aspects to the relationship of vision and faith. Ideally, eyes of faith are necessary to properly see (i.e., interpret rightly) Jesus' signs. There is, however, no uniform usage of "seeing" signs in John, so each instance must be analyzed on a case-by-case basis. On the role of vision in John's Gospel, see Derrett, "Not Seeing," 208–09; Keener, *John*, 1:247–51; Koester, "Hearing, Seeing, and Believing," 327–48; Kysar, *Maverick Gospel*, 86–90; Thompson, *Humanity of Jesus*, 53–86; Thompson, "Signs and Faith," 89–108.

signs (σημεῖα, John 3:2); Jesus refers him to a σημεῖον (3:14; cf. LXX Num 21:8–9) in the OT wilderness narrative, and explains that faith is necessary to properly see σημεῖα (3:15–16), and that either life or judgment follows depending on one's response (3:18–21).

I will now apply the intertextual wilderness reading detailed in the previous chapter to Jesus' dialogue with Nicodemus. My goal in this chapter is to demonstrate that John places Nicodemus in a precarious position by illustrating his fickle faith that is focused on signs. John therefore portrays him as a representative of the Jerusalemites and by analogy, the first wilderness generation.

MANY BELIEVED IN HIM

While illustrating the signs-faith of the Jerusalemites and Nicodemus at the Passover feast (2:23–25), John echoes the shallow faith of the first wilderness generation (Exod 4:1–9, 30–31; Num 14:11). Jesus' dialogue with Nicodemus links back to the setting in Jerusalem at the Passover,[3] and John connects him with the Jerusalemites whose faith centers on Jesus' signs in John 2:23–25. Nicodemus is therefore associated with the many who "believe" in Jesus based on his miraculous signs. John associates Nicodemus with this group on a number of levels. In order to fully understand John's portrayal of the Pharisee Nicodemus, it is helpful to consult the wider context which includes 2:23–25:

> ὡς δὲ ἦν ἐν τοῖς Ἱεροσολύμοις ἐν τῷ πάσχα ἐν τῇ ἑορτῇ, πολλοὶ ἐπίστευσαν εἰς τὸ ὄνομα αὐτοῦ θεωροῦντες αὐτοῦ τὰ σημεῖα ἃ ἐποίει· αὐτὸς δὲ Ἰησοῦς οὐκ ἐπίστευεν αὐτὸν αὐτοῖς διὰ τὸ αὐτὸν γινώσκειν πάντας καὶ ὅτι οὐ χρείαν εἶχεν ἵνα τις μαρτυρήσῃ περὶ τοῦ ἀνθρώπου· αὐτὸς γὰρ ἐγίνωσκεν τί ἦν ἐν τῷ ἀνθρώπῳ.

> Now when he was in Jerusalem at the Passover feast, many people believed in his name after seeing the signs which he did; but Jesus did not entrust himself to them because he knew all people and he had no need that anyone should testify about man; for he himself knew what was in man.

This is the first of several instances in the Gospel where John reports that "many believed in him" (πολλοὶ ἐπίστευσαν εἰς αὐτόν) because of his

---

3. This is in contrast to Gordon, "Final Wilderness," 34, who sees the Nicodemus episode as isolated and not connected to any Jewish feast.

miraculous signs (2:23; 4:39; 7:31; 8:30; 10:42; 11:45; 12:11, 42). I observed in chapter 1 that for John, a signs-based faith, or signs-faith (*Wunderglaube* or *Zeichenglaube*),[4] is not necessarily false but fickle: it is easily swayed, superficial, and ideally should grow into a more mature faith that sees the christological significance of signs more than their miraculous qualities.[5] Edwyn Hoskyns comments, "These casual believers may be the stuff out of which disciples are made, but they are not disciples, and may never become so."[6] More often than not, signs-faith deteriorates into rebellion and rejection, which are the characteristic reactions of the people to Jesus' ministry: εἰς τὰ ἴδια ἦλθεν, καὶ οἱ ἴδιοι αὐτὸν οὐ παρέλαβον ("He came to his own home, yet his own people did not receive him," 1:11).[7] Such embryonic faith fails to grow into mature faith; in fact, quite the opposite: it often degenerates into unbelief. For example, in John 11:45–46, many of the Jews (πολλοὶ ἐκ τῶν Ἰουδαίων) believe in Jesus (ἐπίστευσαν εἰς αὐτόν) after witnessing the raising of Lazarus; but then some of them (τινὲς δὲ ἐξ αὐτῶν) go immediately and report him to the Pharisees who, along with the chief priests, have him arrested and ultimately killed (11:57; 18:3). Simply put, faith that results from merely seeing signs often lacks the persevering nature of firm faith, which John's Gospel demands.

In John 2:23–25, John does not chastise the Jerusalemites[8] for their lack of faith, but instead narrates Jesus' distancing himself from them due to their immature faith that is dazzled by his miracles. Jesus knows their hearts[9] and the fickleness of their faith; the rest of John's Gospel bears this out as many of the people at times believe in Jesus (2:23; 7:31; 8:30; 12:42), while at other times grumble against him (6:41, 43, 61; 7:12, 32). Both belief and grumbling often occur in the face of signs. In short, Jesus does not believe

---

4. Schmidl, *Jesus und Nikodemus*, 89–96.

5. I use the phrase "fickle faith" throughout this study as a synonym for signs-faith. The phrase comes from Carson, *John*, 347–48.

6. Hoskyns, *Fourth Gospel*, 1:215.

7. "His own home" translates the neuter plural τὰ ἴδια; whereas, "his own people" translates the masculine plural οἱ ἴδιοι. The former signifies the coming of the Word to his own possession, property, or domain; whereas, the latter signifies his own people (i.e., Israel). For this distinction, see Köstenberger, *John*, 37; Lincoln, *John*, 102. However, Barrett, *John*, 163, notes that not only was the Word rejected by his own people, but also by the world as stated in John 1:10.

8. I use the term *Jerusalemites* here to refer to the people of Jerusalem who exercise some degree of faith in Jesus, albeit fickle (2:23; 7:31; 8:30; 12:42). They are in contradistinction from "the Jews" who are primarily Jewish leaders who stand in open opposition to Jesus.

9. For Jesus' omniscience in John, see Keener, *John*, 1:531–32; Michaels, *John*, 175; O'Day and Hylen, *John*, 546.

(ἐπίστευεν, 2:24) the people's belief (ἐπίστευσαν, 2:23) because it is based on the miraculous qualities of his signs, rather than their significance.[10]

It is important at this stage to demonstrate where signs-faith leads if it does not flower into firm faith, and this lack of development helps to highlight the precarious position of Nicodemus as one who exhibits signs-faith. John's Gospel demonstrates repeatedly that although "many believed in him" (πολλοὶ ἐπίστευσαν εἰς αὐτόν), such faith is fickle because it fails to see the significance of Jesus' signs. "Many believed in him" is therefore technical terminology for the Jerusalemites' signs-faith, and a cursory reading of the Gospel bears this out in other similar contexts.[11] I have already noted the issue of signs-faith of the Jerusalemites in 2:23-25, but there are additional instances with similar terminology where people believe in Jesus.[12] For example, after reporting Jesus' journey to Jerusalem for the Feast of Tabernacles (7:2, 10), John states that the faith of many of the Jerusalemites is based on signs in 7:31: ἐκ τοῦ ὄχλου δὲ πολλοὶ ἐπίστευσαν εἰς αὐτὸν καὶ ἔλεγον· ὁ χριστὸς ὅταν ἔλθῃ μὴ πλείονα σημεῖα ποιήσει ὧν οὗτος ἐποίησεν; ("Yet many from the crowd believed in him and said, "When the Christ comes, will he do more signs than this man has done?").[13] Again, "many believed in him" but only after seeing signs. The crowd's belief, however, is short-lived; the next verse illustrates the same crowd "grumbling" about Jesus (τοῦ ὄχλου γογγύζοντες περὶ αὐτοῦ, 7:32). As Craig Keener observes, "Such initial signs-faith was no guarantee of perseverance" (2:23-25; 8:30-31).[14] It is important to observe that in John 7:31-32 (cf. 8:30-31), John alludes to the first wilderness generation who "grumbled" (from γογγύζω, Exod 16:2; Num 11:1) against Moses and God.[15] Fickle faith was characteristic of the

---

10. O'Day and Hylen, *John*, 546.

11. Similar terminology appears in John 4:39 where many of the Samaritans believe in Jesus, not because of a sign, but because of the woman's testimony and their own belief in his teaching (4:39, 41). Jesus' disciples come to believe in him as the result of his first miraculous sign at the wedding feast in Cana (2:11). However, their faith fluctuates throughout the Gospel and is strengthened after the resurrection. Therefore, the Samaritans remain the only group who exhibit firm faith in Jesus during his public ministry.

12. John expresses belief in two ways in his Gospel: πιστεύειν plus εἰς plus the accusative (2:23; 4:39; 7:31; 8:30; 10:38; 10:42; 11:45; 12:11; 12:42; 14:1) and πιστεύειν plus the dative (5:24, 46; 8:31). Attempts to distinguish two levels of faith based on these grammatical constructions are unconvincing. For more on this, see Carson, *John*, 346-47; Moloney, *Signs and Shadows*, 103; Morris, *Theology*, 274-76; Reim, *Jochanan*, 138; Ridderbos, *John*, 305.

13. That the crowd expects a negative answer is expressed by μή with an indicative (ποιήσει). For this rule, see Machen, *New Testament Greek*, §505-06, 254-55.

14. Keener, *John*, 1:719.

15. Gordon, "Final Wilderness," 52; Michaels, *John*, 455; Morris, *John*, 368; O'Day

first wilderness generation. They had seen the great things God did among them, yet they failed to trust him.¹⁶ Keener's comments on signs-faith are particularly illuminating for this study as they highlight the issue of signs-faith in the wilderness:

> John here echoes earlier biblical portraits of human nature in general and perhaps of recipients of God's revelations in particular; for instance, the Israelites believed when they saw Moses' signs (Exod 4:31), but their faith collapsed when it was challenged (Exod 5:21–23).¹⁷

The crowds in Jerusalem see Jesus' signs but fail to see their significance. D. A. Carson notes on the Jerusalemites, "There is no hint, however, that these people developed any deep understanding of the significance of the signs, thereby grasping who Jesus really was."¹⁸ Francis Moloney's comment also provides perspective, "A faith inspired by the wonders worked by Jesus often stops at the sign itself."¹⁹ In summary, the phrase "many believed in him" (πολλοὶ ἐπίστευσαν εἰς αὐτόν) is John's tongue-in-cheek way of describing immature signs-faith. It is fickle, superficial, and Jesus has no faith in it.

Nicodemus and Jesus' Signs

The warning against fickle faith that depends merely on the miraculous (John 2:23–25) leads directly into Jesus' dialogue with Nicodemus.²⁰ The Nicodemus episode elaborates on signs-faith as John portrays the Jewish religious leader as a representative of such faith.²¹ Herman Ridderbos notes that Jesus' conversation with Nicodemus offers a very specific elaboration of what was said in a more general sense in 2:23–25.²² Therefore, the Nicodemus pericope is a natural and plausible outgrowth of 2:23–25.²³ Jesus' dialogue with Nicodemus probably takes place in Jerusalem as there has

---

and Hylen, *John*, 85–86.

16. O'Day and Hylen, *John*, 86.
17. Keener, *John*, 1:746.
18. Carson, *John*, 319.
19. Moloney, *Belief in the Word*, 105.
20. Keener, *John*, 1:533.

21. Lincoln, *John*, 145. Michaels, *John*, 172, observes that Nicodemus is the only named individual of the group mentioned in 2:23–25, which again suggests a contextual linkage between the two pericopes.

22. Ridderbos, *John*, 123.
23. Blomberg, *Historical Reliability*, 91.

been no indication that the setting has changed since Jesus' arrival there (2:13, 23).[24] Therefore, John sets Nicodemus in Jerusalem along with other Jerusalemites near the time of the Passover. He then introduces Nicodemus as "a man of the Pharisees" (ἄνθρωπος ἐκ τῶν Φαρισαίων, 3:1) and as a "ruler of the Jews" (ἄρχων τῶν Ἰοθδαίων, 3:1).[25] John later labels him "the teacher of Israel" (ὁ διδάσκαλος τοῦ Ἰσραὴλ, 3:10).[26] In this portrayal, John immediately gives Nicodemus a place of prominence among Israel's leaders as a probable member of the Sanhedrin (7:50–52).[27] However, not only does he represent the Jewish establishment, he also comes to Jesus as a representative Jerusalemite who, like those at the previously-mentioned Passover, has an immature, signs-based faith (3:2). As Craig Koester notes, "Nicodemus speaks for the people who believed in Jesus because of the signs he performed."[28] Martin Schmidl similarly notes that Nicodemus is a representative of the miracle believers; he is typical of one who has signs-faith and serves as an example of the basic phrase.[29] There is also a strong verbal link with the preceding section centering on the word "man" (ἄνθρωπος): Jesus needed no one to testify "about man" (τοῦ ἀνθρώπου), for he knew what was "in man" (ἐν τῷ ἀνθρώπῳ, 2:25). John then introduces Nicodemus as a "man" (ἄνθρωπος, 3:1) of the Pharisees.[30] Indeed, Nicodemus arrives on the scene as the man who represents the kind of fickle faith that Jesus distrusts.

24. Moloney, *Belief in the Word,* 107.

25. The historical identity of Nicodemus does not impact the thesis of this study. See Bauckham, *Testimony,* 137–72; Barrett, *John,* 204; Blomberg, *Historical Reliability,* 91–92; Keener, *John,* 1:535–36; Hylen, "Nicodemus," 4:269–70; Witherington, *John's Wisdom,* 94. For Nicodemus as a character in the Fourth Gospel, see Cotterell, "Nicodemus Conversation," 237–42; Bassler, "Mixed Signals," 635–46; Culpepper, *Anatomy,* 134–36; Koester, *Symbolism,* 45–47; Meeks, "Man from Heaven," 44–72, esp. 53–57; Renz, "Nicodemus," 255–83.

26. These titles will be important later as not only personal identifiers but also as corporate ones.

27. Barrett, *John,* 204; Culpepper, *Gospel and Letters,* 134; Lincoln, *John,* 149; Köstenberger, *Theology,* 198; Martyn, *History and Theology,* 87–89; Ridderbos, *John,* 123; Witherington, *John's Wisdom,* 94. Bultmann, *John,* 133n4, argues that John uses ἄρχων here in a technical sense to refer to a member of the Sanhedrin (e.g., 7:26, 48; 12:42). However, it is by no means certain that Nicodemus was a member of the Sanhedrin; all that is certain is that he was a leader of some kind among the Jewish people (Michaels, *John,* 177). I will discuss a possible wilderness implication of ἄρχων below.

28. Koester, *Symbolism,* 46. See also, Barrett, *John,* 205; Bassler, "Mixed Signals," 637; Culpepper, *Anatomy,* 135; Schmidl, *Jesus und Nikodemus,* 97. Bultmann, *John,* 133, sees 3:1–21 as closely connected to 2:23–25, but he does not see Nicodemus as a representative of the group mentioned in the latter passage. As Bassler comments, most commentators disagree with Bultmann's assessment here ("Mixed Signals," 637).

29. Schmidl, *Jesus und Nikodemus,* 106.

30. Koester, *Symbolism,* 46, makes this same observation. See also, Keener, *John,*

Much has been discussed about Nicodemus's arrival to speak with Jesus "by night" (νυκτός, 3:2).[31] On one hand, discussing Torah at night was the normal routine for Rabbis who typically worked other vocations during the day.[32] On the other hand, it appears more than an incidental reference or chronological marker due to the Fourth Gospel's pervasive symbolism that contrasts light and darkness.[33] Carson observes that based on how John uses "night" elsewhere in the Gospel (9:4; 11:10; 13:30), it always bears some sort of moral and spiritual symbolism.[34] Because John connects Nicodemus so closely with the Jerusalemites who believe in Jesus because of his signs, "by night" is probably yet another subtle clue that he falls short of full-fledged commitment and remains in darkness.

As Jesus' signs prompt "faith" in the Jerusalemites, so also in Nicodemus: ῥαββι, οἴδαμεν ὅτι ἀπὸ θεοῦ ἐλήλυθας διδάσκαλος· οὐδεὶς γὰρ δύναται ταῦτα τὰ σημεῖα ποιεῖν ἃ σὺ ποιεῖς, ἐὰν μὴ ᾖ ὁ θεὸς μετ'αὐτοῦ ("Rabbi, we know that you have come from God as a teacher; for no one is able to do these signs which you do, unless God is with him," 3:2). Here, Nicodemus's opening words immediately identify him with the fickle faith of the Jerusalemites: just as they saw Jesus' signs, Nicodemus has also seen "these signs" (ταῦτα τὰ σημεῖα, 3:2). However, John portrays him as an example of those who believe in Jesus solely because of his signs, and therefore believe inadequately.[35] Further, "we know" (οἴδαμεν) identifies him not only with the Pharisees, but also with the previously mentioned group of Jerusalemites.[36] There is a repetition of the sentiments found in the expressions of insufficient faith based on signs in 2:23–25 in Nicodemus's words.[37] To be sure, Nicodemus's comment does not amount to a rejection of Jesus; quite the opposite: it is at least a superficial acceptance of Jesus and his teachings. His observation that Jesus' signs indicate that God is "with him" (μετ'αὐτοῦ, 3:2) is the kind of respect given to the great figures of Israel in the OT such

---

1:535; Michaels, *John*, 176; Moloney, *Belief in the Word*, 106.

31. For a good summary of the various interpretations, see Carson, *John*, 186.

32. Barrett, *John*, 204; Bultmann, *John*, 133n5; Carson, *John*, 186; Keener, *John*, 1:536; Str-B 2:420. Qumran also reflects the practice of studying Torah at night (1QS 6:6–7).

33. Duke, *Irony*, 108–09; Koester, *Symbolism*, 142–73, esp. 150–52.

34. Carson, *John*, 186.

35. Witherington, *John's Wisdom*, 92.

36. Koester, *Symbolism*, 46.

37. Moloney, *Belief in the Word*, 108. As O'Day and Hylen, *John*, 549, note, based on the response of the "believers" in 2:23–25 to Jesus' signs, John immediately calls into question Nicodemus's assertion of Jesus' identity.

as Moses, Joshua, Jeremiah, and others.[38] While Nicodemus's observation of Jesus implies no disrespect, it nevertheless falls short of complete Christology from the perspective of John's Gospel.[39] To class him with great prophets of Israel's history like Moses or Jeremiah, whom God was also said to be with, does not express the Gospel's stance that Jesus is the Son of God, that the Son is one with the Father, and that whoever sees the Son sees the Father.[40] To recognize Jesus as a teacher not different in kind from other teachers is Nicodemus's error.[41] Similarly, Cyril of Alexandria observes about Nicodemus: "Calling Jesus a teacher from God and a co-worker with him, he does not yet know that Jesus is by nature God. He still approaches Jesus as a mere man and has only a slight conception of who he is."[42] Along these same lines, it is difficult to do better than Andrew Lincoln:

> Getting right in what sense Jesus has come from God is a crucial issue in this Gospel. Its perspective is that Jesus has come from God as God's unique agent, as the Son sent by the Father, as the incarnate Logos. It becomes clear that Nicodemus does not intend this interpretation.[43]

Nicodemus occupies a dangerous position betwixt and between:[44] he recognizes Jesus as a teacher who has come from God, but not as the Teacher who is one with God.

T. David Gordon reports that it was a common assumption among the Rabbis that a teacher sent from God would be able to verify his commission and teaching by performing a sign from heaven.[45] A sign was the verification of a prophet's prophecy: "When a prophet starts to prophesy, if he gives a sign and a miracle, one must listen to him; if, however, not, one need not listen to him" (cf. *Sanh.* 11:6).[46] However, a word of caution is in

---

38. Moloney, *Belief in the Word*, 109. See Exod 3:12; Josh 1:5; Jer 1:8. Witherington, *John's Wisdom*, 94, notes the emphatic position of "from God" which further highlights the respect Nicodemus has for Jesus. However, Lincoln, *John*, 149, sees Nicodemus's statement as reflecting nothing more than traditional categories. Similarly, Derrett, "Correcting Nicodemus," 126, sees the phrase as less than flattering and falls far short of affirming that Jesus' works are worked "in God."

39. The same may be said for Nicodemus's use of "teacher" (Keener, *John*, 1:536).

40. Barrett, *John*, 205. For a similar observation, see Carson, *John*, 186–87.

41. Westcott, *John*, 48.

42. Quoted in Elowsky, ed., *John 1–10*, 109.

43. Lincoln, *John*, 149.

44. Hoskyns, *Fourth Gospel*, 226.

45. Gordon, "Final Wilderness," 27. See also, Edersheim, *Life and Times*, 74–75, 263–64; Koester, *Word of Life*, 87.

46. Str-B 2:480. See also, *m. Taʾan.* 3:8; *b. Ber.* 34b.

order here regarding the use of later rabbinic literature for interpreting the NT. While rabbinic materials at times reflect similar traditions dating back to first-century Judaism (and before),[47] they do not necessarily always do so. The working of miraculous signs as verification by Rabbis is a good case in point. For example, Solomon Schechter states on one hand, "There is hardly any miracle recorded in the Bible for which a parallel might not be found in the rabbinic literature."[48] Some Rabbis clearly performed miraculous signs from time to time according to the rabbinic literature.[49] On the other hand, however, "Only once do we hear of a Rabbi who had recourse to miracles for the purpose of showing that his conception of a certain Halacha was the right one."[50] Therefore, an appeal to the rabbinic literature (à la Gordon, Strack and Billerbeck) need not be the primary recourse for understanding Nicodemus's observation of Jesus' signs as verification of his teaching. It is at best unclear that Nicodemus and other first-century Pharisees had the same belief as the later Rabbis regarding a prophet and his signs.[51] The opposite may be the case. The general Pharisaic view held that prophets were rare or had vanished by the first century, and this may have heightened Nicodemus's awareness to Jesus' signs.[52] Along these same lines, Second Temple Judaism did not generally expect the royal Messiah to be a miracle worker.[53]

47. Brown, *Introduction*, 138; Brown, *John*, 1:LXI; Keener, *John*, 1:191, 194.

48. Schechter, *Rabbinic Theology*, 6.

49. Schecter (ibid.) cites the third chapter of the tractate *Ta'anit* as an example. See also, Edersheim, *Life and Times*, 74–74, 263–64.

50. Schechter, *Rabbinic Theology*, 7. Schechter further adds that in that particular instance (*B. Meṣi'a*, 59b), the majority of onlookers declined to accept the miraculous intervention as a divine demonstration of truth and decided against the rabbi who appealed to it.

51. Hoskyns, *Fourth Gospel*, 226, perceptively comments that Nicodemus does not call Jesus a "prophet," but a "teacher." This somewhat dilutes the previous comment of Strack and Billerbeck regarding a prophet and his signs. Nevertheless, that a connection exists between a teacher who has come from God and his signs is clear from Nicodemus's comment, and whether or not that teacher is regarded as a prophet seems to me irrelevant. One simply cannot ignore the overlapping content of Nicodemus's observation and that of the crowds later in the Gospel: "When the people saw the miraculous sign that he performed, they said, 'This is truly the Prophet who is to come into the world'" (6:14; cf. 7:31).

52. Keener, *John*, 1:534; Lightfoot, *Commentary*, 3:263.

53. Bauckham, *Testimony*, 234; Martyn, *History and Theology*, 90–98; Smith, *John*, 94. I will address the messianic expectations of Second Temple Judaism below. It is sufficient to note here that generally speaking, messianic expectations held that an eschatological prophet like Moses would perform miraculous signs (cf. John 7:31) but this figure was distinct from the royal Davidic Messiah. This latter figure would not primarily be a miracle worker. On these messianic expectations, see Glasson, *Moses*; Meeks, *Prophet-King*; Hunt, *Johannine Problems*, 55–64.

While from the perspective of John's Gospel the Messiah certainly performs miraculous signs (John 7:31; 20:30–31), this is by no means clear in the extant literature from the same period. This perhaps adds even more clarity as to why Nicodemus simply refers to Jesus as a "teacher from God." Simply stated, Nicodemus's comment, "For no one is able to do these signs which you do unless God is with him," reflects the amazement of many in John's Gospel who believed in Jesus because of his signs.

Although my focus throughout this study is on the miraculous signs of Jesus, there is no compelling reason to doubt that "these signs" (ταῦτα τὰ σημεῖα, 3:2) referred to by Nicodemus include both miraculous and non-miraculous deeds.[54] At this point in the Gospel the term σημεῖον includes both elements: the water turned to wine was a miraculous sign (2:11), while the cleansing of temple was a non-miraculous sign (2:18).[55] Plus, John records that Jesus performed "many" signs other than those found in his Gospel, and he has selected those that are significant for his purposes (20:30; 21:24–25).[56] Nicodemus has seen the deeds of Jesus performed in Jerusalem at the Passover and has taken an interest in him as a result. To summarize thus far, there is ample evidence to suggest that John connects Nicodemus to the Jerusalemites by 1) geographical setting, 2) the use of ἄνθρωπος, 3) the use of "we know," and 4) signs-faith. Nicodemus's observation that Jesus is a teacher from God and that God is with him is insufficient and immature because it rests on seeing signs.

Signs-Faith of the First Wilderness Generation

Nicodemus's signs-faith is eerily reminiscent of the first wilderness generation in the OT. Again, according to the Gospel's purpose statement, signs are meant to evoke faith (21:30–31). Therefore, there is nothing inherently wrong with believing in Jesus as a result of witnessing his signs; however, when faith fails to grow into commitment, it lacks the persevering quality of true discipleship. Such is the case in the wilderness narratives in the OT. Before engaging the issue of signs-faith in Numbers, a bit of background from Exodus will help provide a suitable introduction to the phenomenon in ancient Israel. Exodus 4 is fully saturated with signs[57] which are intended

---

54. Michaels, *John*, 172, sees the "signs" mentioned here as being only the temple cleansing incident. This overlooks the use of the plural "signs" (σημεῖα) and is unnecessarily limited.

55. Köstenberger, *Theology*, 323–35.

56. Carson, *John*, 187.

57. Brueggemann, *Exodus*, 721.

to spur the Israelites to believe (πιστεύειν) in Moses as God's spokesperson and delivering agent. Not only do the Israelites need to have their faith encouraged for the long process of redemption from Egypt, Moses also needs a stronger faith for his task. After calling him, God aims to strengthen him. In Exod 4:1, Moses fears that the people will not believe him on the sole basis of his words: ἐὰν μὴ πιστεύσωσί μοι, μηδὲ εἰσακούσωσι τῆς φωνῆς μου ("If they do not believe me nor listen to my voice"). Therefore, Moses perceives that words are not enough to evoke faith in the Israelites. God, then, confirms his call of Moses through a series of three miraculous signs that have the purpose of invoking the people's faith in Moses (Exod 4:1–9).[58] Each sign (σημεῖον) is intended to bring forth faith.

> ἐὰν δὲ μὴ πιστεύσωσίν σοι μηδὲ εἰσακούσωσιν τῆς φωνῆς τοῦ σημείου τοῦ πρώτου πιστεύσουσίν σοι τῆς φωνῆς τοῦ σημείου τοῦ ἐσχάτου·[59] καὶ ἔσται ἐὰν μὴ πιστεύσωσίν σοι τοῖς δυσὶ σημείοις τούτοις ... (Exod 4:8–9).

> And if they do not believe you, nor listen to the voice of the first miraculous sign, they will believe you because of the voice of the last miraculous sign. And it will be that if they do not believe you for these two signs ...

Clearly, Moses' words (i.e., telling the people that he knows God's name and that God appeared to him 4:1; cf. 3:11–17)[60] are not enough to evoke the faith of the Israelites, so signs are then the means through which they will first come to believe in Moses. As Peter Enns observes, "What convinces the people of Moses' divine call are the signs he performs, not the fact that he knows God's name."[61]

God anticipates the people's signs-faith, and the remainder of Exod 4 bears this out, especially vv. 30–31, where the text states unambiguously that the people believed as a result of seeing signs: καὶ ἐποίησεν τὰ σημεῖα ἐναντίον τοῦ λαοῦ. καὶ ἐπίστευσεν ὁ λαὸς καὶ ἐχάρη ("And he did the signs

---

58. Exodus 4:21 states that Moses will perform wonders which God has given (ἔδωκα) into his hands before Pharaoh, thus seemingly referring to a past occurrence of wonders. The implication here is that Moses will perform before Pharaoh the signs already given to him by God in 4:1–9. However, according to Sarna, *Exodus*, 23, the signs in v. 21 are properly the forthcoming plagues rather than the signs mentioned in 4:1–9. Against this, see Enns, *Exodus*, 130. No matter who the recipients of signs are in 4:21, the signs of 4:1–9 are performed before Israel and are for her unbelief.

59. A popular textual variant found in F and M changes ἐσχάτου to δευτέρου. The MT is consistent with the former. For this variant, see Wevers, *Greek Text of Exodus*, 44.

60. Enns, *Exodus*, 100–08.

61. Ibid., 135.

before the people. And the people believed and rejoiced,"). Although there is some debate about who exactly performs the signs, Moses[62] or Aaron,[63] the result is the same in either case—the people believe.[64]

One can only hope that because the people believed (ἐπίστευσεν ὁ λαός), their faith would persevere. Unfortunately, the next chapter reveals the true character of Israel's signs-faith as it collapses when challenged back in Egypt (5:21–23).[65] Moses' chief concern in Exod 4:1 is that the people will not believe and this is born out intermittently throughout the rest of the Pentateuch (cf. Ps 78:22).[66] There is seemingly an endless cycle of miraculous sign, faith, rebellion, repentance; that is, until God himself breaks the cycle when he reveals that signs-faith does not persevere (Num 14:11), and declares that the first wilderness generation will die in the desert (14:22–23). This brief introduction to signs-faith in Exodus sets the stage for its full expression in Numbers.

Signs and faith come together in an anticlimactic way in Num 14. As the signs-faith of the Jerusalemites in John's Gospel degenerates to rebellion, and ultimately rejection, so also the signs-faith of the first wilderness generation met the same ends (Num 14:22–23).[67] Although Moses' signs were intended to build the faith of the embryonic nation in Exod 4, by Num 14 Israel's faith had atrophied to the point of nonexistence. The first generation of wilderness travelers proved to be unfaithful in spite of God's repeated acts of intervention on their behalf. In fact, the structure of the book of Numbers divides along generational lines: Num 1–25 centers on the faithless first wilderness generation, while Num 26–36 focuses on the second, more hopeful generation.[68] While expressions of faith in God are more rare in the OT than in the NT,[69] Num 14:11b rings loudly: ἕως τίνος οὐ πιστεύουσίν μοι ἐν πᾶσιν τοῖς σημείοις οἷς ἐποίησα ἐν αὐτοῖς; ("How long will they not believe me in spite of all the miraculous signs which I have done among them?"). This statement comes after a series of four rebellions by the first generation: one that affects the fringe of the camp (11:1–3); a second involving the people's complaint about manna (11:4–35); a third involving Miriam and

---

62. Sarna, *Exodus*, 27 (cf. Exod 4:17).
63. Enns, *Exodus*, 135; Brueggemann, *Exodus*, 718.
64. Brueggemann, *Exodus*, 718.
65. Keener, *John*, 1:746.
66. Enns, *Exodus*, 109.
67. I will interact with Num 14:22 in more detail below.
68. Olson, *Numbers*, 5. For a good comparison of the two wilderness generations, see ibid., 192–93.
69. Cole, *Numbers*, 229; Wenham, *Numbers*, 137.

Aaron (12:1–16); and a climactic fourth involving the spy story (13–14).⁷⁰ Not only does God indict Israel's lack of faith generally, he does so in spite of the miraculous signs he has performed among them (τοῖς σημείοις οἷς ἐποίησα ἐν αὐτοῖς). Israel finds herself in the same predicament as Pharaoh, who also saw God's miraculous signs yet failed to believe in his power and do what he said.⁷¹ Moses' fear of the people's unbelief in Exod 4:1 is realized in an even greater sense in Num 14:11, as they have not only rejected Moses, but also God. Simply stated, the doing of signs (σημεῖα ποιεῖν) is met with unbelief (οὐ πιστεύουσιν). The signs spoken of in Num 14:11 are no doubt God's mighty deeds performed at the exodus and throughout the wilderness experience: the plagues on Egypt, the crossing of the Red Sea, and the provision of food and water in the arid desert.⁷² Moses' entire ministry, which is unparalleled in ancient Israel's prophetic history according to Deut 34:11, is summarized as σημεῖα ποιεῖν (lit. "to do signs"): ἐν πᾶσι τοῖς σημείοις καὶ τέρασιν ὃν ἀπέστειλεν αὐτὸν κύριος ποιῆσαι αὐτὰ ἐν γῇ Αἰγύπτῳ ("For all the signs and wonders which the Lord sent him to do in the land of Egypt"). What should have been a ministry where the appointed shepherd of God's flock leads the sheep into their own pasture ends as both shepherd and sheep die in the dry desert.

Jesus succeeds as the Good Shepherd who leads his sheep into eternal life (John 10:11, 14), and John parallels his ministry with that of Moses as σημεῖα ποιεῖν.⁷³ While Jesus is greater than Moses in John's Gospel, his signs-ministry is met with similar unbelief as in Num 14:11. A comparison between Num 14:11b and John 12:37 reveals an interesting parallel that highlights the people's unbelief in spite of signs performed on their behalf:

> ἕως τίνος οὐ πιστεύουσίν μοι ἐν πᾶσιν τοῖς σημείοις οἷς ἐποίησα ἐν αὐτοῖς; (Num 14:11b)

> How long will they not believe me in spite of all the miraculous signs that I have performed among them?

> τοσαῦτα δὲ αὐτοῦ σημεῖα πεποιηκότος ἔμπροσθεν αὐτῶν οὐκ ἐπίστευον εἰς αὐτόν (John 12:37)

> Though he performed so many signs in their presence, they did not believe in him.

---

70. Olson, *Numbers*, 81. Olson also notes the progression of rebellion that begins with the fringe, works its way to the people, next to its leaders, and culminates with both the leaders and the people (ibid., 81).

71. Ibid., 80.

72. Cole, *Numbers*, 229; Ashley, *Numbers*, 254–55.

73. Gordon, "Final Wilderness," 30.

Here is an obvious verbal allusion to Num 14:11,[74] which appears at the end of Jesus' public ministry, as does the summary of God's signs performed through Moses appears near the end of his ministry.[75] John's point is not so much that Jesus' signs resembled in appearance those of Moses,[76] but that both signs-ministries were met with signs-faith, which fails in the end. Even though John's Gospel has fewer miracles than the Synoptics, John 12:37 indicates that he did "so many" (τοσαῦτα), and there is no reason to limit this reference only to those recounted in the Gospel.[77] No matter how many signs one finds in John's Gospel, the issue at stake here is that although they were intended to evoke faith (20:31), many who witnessed them failed to move beyond immature signs-faith. As Leon Morris comments, "They might perhaps give occasional evidence of transitory belief, but that is not saving faith."[78] Many believed, but their faith was a short-lived signs-faith. God's people have a history of such reaction to signs that stretches back to the first wilderness generation.

Nicodemus: A Ruler in the Wilderness

John places Nicodemus in the same precarious position as the first wilderness generation: exhibiting signs-faith with no guarantee for further development into heart-felt commitment, and being at risk for not seeing

---

74. Meets the following criteria: Availability: John had access to the whole book of Numbers; Volume: six parallel or synonymous terms/phrases such as τοσαῦτα/πᾶσιν, σημεῖα/σημείοις, πεποιηκότος/ἐποίησα, ἐπίστευον/πιστεύοθσίν, εἰς αὐτόν/μοι, ἔμπροσθεν αὐτῶν/ἐν αὐτοῖς; Recurrence: John appeals to wilderness imagery throughout his Gospel; Thematic Coherence: inadequacy of signs-faith; Historical Plausibility: John's readers knew the wilderness traditions of Israel; History of Interpretation: Brown perceives the echo of Num 14:11 in John 12:37; Satisfaction: satisfies the overall themes of unbelief and rejection in face of miraculous signs. Many thanks to Gary Manning for demonstrating how this allusion fits the criteria.

75. Gordon, "Final Wilderness," 31. See also, Brown, *John*, 1:529. Carson, *John*, 447, sees Deut 29:3-4 as the background to John 12:37: "With your own eyes you saw those great trials, those miraculous signs and great wonders. But to this day the LORD has not given you a mind that understands or eyes that see or ears that hear" (Carson's translation). There is no reason to doubt that both Num 14:11 and Deut 29:3-4, as well as Isa 53:1 (cf. John 12:38) and Isa 6:10 (cf. John 12:39-40) influenced John's text. As Barrett points out, John has absorbed the OT as a whole into his Gospel ("Old Testament," 155-69).

76. Hunt, *Johannine Problems*, 57-64.

77. Moloney, *Signs and Shadows*, 196n65. As Moloney notes, the verse properly refers to the entire ministry of Jesus. Köstenberger, *John*, 390n3, also notes that τοσαῦτα may refer to the quality of signs, being translated as "so great."

78. Morris, *John*, 536.

the eschatological promises of God. If the first wilderness generation is any indication, signs-faith often deteriorates into rebellion and rejection. Nicodemus is on unsure footing at this stage in the dialogue as his faith is one of wonder and amazement; Jesus' signs dazzle him. John presents Nicodemus and the "many who believed" in Jesus because of his signs as echoing the first wilderness generation who similarly exhibited signs-faith. Not only is Nicodemus a representative of those with signs-faith, he is their ruler (ἄρχων, 3:1). The term ἄρχων is translated variously in English translations as "ruler" (ESV, KJV, NAS), or "leader" (NLT, NRSV)[79] in John and is therefore non-specific, probably meaning nothing more than a leader of some kind among the Jews.[80] Nonetheless, John's use of it here may have a tentative connection to the wilderness narratives of LXX Numbers where it is used customarily to translate the Hebrew נשיא, which refers to the leader of an ancestral tribe (נשיא מטת אבתם, Num 1:16, 44; 16:2 and par.).[81] While John attaches no significance to the tribal connotation of ἄρχων as in LXX Numbers (ἄρχοντες τῶν φυλῶν), it may not be a coincidence that the corresponding Hebrew term is densely concentrated in the wilderness and conquest traditions of the Pentateuch.[82] Such "exalted ones" were elevated in the assembly and elected to serve the people,[83] whether it was to supervise the census (1:5–16), to bring dedicatory gifts to the tabernacle (Num 7), or to lead the tribes in war (2:10, 14).[84] R. Dennis Cole remarks similarly, "These men functioned as representatives for their ancestral tribes in matters of military conscription, worship leadership, and general administration."[85] Moreover, as E. A. Speiser notes, "The title [נשיא], in short, stands for a duly elected chieftain."[86] Thus, a נשיא functioned as a representative of the

79. The NIV's "a member of the Jewish ruling council" is superfluous as noted by Michaels, *John*, 177n16.

80. Michaels, *John*, 177. When speaking of human rulers (as opposed to the "ruler of this world" 12:31; 14:30; 16:11) John ordinarily applies the term to rulers of the Jews who are not Pharisees (7:48–49; 12:42), although Nicodemus is an exception in that he is both. For more on the non-specific usage of ἄρχων in the NT, see Delling, "ἀρχηγός, ἄρχων," 1:487–89, esp. 489.

81. Genesis 23:6 appears to be the only exception. For the background of the נשיא, see Speiser, "Background," 111–17.

82. Milgrom, *Numbers*, 335–36.

83. Ashley, *Numbers*, 54. Ashley correctly notes that it is God who does the electing, not the people (contra Speiser, "Background," 113–14). Nonetheless, the representative function of a נשיא should not be ignored.

84. Milgrom, *Numbers*, 335.

85. Cole, *Numbers*, 70. Zeitlin, "The Titles," 1–5, discusses the role of the Nasi as the "president" of the Sanhedrin in the tannaitic literature.

86. Speiser, "Background," 114.

people, and this is precisely how Nicodemus comes to Jesus, e.g., "we know" (John 3:2). Further, his status as a probable member of the Sanhedrin is not irrelevant to the collective, governing function of the נשיאם who occasionally convened to make executive rulings.[87] This is certainly not to suggest that the Second Temple Sanhedrin was in any way identical to the various governing bodies during the wilderness period, nor does it prove to be a clear intertextual allusion. It simply underscores the fact that representative bodies have a long history in Israel, dating from the wilderness period. Nicodemus comes to Jesus, not simply as one of the many who believed in Jesus because of his signs, but also as their representative ruler.

Forfeiting the Eschatological Promises of God

Not only is the faith of the first wilderness generation short-lived, it ends on a disastrous note as God prevents them from not only entering the Promised Land, but even from seeing it:

> πάντες οἱ ἄνδρες οἱ ὁρῶντες τὴν δόξαν μου καὶ τὰ σημεῖα ἃ ἐποίησα ἐν Αἰγύπτῳ καὶ ἐν τῇ ἐρήμῳ ταύτῃ καὶ ἐπείρασάν με τοῦτο δέκατον καὶ οὐκ εἰσήκουσάν μου τῆς φωνῆς, ἦ μὴν οὐκ ὄψονται τὴν γῆν ἣν ὤμοσα τοῖς πατράσιν αὐτῶν (Num 14:22–23).

> All of the men who saw my glory and the signs which I performed in Egypt and in this desert, yet tempted me this tenth time and did not listen to my voice, they will not see the land which I swore on oath to their forefathers.

It is clear from chapter one of this study that God's miraculous signs were meant to test the faith of wandering Israel, but it is also clear from Num 14:22 that Israel's lack of faith has now tested (ἐπείρασάν) God's patience for the tenth time.[88] The signs mentioned above are none other than the

---

87. Milgrom, *Numbers*, 335. Further, it should not be assumed that these representative bodies were democratic as in the United States Congress. That they made rulings as representatives in some fashion is all that can be safely affirmed. For more on this, see Schnabel, "Sanhedrin," 5:102–06.

88. There is some debate as to whether "tenth" (δέκατον) is meant here as a round number indicating an idiomatic expression meaning "over and over," or a specific tenth test. Ashley, *Numbers*, 260–61, sees it as the former, but also notes that the Babylonian Talmud (*Arak* 15b) lists ten specific occasions where Israel tested God: at the Red Sea (Exod 14:11–12), at Marah (15:23), in the wilderness of Sin (16:2), twice at Kadesh (16:20, 27), at Rephidim (17:2–7), at Sinai (ch. 32), at Taberah (Num 11:1), at Kibroth-Hattaavah (11:4), and the present situation (chs. 13–14). See also, Budd, *Numbers*, 158; Cole, *Numbers*, 232–33.

miraculous deeds that God worked through Moses at the exodus and throughout the wilderness.[89] Israel's failure to believe in God in spite of his miraculous signs caused them to forfeit the eschatological promise of land which God swore on oath to their forefathers. In short, the first generation's signs-faith, instead of growing and flowering into firm faith, degenerated into unbelief thus causing them not to even have a glimpse of the Promised Land.

John presents Nicodemus as being in yet another analogous situation as the first wilderness generation: he exhibits signs-faith which threatens to compromise his own experience of the eschatological promises of God: ἀπεκρίθη Ἰησοῦς καὶ εἶπεν αὐτῷ· ἀμὴν ἀμὴν λέγω σοι, ἐὰν μή τις γεννηθῇ ἄνωθεν, οὐ δύναται ἰδεῖν τὴν βασιλείαν τοῦ θεοῦ ("Jesus answered and said to him, 'Truly, truly, I say to you, unless someone is born from above, he is not able to see the kingdom of God,'" John 3:3). While I will interact with "born from above" in more detail later in this chapter, it is sufficient to note here that Jesus' words reflect spiritual rebirth, which comes from God and is in contrast to fickle human faith, and is essential for seeing (i.e., interpreting) Jesus' signs rightly. It is the very opposite of the fickle faith Nicodemus exhibits so far in the narrative. Jesus here calls Nicodemus to a higher level of faith than signs-faith, and calls him to recognize that a complete overhaul of his inclinations must take place in order for him to experience the eschatological promises of God. There is probably no substantive difference between the phrases "to see" (ἰδεῖν, 3:3) and "to enter into" (εἰσελθεῖν εἰς, 3:5) the kingdom of God.[90] For John, the overall experience of the kingdom is what matters. As R. Alan Culpepper observes, "Like the scribe in Mark 12:28–34, Nicodemus is 'not far from the kingdom of God,' but he remains outside."[91]

Kingdom of God and Jesus' Kingship in John's Gospel

John expresses his eschatological expectation here in terms of the "kingdom of God" (βασιλεία τοῦ θεοῦ, John 3:3).[92] While this may not appear

89. Ashley, *Numbers*, 260; Cole, *Numbers*, 229.

90. Köstenberger, *John*, 122n20, notes John's penchant for stylistic variation. Both express the overall notion of experiencing the eschatological promises of God although entering the kingdom may express a slightly stronger notion.

91. Culpepper, *Anatomy*, 136.

92. Although a few Greek MSS (1009 472 291 245 *א* *l*26) replace τοῦ θεοῦ with τῶν οὐρανῶν ("of heaven"), the first reading is preferred due to the age and diversity of witnesses supporting it, and the likelihood of copyists introducing τῶν οὐρανῶν in an effort to imitate the recurring phrase in Matthew's Gospel. For more, see Metzger, *Textual Commentary*, 174.

at first to be directly relevant to a study of John's wilderness motif, in reality, the Pentateuch's wilderness narratives provide early evidence of an eschatological kingly Messiah (Num 24:17). Therefore, embedded in John's use of "kingdom of God" is his portrayal of Jesus as Judaism's eschatological kingly Messiah—a tradition that is firmly rooted in the wilderness traditions of Numbers. What is more, this eschatological expectation is prevalent in the literature of the Second Temple period, notably the Qumran Scrolls and *Psalms of Solomon*, as well as in later rabbinic materials like *Targum Onqelos*. I will comment on each of these in turn. Before addressing John's kingly messianic expectations, however, I will briefly discuss his use of "kingdom of God" (βασιλεία τοῦ θεοῦ, 3:3, 5). How might Nicodemus have understood this phrase? What were his assumptions about the kingdom? "Kingdom of God," while prominent in the Synoptics, is largely replaced with "eternal life," or "life" in John's Gospel as an eschatological emphasis.[93] In fact, "kingdom of God" occurs only twice (John 3:3, 5; cf. 18:36), but the idea of Christ as king is present throughout.[94] Raymond E. Brown observes, "John refers to Jesus as king fifteen times, almost double the number of times that this reference occurs in any of the other Gospels."[95] He states further, "The Synoptic emphasis on the *basileia* ("kingdom") making itself felt in Jesus' activity seems to have become in John an emphasis on Jesus who is *basileus* ("king") and who reigns."[96] Brown also notes that in spite of the minimal use of "kingdom of God," John makes it obvious that Jesus is "the King of Israel" (1:49): he has an Israel of believers to reign over; if Jesus is the shepherd, he has a flock that has to be gathered; if Jesus is the vine, there are branches on the vine.[97]

By "kingdom of God," John points to God's active reign in people's lives, as opposed to a static realm or earthly kingdom.[98] This kingdom is

---

93. Köstenberger, *Theology*, 285; Köstenberger, *Encountering John*, 41; Köstenberger, *John*, 122–23; Morris, *John*, 190. For John's synonymous use of "eternal life" and "life," see Dodd, *Interpretation*, 144–50; Keener, *John*, 1:385–86; Ladd, *Theology*, 290–95; Smith, *Theology*, 149–51; Morris, *Theology*, 266–69; Thielman, *Theology*, 171–73. I will discuss Johannine eternal life in more detail in chapter 4 when discussing John 3:16.

94. Brown, *Introduction*, 228–29. For more on the kingdom of God in John, see Brown, *John*, 1:CX; Koester, *Word of Life*, 91–96; Leung, *Kingship-Cross Interplay*; Meeks, *Prophet-King*. Köstenberger, *Theology*, 285–86, aptly illustrates the non-traditional portrait of Christ's kingdom in John. For perhaps the most comprehensive and current analysis of Jesus' kingship that considers the NT as a whole, see Wright, *Jesus and the Victory of God*, 198–663.

95. Brown, *John*, 1:CX.

96. Brown, *Introduction*, 229.

97. Ibid.

98. Ibid.

both a present possession and a future promise in John, and this reflects the two prevailing conceptions of the kingdom in first-century Judaism: the present reign of God and the future eschatological kingdom of God.[99] That John *substitutes* "eternal life" for "kingdom of God" elsewhere is probably the best way of stating the matter, for they are equivalents. Morris notes that for John "the possession of eternal life appears to mean very much the same as entering the kingdom of God as the Synoptists picture it."[100] F. F. Bruce summarizes the relationship between kingdom of God and eternal life in the context of the Nicodemus dialogue: "To a Jew with Nicodemus's upbringing, seeing the kingdom of God would mean participation in the age to come, the resurrection life. In this Gospel as in the others, 'the kingdom of God' in this sense is interchangeable with 'eternal life.'"[101]

The question arises as to the reason for John's change in phraseology from "kingdom of God" to "eternal life." Andreas Köstenberger proposes that it is possible that John sees the notion of "kingdom" as being too political and worldly. That is, it is rooted in the realm of this world and looks back to earthly kings in Israel's history, such as David and Solomon. Eternal life, on the other hand, is a more transcendent, universal category for all humanity, not merely Israel.[102] Further, Jesus' understanding of "kingdom" is somewhat different from that of the Jews in John's Gospel: the former has a predominantly sacrificial understanding where the king sacrifices his life in order to give life to his people, while the latter has more nationalistic overtones (John 6:15; 12:13–15).[103] Jesus is markedly ambivalent when confronted about the notion of kingship throughout John's Gospel, indicating his reticence to accept the title as understood by the people.[104] Nevertheless, there was enough diversity among Second Temple Judaism regarding the Messiah (or anointed king),[105] that Jesus was able to find a nucleus of contemporary messianic assumptions appropriate to defining his mission,

---

99. Belleville, "Born," 125–41. For more on this dual nature of the kingdom of God in the NT, see VanGemeren, *Progress of Redemption*, 347–55; Vos, *Biblical Theology*, 381–86.

100. Morris, *John*, 190. For an example, see Matt 19:16, 24.

101. Bruce, *John*, 83. Similarly, see Carson, *John*, 188. Further, as Belleville notes, the OT prophets bear out this future eschatological expectation alongside the kingdom as a present reality ("Born," 136). Belleville cites Mic 4:7–8; Pss 102:19; 144:11, 13; cf. Wis 6:4; 10:10; Dan 3:54; 4:3. See also, Isa 9:1–7; 11.

102. Köstenberger, *Theology*, 285.

103. Similarly, ibid., 285–86.

104. Ibid., 285.

105. Keener, *John*, 1:284.

especially in regards to the eschatological Prophet like Moses and the Davidic Messiah.[106]

The notion of *kingship* is implicit in the idea of kingdom for John. While the picture of Second Temple Jewish messianic hopes was varied, there was nonetheless a common denominator that centered on the arrival of a Davidic king.[107] The general view of Second Temple Judaism held that the Messiah, as the anointed king of Israel, would ascend to the throne in the eschatological kingdom of God. Mark Black's brief summary helps to identify the general parameters of Second Temple Judaism's messianism: "The expectation of the Messiah was most often a royal (kingly) role, occupied by a human being who would be a new (and better) David: a great warrior, a righteous man of God, a wise and just ruler who would bring back the days of glory and power to oppressed Israel."[108]

The Pentateuch contains two of the most popular and ancient prophecies of the royal Messiah: Gen 49:9–10 and Num 24:17.[109] Given the present intertextual study of John 2:23—3:21 and Numbers, the latter verse is significant: "I see him, but not now; I behold him, but not near: a star shall come out of Jacob, and a scepter shall rise out of Israel" (Num 24:17 ESV). Balaam's prophecy involves the destruction of Moab and Edom, and in one sense, King David accomplished this (2 Sam 8:2, 13–14; 1 Kgs 11:15–16).[110] However, it was only a partial victory because both Moab and Edom regained their independence and were reconquered several times through Israel's history.[111] Therefore, this lack of permanent possession of these enemies led the prophets of Israel to anticipate a future conquering of both

---

106. Ibid., 1:289–90. For more on John's portrait of the Messiah, see Bauckham, *Testimony*, 207–38; Dodd, *Interpretation*, 228–40; Köstenberger, *Theology*, 311–35; Pryor, *Covenant People*, 131–37. For more on the various messianic expectations of Second Temple Judaism, see Achtemeier et al., *Introducing*, 229–30; Bauckham, *Testimony*, 207–38; Collins, "Messiah, Jewish," 4:59–66; Collins, *Scepter and Star*; Cullmann, *Christology*, 113–17; Ferguson, *Backgrounds of Early Christianity*, 551–54; Horbury, "Jewish Messianism," 3–24; Keener, *John*, 1:284–90; Köstenberger, *Theology*, 313–14; Martyn, *History and Theology*, 90–98; Neusner et al., *Judaisms and Their Messiahs*; Schürer, *History of the Jewish People*, 2:126–87; VanderKam, *Dead Sea Scrolls Today*, 117–19; Wright, *Knowing Jesus Through the Old Testament*, 137–40. For the Davidic Messiah in the OT generally, see Gowan, *Eschatology*, 32–39.

107. Achtemeier et al., *Introducing*, 229–30; Collins, *Scepter and Star*, 209; Martyn, *History and Theology*, 94.

108. Black, *Luke*, 88.

109. Bauckham, *Testimony*, 213.

110. Ashley, *Numbers*, 503; Dozeman, *Numbers*, 191; Milgrom, *Numbers*, 207; Olson, *Numbers*, 150; Wenham, *Numbers*, 200–01.

111. Ashley, *Numbers*, 503.

(Isa 11:14; 25:9–11).¹¹² The prophetic eschatological anticipation eventually became a fuller messianic expectation of a royal Messiah in the Second Temple period.¹¹³ Dennis Olson's summary is helpful, "In the history of Israel, the promise of a new king or messiah was extended beyond King David to a future hope for a messiah who would usher in God's kingdom in a new apocalyptic age."¹¹⁴ That this eschatological figure would be a royal ruler is indicated clearly in the MT, where he is referred to as a "star" (כוכב) and a "scepter" (שבט).¹¹⁵ The Greek version of Num 24:17 also points to a human royal figure, but in a more specific sense as it substitutes "man" (ἄνθρωπος) for "scepter": δείξω αὐτῷ καὶ οὐχὶ νῦν μακαρίζω καὶ οὐκ ἐγγίζει ἀνατελεῖ ἄστρον ἐξ Ιακωβ καὶ ἀναστήσεται ἄνθρωπος ἐξ Ισραηλ ("I will reveal him, but not now; I bless him, but he is not near; a star will rise out of Jacob, and a man will rise out of Israel").¹¹⁶ The messianic interpretation of Num 24:17 is clear in both Hebrew and Greek traditions.

The expectation of a royal messianic figure based on Num 24:17 extended into the Second Temple period, and even later into the rabbinic period. The Qumran Scrolls show evidence that Num 24:17 was interpreted messianically in the Second Temple period.¹¹⁷ The editor of 4QTestimonia evidently saw the text as an allusion to the royal Messiah (4Q175).¹¹⁸ The

112. Ibid.

113. Ibid. Dozeman, *Numbers*, 191; Milgrom, *Numbers*, 207; Olson, *Numbers*, 150; Wenham, *Numbers*, 201.

114. Olson, *Numbers*, 150.

115. Ashley, *Numbers*, 500, notes that although rare, a star is used in Israel to refer to a royal figure (Isa 14:12). Milgrom, *Numbers*, 207n17, notes the tradition where Rabbi Akiba identified this eschatological king as Bar Kokhba ("star"), thereby proclaiming him to be the Messiah. However, Milgrom also notes that כוכב can be translated as "host" yielding, "a host will march forth from Jacob." Further, he notes that in ANE mythology, it can refer to a literal comet or shooting star directed by gods to destroy their enemies. A scepter is a more common royal metaphor in Israel (Ps 45:6; Amos 1:5, 8; cf. Gen 49:10). Olson, *Numbers*, 150, comments that a royal staff or scepter symbolizes royal authority. He also notes that a staff can also symbolize authority in general as with Moses and Aaron in the exodus/wilderness tradition (Exod 4:2–5; 7:8–13; 17:5–6). On the staff (שבט) of both Moses and Aaron, see Cole, *Numbers*, 426.

116. Cathcart, "Numbers 24:17," 511–20, sees the Greek text as more messianic than the Hebrew. Lust, "Greek Version," 233–57, esp. 241, argues that the Greek text is no more messianic than the Hebrew, in spite of the former's use of ἄνθρωπος. I agree that both versions have messianic implications; however, it is safer to suggest that the LXX points more specifically to a human messianic figure where the MT points to a messianic notion in a vague, general sense. Ashley, *Numbers*, 500, notes (although not suggesting) that Balaam's oracle may apply to the nation of Israel as a whole rather than an individual Messiah.

117. Cole, *Numbers*, 426.

118. Brooke, "Thematic Commentaries," 134–57; Cathcart, "Numbers 24:17," 514;

use of the text in the *Damascus Document* is interesting in that the prophecy of the star is applied to the community's Interpreter of the Law, and the scepter with the prince of the whole congregation (CD 7:19–20), highlighting Qumran's multiple messianic expectation.[119] The "Interpreter of the Law" was the expected priestly Messiah, and the "Prince of the Congregation" was the Davidic Messiah.[120] Finally, in the *War Scroll*, the commentary on Num 24:17 is focused on God himself as the agent of destruction (1QM 11:5–7).[121] George Brooke's summary helps collate the various views of the prophetic figure of Num 24:17: "Whatever the case, it can be seen that this prophetic text is understood as concerning one or more eschatological figures."[122] The same interpretive trend regarding the royal Messiah of Num 24:17 is found in the Targums as well where *Targum Onqelos* translates "star" with "king" (מלכא) and "scepter" with "anointed one/Messiah" (משיחא).[123] It is clear that Num 24:17 was interpreted messianically throughout Israel's history by various groups, offering very early glimpses at the eschatological royal Messiah. John Collins observes, "We may speak of a strong and widespread tradition that identified the scepter with the Davidic messiah."[124] In summary, Balaam's prophecy in Num 24:17 speaks of the eschatological royal Messiah, and this interpretative tradition was more or less fixed in Second Temple Judaism. This messianic interpretation likely undergirds John's portrait of Jesus as the eschatological Messiah who reigns in the kingdom of God.[125]

The royal expectation of Balaam's oracle is paralleled in other literature of the Second Temple period, but with one additional detail: the royal

---

Collins, *Scepter and Star*, 65.

119. Brooke, "Thematic Commentaries," 139.

120. Cathcart, "Numbers 24:17," 515. I will interact more with the Davidic Messiah below.

121. Brooke, "Thematic Commentaries," 139; Collins, *Scepter and Star*, 65.

122. Brooke, "Thematic Commentaries," 139. For discussions of the multiple Messiahs of Qumran, see Cathcart, "Numbers 24:17," 514; Collins, "Messiah, Jewish," 4:63; Collins, *Scepter and Star*, 11, 78; VanderKam, *Dead Sea Scrolls Today*, 177–80. On the use of Balaam's oracle at Qumran, see Gordley, "Seeing Stars," 107–19.

123. Ashley, *Numbers*, 503; Cathcart, "Numbers 24:17," 512. Cathcart also notes that *Targum Neofiti* and *Targum Pseudo-Jonathan* share a similar messianic interpretation of Num 24:17.

124. Collins, *Scepter and Star*, 66. Collins also notes that there was quite a bit variation regarding this messianic expectation.

125. The interpretive tradition of Num 24:17 also undergirds other messianic passages in the NT such as the Star of Bethlehem (Matt 2:1–10), Jesus as the Root and Offspring of David, and the bright Morning Star of Rev 22:16. For more on these other NT connections, see Ashley, *Numbers*, 503; Cathcart, "Numbers 24:17," 516, 519; Cole, *Numbers*, 426; Duguid, *Numbers*, 286–88; Gane, *Leviticus, Numbers*, 712–13; Olson, *Numbers*, 150; Wenham, *Numbers*, 201.

Messiah would be specifically a *Davidic* king (Gen 49:10; 2 Sam 7:14), not any royal figure. *Psalms of Solomon* 17 is another notable example of the kingly expectation in the extant literature of the Second Temple period. Probably written around the middle of the first century BCE, it reflects the desire for a Davidic king to ascend to the throne to dispose of the Hasmoneans who had renewed native Jewish kingship, but they themselves were not descendants of David (*Pss. Sol.* 17:4-6).[126] What is more, it is likely a product of Pharisaism,[127] making it relevant to Nicodemus's own eschatological expectation. The desire for a descendent of David to ascend to the throne is explicitly stated:

> See, Lord, and raise up for them their king, the son of David, to rule over your servant Israel in the time known to you, O God. Undergird him with the strength to destroy the unrighteous rulers, to purge Jerusalem from gentiles who trample her to destruction; in wisdom and in righteousness to drive out the sinners from the inheritance; to smash the arrogance of sinners like a potter's jar; to shatter all their substance with an iron rod; to destroy the unlawful nations with the sword of his mouth; at his warning the nations will flee from his presence; and he will condemn sinners by the thoughts of their hearts (*Pss. Sol.* 17:21-25).[128]

Further, *Psalms of Solomon* refers to this Davidic king as the eschatological Messiah in titular fashion: "There will be no unrighteousness among them in his days, for all shall be holy, and their king shall be the Lord Messiah" (*Pss. Sol.* 17:32). Paul Achtemeier, Joel Green, and Marianne M. Thompson note regarding the messianic expectation of *Psalms of Solomon*, "This figure is called the anointed one of the Lord and son of David; he is expected to defeat Israel's enemies, gather the dispersed Jews together, and settle the tribes of Israel in the land."[129] Therefore, the paucity of the phrase "kingdom of God" in John's Gospel does not dilute the reality of the reign of God in a present and future sense, and the Pharisee Nicodemus would have been familiar with the concept even if he had a somewhat different understanding

---

126. Collins, "Messiah, Jewish," 4:63.

127. Ibid. Collins, *Scepter and Star*, 6. Collins also notes that the Pharisaic character of *Psalms of Solomon* has been questioned (ibid., 51, 69n23).

128. Translated by Wright. All quotations of the Pseudepigrapha are taken from Charlesworth, ed., *Old Testament Pseudepigrapha*.

129. Achtemeier et al., *Introducing*, 230.

of it than Jesus. The Messiah is a Davidic royal figure throughout John's Gospel,[130] and this is implied in John's "kingdom of God" language.

As stated earlier, Nicodemus is at risk of not experiencing the eschatological promises of God because of his signs-faith, which tends to run shallow in John. John 3:3 thematically echoes[131] Num 14:22–23. As the first wilderness generation was forbidden to enter, or even to see, the Promised Land due to their unbelief, Nicodemus similarly stands in jeopardy of not experiencing the kingdom of God. B. F. Westcott hears the verbal echo in the notion of entering the kingdom: "The image suggested by the words *enter into* is that of entering into the Promised Land—the type of the kingdom of heaven."[132] To be sure, this does not suggest an exact correspondence between the Pentateuch's eschatological expectation of life in the land and John's eschatological expectation of life eternal.[133] It simply highlights that those with fickle faith run the risk of not seeing (i.e., experiencing) the eschatological promises of God. A portion of the Pentateuchal eschatological expectation held that Israel would experience abundant life in the land of Canaan. God's promise to Abraham included the land (Gen 12:7; 13:14–17; 15:18–21), and this expectation would not have been lost on Nicodemus, who, as a Jewish ruler in the Second Temple period, expected the kingdom of God to include the land of Palestine.[134] As Emil Schürer notes, "The Holy Land [Palestine] forms the central point of this kingdom."[135] Ancient Israel's eschatological expectation held that the nation would dwell in its own land

---

130. Bauckham, *Testimony*, 213.

131. Meets the following criteria: Availability: John had access to the whole book of Numbers; Volume: use of verbal forms of ὁράω; Recurrence: John repeatedly appeals to wilderness imagery throughout his Gospel; Thematic Coherence: forfeiting the eschatological promises of God; Satisfaction: illuminates the larger discussion of the detriments of signs-faith.

132. Westcott, *John*, 50.

133. Burge has recently published an insightful study on "holy land" theology arguing that Christians should reexamine the claim that the land of Palestine is in and of itself holy (*Jesus and the Land*). In fact, the Fourth Gospel's replacement motif calls into question any notion of holy land theology: "What Judaism sought in its festivals and institutions, it can now find in Christ. What is sought in its Temple is now fulfilled in Christ. And the energies Judaism directed to the land must now be redirected to the One Vine of the vineyard who encompassed in his life the very promises life in the land had to offer" (ibid., 57). For more on the OT eschatological expectation of land, see Brueggemann, *The Land*; Gowan, *Eschatology*, 21–29.

134. For the Jewish expectation of land during the NT era, see Burge, *Jesus and the Land*, 10–11, 13–14; Schürer, *History of the Jewish People*, 2:172–75.

135. Schürer, *History of the Jewish People*, 2:172. Schürer also notes that the kingdom is not confined to Palestine, but ultimately comprises the whole world.

based on the promises of God to Abraham, Isaac, and Jacob,[136] and this expectation is especially prominent in Numbers, given that the fulfillment of land for an inheritance remains elusive.[137] In fact, the whole book of Numbers looks forward to the eventual occupation of the land of Canaan.[138] While the OT uses the phrase "kingdom of God" only once (Wis 10:10), the notion of God as King is prevalent nevertheless (Exod 15:18; Pss 93:1; 103:19). God's reign was global, encompassing the entire earth, which of course included the land of Canaan.[139] As C. C. Caragounis notes, "In the conquest of Canaan Yahweh as king apportions to his people a country; a country, moreover, which he, as the creator and king of the earth, can dispose as he pleases."[140] In John, Nicodemus is in danger of forfeiting not the land, as was the case with the first wilderness generation, but the kingdom of God in its more comprehensive sense, that is, eternal life under the reign of the royal Messiah. Nicodemus's signs-faith places him in the precarious position of not even seeing the eschatological promises of God.

It is clear from this study so far that John intends to introduce Nicodemus as a representative of those who demonstrate signs-faith. He is not only one of them, but is in fact their leader. John echoes the wilderness tradition in three ways as he introduces Nicodemus. First, his signs-faith reflects that of the older wilderness generation. Second, his representative leadership (ἄρχων) of the Jews has its roots in the wilderness tradition. Third, he is at risk for not being able to see the eschatological promises of God, (i.e., "kingdom of God"), much like the first wilderness generation. For John, signs-faith (*Zeichenglaube*) is tenuous at best, and at worst leads to outright rebellion and rejection. Unfortunately, the latter is often the normal course of events (Num 14:22; John 12:37). Therefore, John places Nicodemus in a precarious position as someone who has seen Jesus' miraculous signs and exhibits a measure of faith but not enough for Jesus to have faith in him. In short, by witnessing Jesus' signs, he has been put to the test by them. The signs that God worked through Moses (Deut 4:34; 8:2, 16) tested the first wilderness generation; consequently, those signs worked by Jesus tested Nicodemus and the Jerusalemites. It remains to be seen whether or

---

136. For more on the Pentateuch's eschatological expectation of land, see Alexander, *From Paradise to the Promised Land*; Burge, *Jesus and the Land*, 1–14.

137. Cole, *Numbers*, 56.

138. Wenham, *Numbers*, 48.

139. For more on the kingdom in the OT, see Achtemeier et al., *Introducing*, 215–17; Caragounis, "Kingdom of God/Heaven," 417–30, esp. 417–18; Carson, *John*, 188; Childs, *Biblical Theology*, 631–36; Beasley-Murray, *Jesus and the Kingdom of God*, 17–25; Ridderbos, *Coming of the Kingdom*, 3–8; Vos, *Biblical Theology*, 372–74.

140. Caragounis, "Kingdom of God/Heaven," 417–18.

not Nicodemus's faith will mature beyond signs-faith. Jesus will continue to test him throughout the remainder of the dialogue to see whether he has a hard or soft heart.

SPIRITUAL REBIRTH REQUIRED FOR FAITH

What will it take for Nicodemus to experience the kingdom of God? What will it take for him to grow beyond signs-faith to full commitment to Christ? John develops an elaborate answer to these questions in John 3:3–8, building on Jesus' authoritative declaration in vv. 3 and 5: ἀμὴν ἀμὴν ("Truly, truly" ESV).[141] In short, it will take a miraculous rebirth from God, through his Spirit, to effect a radical change of Nicodemus's heart and orientation (John 3:3, 5). Only those who are born from above can experience or enter the kingdom.[142] Nicodemus must be born from above; that is, he must undergo a circumcision of the heart, a spiritual renewal that leads him beyond signs-faith to a more heart-felt commitment to Christ. While the doctrine of "regeneration"[143] is most often associated with systematics, it is not altogether different from John's emphasis on spiritual rebirth. Simply stated, rebirth must take place in order for Nicodemus to truly believe in Jesus' miraculous signs and thus grasp the deeper realities of his messianic identity. Otherwise, he remains an obtuse Jewish leader who represents those who have signs-faith. When speaking of Nicodemus and those whom he represents, Köstenberger comments: "The Messiah (Jesus) is met with a spiritually unregenerate Jewish leadership that opposes his messianic mission."[144] I am more hesitant than Köstenberger at suggesting that Nicodemus "opposes" Jesus, but he certainly lacks spiritual clarity. John, then, confronts his ignorance and obtuseness with his need to experience rebirth. I will now demonstrate that John grounds various aspects of spiritual rebirth in the events of the exodus and wilderness: "rebirth," "water and Spirit," and the outpouring of the eschatological Spirit.

---

141. Köstenberger, *Encountering John*, 82–83.

142. Ladd, *Theology*, 326.

143. On the doctrine of spiritual regeneration, see Brooks, "New Birth," 149–64; Burge, *Anointed Community*, 165–69; Dodd, *Interpretation*, 223–24; Grenz, *Theology for the Community of God*, 536–41; Grudem, *Systematic Theology*, 699–706; Koester, *Word of Life*, 137–39; Köstenberger, *Theology*, 470–79; Murray, *Collected Writings*, 2:167–201; Russell, "Holy Spirit's Ministry," 227–39, esp. 230–32; Smith, *Theology*, 93–94, 163; VanGemeren, *Progress of Redemption*, 409.

144. Köstenberger, *Theology*, 199.

John first describes rebirth as γεννηθῇ ἄνωθεν (3:3). He has a well-documented penchant for double entendre[145]—using two meanings of a word, both of which are distinct enough that they cannot convey one aspect of thought.[146] This is evident in John's use of ἄνωθεν, which can be translated "again," "anew," "from the beginning," or "from above" in 3:3.[147] Translating ἄνωθεν as "from above" accounts best for Jesus' meaning and emphasis on the divine birth.[148] In fact, every other instance of the term in John's Gospel bears this meaning (3:31; 19:11, 23). However, translating ἄνωθεν as "again" accounts best for Nicodemus's misunderstanding. As Köstenberger keenly observes, "The popular phrase 'to be born again' is thus based on a misunderstanding."[149] Nevertheless, given John's quite sophisticated use of double entendre, "again" best preserves the ambiguity of ἄνωθεν.[150] It is obvious that Nicodemus (mis)understands ἄνωθεν as "again," as a second (i.e., literal) physical birth[151] (πῶς δύναται ἄνθρωπος γεννηθῆναι[152] γέρων ὤν; μὴ δύναται εἰς τὴν κοιλίαν τῆς μητρὸς αὐτοῦ δεύτερον εἰσελθεῖν καὶ γεννηθῆναι; ("How can a man be born being old? Is he able to enter into his mother's womb a second time and be born?" 3:4); therefore, he clearly misses Jesus' emphasis on the necessity (ἐὰν μή 3:3, 5) of being born from "above," i.e., from God.

Exodus as Rebirth

Rebirth, or birth from above, is used in certain Jewish exegetical traditions to describe Israel's experience during the exodus, therefore grounding the

---

145. Richard, "Expressions," 96–112; Wead, "Double Meaning," 106–20; Van Der Watt, "Double Entendre," 463–81. On other literary features in John 3:1–21, see Born, "Literary Features," 3–17.

146. Wead, "Double Meaning," 106.

147. Belleville, "Born," 138n75; Koester, *Word of Life*, 138; Morris, *Theology*, 256; Murray, *Collected Writings*, 2:176–78; Schnackenburg, *John*, 1:367; Smith, *Theology*, 163. That Jesus and Nicodemus's conversation may have originally been in Aramaic, where the wordplay did not exist, is immaterial given the Greek text of John is all we have. For more on this, see Carson, *John*, 191n1.

148. Murray, *Collected Writings*, 2:177.

149. Köstenberger, *Encountering John*, 84.

150. Barrett, *John*, 205; Koester, *Word of Life*, 138; Köstenberger, *Encountering John*, 84; Moloney, *Belief in the Word*, 109; Morris, *Theology*, 256n2.

151. Culpepper, *Anatomy*, 135; Schmidl, *Jesus und Nikodemus*, 169. Westcott, *John*, 49, sees here an intentional probing by Nicodemus of the difficult image at hand.

152. P66 adds ἄνωθεν to reflect the quote of v. 3.

notion in the wilderness.[153] While not an intertextual connection to Numbers per se, rebirth does stem from a wilderness context, and John is likely hinting at this in Jesus' dialogue with Nicodemus. Matthew Vellanickal draws attention to the notion of the exodus experience as that of the divine sonship of Israel as a nation based on Exod 4:22: "Israel is my first-born son" (ESV).[154] In the same way, he explains the covenant at Sinai as a "begetting" of Israel by God based on Deut 32:18: "You were unmindful of the Rock that bore you, and you forgot the God who gave you birth" (ESV).[155] After a brief survey of the OT material on the begetting of Israel, Vellanickal concludes: "Israel becomes 'son of God' as a result of their creation as 'people of God' through the saving act of Yahweh in Exodus and through the Covenant."[156] Peder Borgen also captures the relationship between begetting and the exodus tradition when commenting on John 3: "Drawing on the assumption that Moses and Israel experienced rebirth at Mt. Sinai, Jesus states that birth from above is a condition for entry into heaven. This birth does not take place by man's ascent into heaven. It is brought about by the descent and exaltation by the divine and royal Son of Man."[157] Two brief examples from Borgen's article will suffice. First, Philo views Moses' ascent on Sinai in Exod 24:16 as a second birth: "But the calling above of the prophet is a second birth better than the first" (QE 2:46). Moses' rebirth is identified with his experience at Mt. Sinai.[158] Second, the Rabbis make the connection between new birth and Sinai:

> I would lead thee, and bring thee: *I would lead Thee from the upper world to the lower.* I would bring thee into my mother's house: *this is Sinai. R. Berekiah said: Why is Sinai called* my mother's house? *Because there Israel became like a new-born child . . ."* (Song. Rab. 8:2, §1)[159]

A totally new beginning had taken place for Israel at Sinai, and their old identity in Egypt no longer had meaning.[160] This change of identity must

---

153. Borgen, "Exegetical Traditions," 243–58; Keener, *John*, 1:542, cites *b. Šabb.* 145b–146a; *Song. Rab.* 8:2, §1; Vellanickal, *Divine Sonship*, 38–39. I will discuss ἄνωθεν in more detail below.

154. Vellanickal, *Divine Sonship*, 10.

155. Ibid., 23–24. Thus, the redemption of Israel from Egypt is expressed as the begetting of Israel.

156. Ibid., 26.

157. Borgen, "Exegetical Traditions," 246.

158. Ibid., 256.

159. Taken from ibid. Targumic expansion italicized.

160. Ibid.

happen to Nicodemus. John's language of rebirth (γεννηθῇ ἄνωθεν, John 3:3) is important, not simply because Nicodemus needs a divine birth to grasp who Jesus is and what he teaches, but also because it reflects a connection with the exodus/wilderness event which was seen by Jewish exegetes as a new birth for Moses and Israel. The late date of the rabbinic materials is of little concern given that Philo likely relies on Jewish exegesis as a basis for his understanding of the Sinai ascent as rebirth; Philo supports the hypothesis that the core of many rabbinic passages goes back to the beginning of the first century or earlier.[161] Therefore, John's language of rebirth has foundational roots in the exodus/wilderness tradition of ancient Israel and this serves as a plausible explanation for his use of γεννηθῇ ἄνωθεν. For John, Nicodemus must experience rebirth in much the same way as Moses and Israel at the exodus event. God must give him a fresh start.

John Murray explains the inner dynamics of spiritual rebirth: "There is a change that God effects in man, radical and reconstructive in its nature, called new birth, new creation, regeneration, renewal—a change that cannot be accounted for by anything that is in lower terms than the interposition of the almighty power of God."[162] Rebirth is a miracle in the strictest sense of the word because God's Spirit is the active agent.[163] The source of spiritual rebirth is the grace, mercy, and love of God; it does not take its starting point from anything in mankind.[164] It will take this miracle for Nicodemus to truly see Jesus' miracles as pointers to his messianic mission. Therefore, John discusses rebirth as the requirement for Nicodemus to grow beyond signs-faith.

In addition to being born ἄνωθεν (3:3), John also describes the process of rebirth as γεννηθῇ ἐξ ὕδατος καὶ πνεύματος ("born of water and Spirit," 3:5).[165] The second phrase is an explanation of the first so that they should properly be seen as paralleling one another and differing only in terminology. Gary Burge helpfully illustrates the parallelism of vv. 3 and 5:[166]

161. Ibid., 257.
162. Murray, *Collected Writings*, 2:171.
163. Similarly, Smith, *Theology*, 163.
164. Murray, *Collected Writings*, 2:189. This does not eliminate Nicodemus's responsibility for it is presumed throughout the dialogue. He has the responsibility to believe what Jesus tells him. Burge, *Anointed Community*, 169n80, observes that πιστεύειν is the most repeated term in the discourse (eight times), surpassing even πνεῦμα. Simply put, faith is both a gift from God and a human responsibility in John's Gospel.
165. Bultmann, *John*, 138–39n3, sees ὕδατος καὶ as an insertion by the ecclesiastical redactor. This stems from Bultmann's anti-sacramental understanding of the Fourth Gospel. Nevertheless, there is no MS evidence to support Bultmann's contention of ὕδατος καὶ being an intrusion to the text.
166. Burge, *Anointed Community*, 167. On John 3:3, 5 as parallel expressions, see

3:3 ἀμὴν ἀμὴν λέγω σοι, ἐὰν μή τις γεννηθῇ ἄνωθεν,
οὐ δύναται ἰδεῖν
τὴν βασιλείαν τοῦ θεοῦ.

3:5 ἀμὴν ἀμὴν λέγω σοι, ἐὰν μή τις γεννηθῇ ἐξ ὕδατος καὶ πνεύματος,
οὐ δύναται εἰσελθεῖν
εἰς τὴν βασιλείαν τοῦ θεοῦ.

The idea of rebirth that is expressed in these two verses is a well-known interpretive crux. Nicodemus is confused by "rebirth" terminology and takes Jesus' comment as literally pertaining to physical birth. However, the reader of John's Gospel has encountered similar language in 1:13 when speaking of believers as children born not of natural descent, but born of God: οἳ οὐκ ἐξ αἱμάτων οὐδὲ ἐκ θελήματος σαρκὸς οὐδὲ ἐκ θελήματος ἀνδρὸς ἀλλ᾽ ἐκ θεοῦ ἐγεννήθησαν ("Those born not of blood, nor of the will of the flesh, nor of the will of man, but of God"). Nevertheless, γεννηθῇ ἄνωθεν and γεννηθῇ ἐξ ὕδατος καὶ πνεύματος have added to the confusion not only for Nicodemus but also for Johannine scholars throughout church history. As Schmidl remarks, "The words 'water and spirit' are the most-discussed of the third chapter."[167] Much of the debate swirls around whether or not γεννηθῇ ἐξ ὕδατος καὶ πνεύματος ("born of water and Spirit") should be taken as a Johannine reference to the sacrament of baptism.[168] Since in 3:5 ὕδατος καὶ πνεῦμα are governed by the single preposition ἐκ, "born of water and Spirit" should be seen as a hendiadys expressing one grand event, namely, rebirth.[169] Put differently, water and Spirit are not exclusive referents, one

---

Carson, *John*, 191; Köstenberger, *Encountering John*, 84; Köstenberger, *Theology*, 474; Murray, *Collected Writings*, 2:179; Schnackenburg, *John*, 1:366.

167. Schmidl, *Jesus und Nikodemus*, 144.

168. For more on this complex and multiperspectival discussion, see Anderson, "Born to Better Living," 165–69; Bernard, *John*, 1:CLXII–CLXVI; Belleville, "Born," 125–41; Beasley-Murray, *Baptism in the New Testament*, 226–32; Burge, *Anointed Community*, 159–64; Carson, *John*, 191–96; Keener, *John*, 1:548–50; Koester, *Symbolism*, 183–86; Koester, *Word of Life*, 18–21, 137–46; Kysar, *Maverick Gospel*, 122–26; McCabe, "The Meaning," 85–107; Morris, *Theology*, 256–58; Murray, *Collected Writings*, 2:180–81; Osburn, "Exegetical Observations," 129–38; Robinson, "Born of Water and Spirit," 15–23. On the sacraments in John in general, see Barrett, *John*, 82–85; Beasley-Murray, *Gospel of Life*, 85–101; Brown, *John*, 1:CXI–CXIV; Brown, *Introduction*, 229–34; Burge, *Anointed Community*, 150–90; Koester, *Symbolism*, 301–09; Kysar, *Voyages with John*, 247–50; Morris, *Theology*, 285–86; Ladd, *Theology*, 319–21; Paschal, "Sacramental Symbolism," 159–61; Schmidl, *Jesus und Nikodemus*, 144–91; Smalley, *Evangelist and Interpreter*, 204–10; Smith, *Theology*, 155–60; Witherington, *John's Wisdom*, 95–99. For my view, see Appendix 2.

169. Burge, *Anointed Community*, 166; Köstenberger, *Theology*, 474–75; Murray, *Collected Writings*, 2:179. I take the καὶ epexegetically, thus rendering the idea that water is Spirit as in 7:37–39 (cf. Isa 44:3–5; Ezek 36:25–27. Put differently, water is symbolic

referring to water baptism and the other to the Spirit. Instead, John uses water as a metaphor for the Spirit in his function of imparting life.[170] John 3:5, therefore, symbolizes the life-giving operation of the Spirit.[171]

"Water and Spirit" as Wilderness Imagery

John's water-spirit symbolism[172] is firmly rooted in his wilderness motif. Johannine commentators have not always noted this. For example, when commenting on John's use of "water and Spirit" (3:5), they propose strong connections to OT prophetic passages regarding the outpouring of the eschatological Spirit (Isa 44:3-4; Ezek 36:25-27; Joel 2:28-29).[173] I agree that there are indeed connections to be made with these prophetic texts, and I will survey a couple of these below. However, strong connections should also be made between the wilderness narratives of the Pentateuch and John's water-spirit symbolism. Given the prominent role that Mosaic traditions play in John's Gospel, and given the prevalent wilderness imagery that I have argued for so far in this study, water-spirit symbolism is equally suited to these traditions.

Jesus' discourse at the Feast of Tabernacles (John 7:37-39) is of prime importance for John's wilderness motif, and also contributes significantly to his water-Spirit symbolism. That Jesus fulfills the symbolism of Jewish feasts in John's Gospel is well documented.[174] His provocative discourse at Tabernacles demonstrates his fulfillment of the water and light ceremonies toward the end of the festival week.[175] My interest here is on the water ritual that, while not prescribed in the OT, became standardized by the first

---

of the Spirit. For this view, see Belleville, "Born," 129; Culpepper, *Anatomy,* 193-94; Keener, *John,* 1:550; Koester, *Symbolism,* 176-203; McCabe, "Born of Water and the Spirit," 90, 93; Murray, *Collected Writings,* 2:182-84; Robinson, "Water and Spirit," 19. I will interact with additional OT antecedents associated with this view below.

170. McCabe, "Born of Water and the Spirit," 93.

171. Ibid.

172. Burge, *Anointed Community,* 161-71; Glasson, *Moses,* 48-59; Koester, *Symbolism,* 175-206.

173. Belleville, "Born," 140; Carson, *John,* 195; Keener, *John,* 1:551; Köstenberger, *John,* 124.

174. For a good summary treatment, see Köstenberger, *Theology,* 413-22.

175. For more on the Feast of Tabernacles and its attendant symbolism in John, see Brown, *John,* 1:306, 320-29; Burge, *Anointed Community,* 88-93; Carson, *John,* 305, 326-28; Edersheim, *The Temple,* 212-28; Glasson, *Moses,* 48-64; Keener, *John,* 1:703-04, 721-25; Köstenberger, *Theology,* 420-22; Kurtz, *Offerings,* 381-85; Ridderbos, *John,* 272-76; Thompson, "John," 182-200, esp. 194; Wise, "Feasts," 234-41.

century CE.[176] The Feast of Tabernacles, or Feast of Booths, commemorates the sojourn of Israel in the wilderness after the exodus from Egypt.[177] It was originally a harvest festival that recalled the provisions of God in the wilderness, itself a place of desolation and lack of water.[178] The water ritual, which occurred toward the end of the feast, recalled God's miraculous provision of water in the wilderness (Exod 17:1-6; Num 20:2-13; 21:16-18). As an aside, particularly noteworthy are the two passages from Numbers. The first recalls the miraculous outpouring of water from the rock struck by Moses: ἐπάταξεν τὴν πέτραν τῇ ῥάβδῳ δίς καὶ ἐξῆλθεν ὕδωρ πολύ ("He struck the rock twice with the staff and much water came out," Num 20:11). The second remembers the "song of the well" (Num 21:16-18). Both passages recall God's provision of water in the wilderness and both have been proposed as possible backgrounds for John's reference to ὕδατος ζῶντος ("living water," John 7:38) at Tabernacles.[179] The water ritual at Tabernacles recalled these events. It consisted of a daily procession where the priest would fill a golden pitcher with water from the Pool of Siloam; he would then march to the temple where he would pour out the water onto the altar.[180] A special water-pouring rite, as well as a lighting ceremony at the temple, marked the seventh day of the festival (*m. Sukkah* 4:1, 9-10).[181] While the water ritual recalled the events of the past, it also anticipated God's abundant provision in the immediate future for the upcoming harvest. As Koester observes, "The outpouring of the water was a visible petition that as God provided water for the people in the past, he would send the rains again and grant prosperity to his people during the coming year."[182] However, not only did the ceremony petition God to act in the immediate future, it also anticipated the outpouring of his blessings, symbolized as "living waters" (ὕδωρ ζῶν) in the eschatological era as foretold by the prophet Zechariah: "On that day living waters shall flow out from Jerusalem," (Zech 14:8 ESV; cf. Isa 43:19; 44:3; Ezek 47:1-11). T. F. Glasson notes the dual aspect of looking backward and forward in the symbolic events associated with the festival: "It would be difficult for those who witnessed the water ceremony to avoid thinking of

---

176. Köstenberger, *Theology*, 421.
177. Kurtz, *Offerings*, 382.
178. Similarly, ibid.
179. Hanson, *Prophetic Gospel*, 107-09.
180. Carson, *John*, 321-22; Koester, *Symbolism*, 197; Köstenberger, *Theology*, 421.
181. I will discuss this lighting ceremony below.
182. Koester, *Symbolism*, 197.

the waters in the desert as well as the promised streams of the Messianic era especially as the latter were derived from the events of the desert period."[183]

John illustrates that on the last great day of the feast[184] Jesus applies the symbolism of the water ceremony to himself: ἐάν τις διψᾷ ἐρχέσθω πρός με καὶ πινέτω, ὁ πιστεύων εἰς ἐμέ. καθὼς εἶπεν ἡ γραφή, ποταμοὶ ἐκ τῆς κοιλίας αὐτοῦ ῥεύσουσιν ὕδατος ζῶντος ("If anyone thirsts, let him to come me and drink, whoever believes in me. Just as the Scripture says, rivers of living water will flow from his belly," John 7:37–38).[185] Jesus, therefore, invites his audience to come to him, the source of eschatological water, i.e., the Spirit. John makes the connection between water and Spirit clear for his audience with his own commentary on Jesus' invitation: τοῦτο δὲ εἶπεν περὶ τοῦ πνεύματος ("Now he said this concerning the Spirit," 7:39). What is more, John clarifies that his comment is about the outpouring of the Spirit in the eschatological era: ὃ ἔμελλον λαμβάνειν οἱ πιστεύσαντες εἰς αὐτόν· οὔπω γὰρ ἦν πνεῦμα, ὅτι Ἰησοῦς οὐδέπω ἐδοξάσθη ("Which those who believed in him were about to receive; for the Spirit had not yet been given, because Jesus was not yet glorified," 7:39). John, therefore, builds on the symbolism of the feast that both remembers the wilderness sojourn and anticipates the eschatological provision of God in the messianic era. As water is a dominant symbol at the feast, so it is also in John's Gospel. While 7:37–39 is only one instance where "water" carries a wilderness connotation, Glasson observes similar usage elsewhere, "The influence of the wilderness experiences can be traced in other Johannine references to water."[186] He has in mind 4:14

---

183. Glasson, *Moses*, 50.

184. For more on the timing of Jesus' words in relation to the feast, see Carson, *John*, 321.

185. I have opted for the Western, or christological interpretation which sees Jesus as the source of living water rather than the believer (Eastern interpretation represented in P66 and P67). While John does report that water wells up within the believer (John 4:14), his use of Scripture in 7:37–38 begs for a christological application. Put differently, John usually uses Scripture to point to Christ, not believers. Further, it would seem strange based on the connection with the Holy Spirit immediately following (v. 39) that believers could dispense the Spirit. Equally difficult is Jesus' citation of "the Scripture" (ἡ γραφή) which reflects no single OT passage. Jesus seems to refer to a matrix of passages which are associated with the outpouring of water (which John identifies as the Spirit in v. 39) in the messianic era (Num 20:11; 21:16–18; Neh 8:5–18; Isa 12: 3; 44:3; 49:10; 58:11; Ezek 36:25–27; 47:1; Joel 2:28; 3:18; Amos 9:11–15; Zech 13:1; 14:8). For more on the complexities of the grammar and theology associated with both Western and Eastern views as well the scriptural proofs associated with this passage, see Brown, *John*, 1:320–23; Burge, *Anointed Community*, 88–93; Carson, *John*, 322–29; Glasson, *Moses*, 50–51; Hanson, *Prophetic Gospel*, 99–115; Keener, *John*, 1:726–30; Köstenberger, *Theology*, 420–22; Michaels, *John*, 463–67.

186. Glasson, *Moses*, 55.

where living water is said to "leap up" within the believer, a text that recalls the song of the well in the wilderness (Num 21:17ff). This is another instance of John's water-spirit symbolism, and this becomes apparent as the dialogue with the Samaritan women unfolds and culminates in the Spirit's role in true worship (4:24). To be sure, the wilderness connotations of water in 4:14 and 7:37–39 are more explicit than in 3:5. Nonetheless, given John's pervasive water-spirit symbolism, these passages should not be read in isolation of each other; they mutually illuminate one another other. That is, water-spirit symbolism is a connecting link between 3:5, 4:14, and 7:37–39.[187] It is therefore safe to conclude that John's use of "water" often carries a wilderness connotation as well as an eschatological one and our current passage (3:5) is yet another occurrence of both.

The Spirit Evokes Belief

If Nicodemus is ever to move beyond fickle faith to firm faith, he will need God's Spirit to do so. John's focus in this section is undoubtedly not on the water but rather on the Spirit, as he is at the center of the dialogue through v. 8. While ὕδωρ occurs only once in the pericope, πνεῦμα occurs five times, thereby solidifying it as Jesus' emphasis.[188] Yet the two cannot be easily separated. Westcott states the relationship between water and Spirit succinctly: "The two are coordinate, correlative, complimentary."[189] It is probably best to see here a reference to the third person of the Trinity as Murray boldly states: "There is no room for question but that *Pneumatos* is the Holy Spirit."[190] On this understanding, John emphasizes the need for a *Spiritual* rebirth, i.e., a birth that results specifically from the life-giving Spirit.

The role of the Spirit in John's Gospel is a formidable study in its own right.[191] Frank Pack states it succinctly as he writes, "The Fourth Gospel

---

187. Lincoln, *John*, 174. Similarly, Köstenberger, *Theology*, 165.

188. McCabe, "Water and the Spirit," 89. See also, Burge, *Anointed Community*, 165–67; Koester, *Symbolism*, 183; Schmidl, *Jesus und Nikodemus*, 146.

189. Westcott, *John*, 49.

190. Murray, *Collected Writings*, 2:183 (cf. 2:171). The absence of the definite article (τό) is inconsequential because an anarthrous noun may be definite (McCabe, "Water and the Spirit," 97). Against this, see Carson, *John*, 195; Köstenberger, *Theology*, 393–94.

191. Barrett, *John*, 88–92; Barrett, "Holy Spirit," 1–15; Beare, "Spirit of Life," 110–25; Beasley-Murray, *Gospel of Life*, 59–84; Brown, "Paraclete," 113–32; Burge, *Anointed Community*; Bultmann, *John*, 139–40n1; Culpepper, *Gospel and Letters*, 103–05; Dodd, *Interpretation*, 213–27; Koester, *Word of Life*, 133–60; Köstenberger, *Theology*, 393–400; Kysar, *Maverick Gospel*, 106–12; Ladd, *Theology*, 322–33; Martyn, *History and Theology*, 136–43; Morris, *John*, 587–91; Morris, *Theology*, 256–65; Frank Pack, "Holy Spirit in the Fourth Gospel," 139–48; Ridderbos, *John*, 14–16; Russell, "Holy Spirit's Ministry";

presents the fullest account of the Holy Spirit and his activities of any of the Gospels."[192] Primarily for the present purpose, the Spirit moves people to faith. As the Spirit gives life (τὸ πνεῦμά ἐστιν τὸ ζῳοποιοῦν, 6:63), he also evokes faith, enabling recipients to see the identity and mission of Christ with eyes of faith. Eduard Schweizer states it perhaps most profoundly, "For John the supreme miracle is when a person is brought to faith. When that happens a new world dawns, a new kind of life begins . . . it is the Creator-Spirit that summons us into life."[193] The Spirit brings people to faith and enables them to believe, and this is embedded in the John's presentation of spiritual rebirth.[194] John does not describe *how* the Spirit engenders faith; there is no systematic elaboration on this complex dynamic. However, he does illustrate *that* the Spirit engenders faith by providing evidence of the Spirit's presence at numerous, critical encounters where subjects begin to grasp Jesus' identity. For example, John the Baptist confesses to not knowing that Jesus was the Son, the Lamb of God (1:31, 33), until he saw the Spirit descend and remain on Jesus (τεθέαμαι τὸ πνεῦμα καταβαῖνον ὡς περιστερὰν ἐξ οὐρανοῦ καὶ ἔμεινεν ἐπ' αὐτόν, 1:32). Jesus describes to the Samaritan woman at the well the kinds of worshipers whom God seeks to worship him "in Spirit and truth" (ἐν πνεύματι καὶ ἀληθείᾳ, 4:23-24).[195] She then becomes a model of discipleship as well an evangelist to her fellow townspeople (4:28-29, 39-42). After feeding the 5,000, Jesus challenges many of his disciples to believe in him not simply because of the miraculous feeding, but also because his words are Spirit and life (τὰ ῥήματα ἃ ἐγὼ λελάληκα ὑμῖν πνεῦμά ἐστιν καὶ ζωή ἐστιν, 6:63).[196] While it is true that some disciples abandoned Jesus after hearing him elaborate the meaning of the feeding miracle thus proving their unbelief, Peter's great confession immediately follows: ῥήματα ζωῆς αἰωνίου ἔχεις, καὶ ἡμεῖς πεπιστεύκαμεν καὶ ἐγνώκαμεν ὅτι σὺ εἶ ὁ ἅγιος τοῦ θεοῦ ("You have words of eternal life, and we have come to believe and know that you are the Holy One of God," 6:68-69). After Jesus speaks of the thirst-quenching power of the Spirit at

---

Smalley, "Pneumatology," 289-300.

192. Pack, "Holy Spirit in the Fourth Gospel," 139.
193. Quoted in Morris, *Theology*, 258n6.
194. Similarly, Brown, *John*, 1:140.
195. For πνεῦμα as a reference to the Holy Spirit in John 4:23-24, see Barrett, *John*, 238; Beasley-Murray, *Gospel of Life*, 69-70; Burge, *Anointed Community*, 192-93; Carson, *John*, 224-25; Ridderbos, *John*, 163-64. Against this, see Köstenberger, *John*, 156.
196. The first clause in v. 63 (τὸ πνεῦμά ἐστιν τὸ ζῳοποιοῦν) demonstrates that it is none other than the Spirit that Jesus speaks of in connection with his own words. For this as a reference to the Spirit, see Barrett, *John*, 305; Carson, *John*, 301-02; Ridderbos, *John*, 246. Against this, see Köstenberger, *John*, 219n94.

the water ceremony of the Feast of Tabernacles (7:37-39), many acclaimed him as "the Prophet" (ὁ προφήτης, 7:40). One final example involves Jesus' glorification on the cross in 19:30. The Gospel's pervasive water-Spirit symbolism likely undergirds John's account of Jesus' death. For example, he first gives up the Spirit (παρέδωκεν τὸ πνεῦμα, 19:30), which may be an anthropological statement (i.e., "He gave up his spirit") or a pneumatological one ("He gave up the Spirit").[197] Secondly, the outpouring of blood and water (αἷμα καὶ ὕδωρ, 19:34) from Jesus' pierced side probably symbolizes his giving forth the life-giving Spirit to those who believe (cf. 7:37-39).[198] As Burge perceptively notes, "The Spirit is thus closely tied with Jesus' death. There is in 19:34 a proleptic symbol of the [eschatological] release of the Spirit."[199] It is in this connection that John writes his own commentary on the cross: ἵνα καὶ ὑμεῖς πιστεύ[σ]ητε ("so that you also may believe," 19:35). Examples could be multiplied, but these help to illustrate the Spirit's role in bringing people to believe in Jesus throughout John's Gospel.

The entire discussion of being born from above is one and the same with coming to faith. Donald Miller expresses the idea that to be born from above/again "is to receive the gift of faith."[200] Put differently, being brought to faith is expressed in the present passage as γεννηθῇ ἄνωθεν.[201] Being born anew means coming to faith, and faith is the primary manifestation of the Spirit's work.[202] The main issue in Jesus' dialogue with Nicodemus is wheth-

197. Barrett, *John*, 554; Carson, *John*, 621; Köstenberger, *John*, 551, take the anthropomorphic view, although τὸ πνεῦμα makes this view tenuous. The addition of the definite article and the lack of a personal pronoun cause serious difficulties for the anthropological view. Given John's penchant for double-meaning, it may be a symbolic giving of the Spirit, which proleptically points to the climactic giving of the Spirit in 20:22. For this view, see Burge, *Anointed Community*, 133-35; Lincoln, *John*, 478; Michaels, *John*, 965.

198. Burge, *Anointed Community*, 93-95; Michaels, *John*, 969. Commentators debate the source of the phrase, "Out of his heart will flow rivers of living water," in John 7:38. Does living water come from within the invigorated believer or from Christ? I agree with Burge that Christ is the source of this living water (ibid., 95). Dodd, *Interpretation*, 428, and Pryor, *Covenant People*, 39-40, also support the view that Christ is the source of living water, not the believer. Against this, as well as for a detailed discussion of the complexities of John 7:37-38, see Carson, *John*, 321-28.

199. Burge, *Anointed Community*, 95.

200. Miller, "John 3:1-21," 174-79.

201. Similarly, Koester, *Word of Life*, 137, 142-43. In an effort not to reduce coming to faith to a punctiliar moment in time, Koester aptly notes the complexity of Nicodemus's faith journey throughout the Gospel. In short, the movement from unbelief to belief can take different forms in different characters; the Gospel seems to appreciate this diversity while at the same time pressing for clarity in one's commitment to Jesus.

202. Koester, *Symbolism*, 184.

er or not he believes, or better, the focus of his faith—Jesus' miraculous signs or his messianic identity. If flesh gives birth to flesh (τὸ γεγεννημένον ἐκ τῆς σαρκὸς σάρξ ἐστιν, "That which is born of flesh is flesh," 3:6) and if like begets like,[203] then what is needed for Nicodemus to truly believe is a miraculous outpouring of faith through God's Spirit. For John, "flesh" (σάρξ) is not inherently evil—after all, God's Word became flesh (1:14)—but it is limited.[204] Flesh is frail, mortal, and creaturely.[205] John has already distinguished in the Prologue the difference between being born of the flesh and being born of God: "Those born not of blood, nor of the will of the flesh, nor of the will of man, but of God," 1:13). John's concern in both 1:13 and 3:6 is to contrast those who remain part of the natural human order with those who have been transformed by God's Spirit.

Spiritual rebirth is so important for Nicodemus to grasp that Jesus repeats with stronger, more direct language in v. 7 what he introduced in v. 3: δεῖ ὑμᾶς γεννηθῆναι ἄνωθεν ("You must be born from above," 3:7).[206] Being born from above points to a divine necessity expressed by the typical Johannine impersonal verb δεῖ (3:14, 30; 4:4, 24; 9:4; 10:16; 12:34; 20:9).[207] Granted, it is not inevitable that Nicodemus will be born from above. Jesus is not promising him that he will be illuminated by God's Spirit and transformed. He simply states it as a divine necessity and as the means through which one experiences the eschatological kingdom of God.[208]

In classic Johannine double-meaning fashion, Jesus offers an analogy, or a short parable,[209] between those who are born of the Spirit and the blowing of the wind: τὸ πνεῦμα ὅπου θέλει πνεῖ καὶ τὴν φωνὴν αὐτοῦ ἀκούεις, ἀλλ' οὐκ οἶδας πόθεν ἔρχεται καὶ ποῦ ὑπάγει· οὕτως ἐστὶν πᾶς ὁ

---

203. Murray, *Collected Writings*, 2:194.

204. Koester, *Word of Life*, 138.

205. Keener, *John*, 1:553. As Gregory of Nyssa states: "We know too that the flesh is subject to death because of sin, but the Spirit of God is both incorruptible and life-giving and beyond death." Quoted in Elowsky, *John 1–10*, 114. To be sure, flesh does not carry the negative connotations in John as it often does in Paul (Rom 8:3–8; 1 Cor 3:3), nor is it to be despised as in Gnosticism (Burge, *Anointed Community*, 168n74). For more on the flesh and spirit dualism in John, Murray, *Collected Writings*, 2:184–86; Ridderbos, *John*, 128–32.

206. The plural "you" (ὑμᾶς) in v. 7 has been variously explained, but harks back to Nicodemus's "we know" (οἴδαμεν) in v. 2. Perhaps the best option is to see it as reflecting Nicodemus's representative role as member of the Pharisees, possibly the Sanhedrin, the Jerusalemites in 2:23–25, or the Jewish nation as a whole (Barrett, *John*, 210; Köstenberger, *John*, 124; Michaels, *John*, 186).

207. Michaels, *John*, 186.

208. Ibid.

209. Schnackenburg, *John*, 1:373.

γεγεννημένος ἐκ²¹⁰ τοῦ πνεύματος ("The wind blows where it wills and you hear its sound, but you do not know from where it comes or where it goes; so it is with all who have been born of the Spirit," 3:8; cf. Eccl 11:5). Commentators frequently point out that "Spirit," "wind," and "breath" translate the same Greek term πνεῦμα, so there is an obvious wordplay at work, but it cannot be duplicated precisely in English.²¹¹ There is also a play on the "sound" (φωνή) of the wind, which is also the "voice" (φωνή) of the Spirit.²¹² The comparison is not between the Spirit and the wind but rather between those born of flesh and those born of Spirit. Nevertheless, comparing the Spirit to the wind is not far from John's point: those born of the Spirit replicate the Spirit's character, making their origin and destiny as mysterious to outsiders.²¹³ The imagery is meant in part to further the contrast between those born of flesh and those born of the Spirit. The wind is observable only by the effect it has on the environment as it blows. People hear and feel the wind; they see what it passes, but do not see the wind itself. It cannot be pinned down by human determination; it cannot be tamed. John Chrysostom noted how ineffectual humans are at controlling the wind: "No one can hold the wind; it moves where it pleases. And so, whether it is the laws of nature or the limits of bodily generation or anything else like this—they have no ability to restrain the operations of the Spirit."²¹⁴ The wind is in a sense mysterious, and so it is with those born of the Spirit. They participate in the divine nature and have begun to experience an unbound and unlimited existence (i.e., eternal life). As Herman Ridderbos helpfully summarizes, "Wind is observable, but it goes sovereignly where it pleases and is untraceable in its origin and disappearance. Also free, mighty, and untraceable in its movements is the Spirit in a person who is born of the Spirit."²¹⁵

Spiritual Rebirth not a Novel Concept

The entire description of new birth from above through the Spirit is utterly unrecognizable to Nicodemus the Pharisee who asks: "How are these things

---

210. א adds τοῦ ὕδατος καὶ in v. 8 as an assimilation to v. 5. Westcott, *John*, 51, properly sees this as a gloss.

211. Barrett, *John*, 210–11; Brown, *John*, 131; Michaels, *John*, 187, among others. The same wordplay appears with the Hebrew רוח.

212. Keener, *John*, 1:558.

213. Ibid., 1:555.

214. Quoted in Elowsky, *John 1–10*, 116.

215. Ridderbos, *John*, 129. For additional parallels between the Spirit and wind, see Murray, *Collected Writings*, 2:187; Westcott, *John*, 51.

able to be?" (πῶς δύναται ταῦτα γενέσθαι; John 3:9). Jesus chastised him earlier for being so obtuse to the idea of spiritual rebirth: "Stop being surprised that I said to you, 'You all must be born from above,'" (μὴ θαυμάσῃς ὅτι εἶπόν σοι· δεῖ ὑμᾶς γεννηθῆναι ἄνωθεν, 3:7).[216] Jesus' frustration with Nicodemus's lack of spiritual clarity is even more evident in v. 10: "*You* are the teacher of Israel and you do not know these things?" (σὺ εἶ ὁ διδάσκαλος τοῦ Ἰσραὴλ καὶ ταῦτα οὐ γινώσκεις;).[217] Jesus' observation is saturated with irony.[218] First, Nicodemus is "the teacher" (ὁ διδάσκαλος) of his people, which highlights once again his representative role as a "ruler of the Jews" (3:2).[219] Where Nicodemus originally hailed Jesus as a "teacher" who has come from God, Jesus in a kind of mock confession now reminds Nicodemus of his own authoritative status.[220] Second, the idea that a Pharisee, a ruler of the Jews, a teacher of Israel, could be even slightly ignorant of the OT prophetic promises of the outpouring of the Spirit in the eschatological era, adds to the thick irony of the dialogue. As Robert V. McCabe observes, "As a recognized Jewish teacher, Nicodemus should have been familiar with eschatological contexts, such as Isaiah 44 and Ezekiel 36–37, affirming the cleansing and transformation produced by the Spirit."[221] The Pharisees not only acknowledged the Torah as divine Scripture, but also the Prophets.[222] This latter corpus, with which I will interact in more detail below, repeatedly anticipates the eschatological outpouring of the Spirit (Isa 44:3–5; Ezek 36:25–27; Joel 2:28–29). Nevertheless, C. K. Barrett perceives Nicodemus's apparent ignorance and the irony of the situation: "Nicodemus, therefore, as the representative of the people of God ought above all men to have understood the meaning of the Spirit and birth from above, since his own authoritative Scripture, the Old Testament, bears witness to these themes."[223]

---

216. "Stop being surprised," reflects Köstenberger, *Theology*, 475.

217. Note the emphatic placement of σὺ. In addition, while I have opted to translate Jesus' statement as a question, it can be translated as a simple statement of fact: "You are the teacher of Israel, and you do not know these things" (Michaels, *John*, 189).

218. Michaels, *John*, 189; Duke, *Irony*, 45–46; Köstenberger, *Theology*, 198. For more on Johannine irony, see Carter, *Storyteller*, 118–22; Duke, *Irony*; O'Day and Hylen, *John*, 9–10; Köstenberger, *Encountering John*, 83.

219. Duke, *Irony*, 46.

220. Michaels, *John*, 189.

221. McCabe, "Water and the Spirit," 99. For my view on Nicodemus's apparent confusion, see Appendix 3.

222. Albert Bell, *Exploring the New Testament World*, 35.

223. Barrett, *John*, 211. On spiritual rebirth as an OT reality, and as such, readily recognizable to Nicodemus in theory, see Lewis, "New Birth," 35–44.

This raises the issue regarding the background of spiritual rebirth and Nicodemus's familiarity (or lack of) with it. I have already noted that "rebirth" has roots in the Sinai experience of Moses and Israel, therefore providing a wilderness background for the idea of rebirth. I have also illustrated a wilderness background for "water and Spirit" in the Feast of Tabernacles. These motifs are bound tightly together in the prophetic corpus, a division of the OT with which Nicodemus must have been familiar. His ineptitude regarding the outpouring of the Spirit once again adds to the thick irony of John's portrait of him as a Pharisee and ruler of the Jews.

There are parallels in Hellenism that may form the background of John's thought regarding rebirth;[224] however, more relevant are the plethora of OT passages which speak directly to the outpouring of God's Spirit on his covenant people for their rebirth. To be sure, the phrases, γεννηθῇ ἄνωθεν and γεννηθῇ ἐξ ὕδατος καὶ πνεύματος are scripturally unprecedented;[225] however, there are key prophetic passages that proleptically point to the miraculous phenomenon of spiritual rebirth in the eschatological era. These prophetic passages that speak of water and Spirit in the same breath are especially relevant to the Johannine emphasis on spiritual rebirth in the eschatological era. For example, water and Spirit are correlated in Isa 44:3–5 and Ezek 36:25–27 (cf. Joel 2:28–29; *Jub.* 1:23).[226] The cleansing and purifying metaphor of water parallels the restorative work of the Spirit in the eschatological era. Both passages likely stand behind John's understanding of rebirth expressed in John 3:3–8.[227] Given the Pharisaic affirmation of the prophetic corpus of the OT, McCabe presents some startling statistics regarding its emphasis on the eschatological outpouring of the Spirit:

---

224. Bultmann, *John*, 133–43, emphasizes a Gnostic influence. Dodd, *Interpretation*, 223–27, emphasizes the influence of Hermetic literature. For more on the Hellenistic background of rebirth, see Barrett, *John*, 207; Keener, *John*, 1:539–41. Barrett's understanding is that rebirth, while having roots in both Judaism and Hellenism, is uniquely Christian as John presents it. While I agree with Barrett given the christological affirmations that run throughout the pericope, this does not alter the fact that Jesus apparently felt that Nicodemus had enough of a biblical template to be able to make sense of the eschatological expectation of the Spirit and its regenerating effect on God's people. Keener notes that all of the sources available for placing rebirth in a Hellenistic context of some kind are late (*John*, 1:541).

225. Belleville, "Born," 137.

226. McCabe, "Water and the Spirit," 90. For more on the OT parallelism of water and Spirit, see Hildebrandt, *Theology*, 62–66.

227. Barrett, *John*, 208; Belleville, "Born," 137–39; Brown, *John*, 139–40; Carson, *John*, 191–96; Keener, *John*, 1:542–44, 552; Köstenberger, *John*, 124; McCabe, "Water and the Spirit," 90; Moloney, *Belief in the Word*, 115; Pryor, *Covenant People*, 19; Robinson, "Born of Water and Spirit," 17; Ridderbos, *John*, 132; Russell, "Holy Spirit's Ministry," 231–32; Schnackenburg, *John*, 1:371.

Both Isaiah and Ezekiel use the Old Testament term רוח ("breath, spirit, wind") over 50 times. Of the 377 or 378 uses of רוח in the Masoretic Text, רוח is found in Isaiah 51 times and Ezekiel 52 times. Because of the major emphases of Isaiah and Ezekiel, these are texts with which a Jewish teacher such as Nicodemus should have been acquainted.[228]

The parallelism of water and Spirit in Isa 44:3–4 describes the eschatological era of blessing:

"For I will pour water on the thirsty land
   and streams on the dry ground;
I will pour my Spirit upon your offspring
   and my blessing on your descendants.
They shall spring up among the grass,
   Like willows by flowing streams" (ESV).

Even more to the point in Jesus' dialogue with Nicodemus, Ezek 36:25–27 demonstrates the same parallelism as Isaiah, but touches more specifically on renewal and personal moral transformation:

"I will sprinkle clean water on you,
   And you shall be clean from all your uncleannesses,
   And from all your idols I will cleanse you.
And I will give you a new heart, and a new spirit I will put within you.
   And I will remove the heart of stone from your flesh and give you a heart of flesh.
   And I will put my Spirit within you,
And cause you to walk in my statutes and be careful to obey my rules" (ESV).

As in John, the emphasis in both prophetic passages is on divine intervention which effects a change in human nature itself.[229] This emphasis on divine rebirth is part and parcel of the larger eschatological expectation of the prophets. Put differently, it is not as if renewal and rebirth were peripheral blessings of the messianic era, so that perhaps they received little attention in Second Temple Judaism's eschatological outlook. On the contrary, Benjamin Warfield goes so far as to suggest that "The recreative activity of the Spirit of God is made the *crowning* Messianic blessing; and this is as much

---

228. McCabe, "Water and the Spirit," 90.

229. Gowan, *Eschatology*, 73. See ibid., 73–75 for a more detailed discussion of spiritual rebirth in OT prophetic works.

as to say that the promised Messianic salvation included in it provision for the renewal of men's hearts."[230] While the intricacies of Isa 44:3–4 and Ezek 36:25–27 are beyond the scope of this study, these passages nevertheless reveal an OT context for "water and Spirit" in the eschatological era.

The fact that Nicodemus is a Pharisee, a member of a scholar class[231] devoted to the interpretation and application of Scripture, makes it extremely doubtful that he was wholly ignorant of these prophetic passages, not to mention similar ones in the Torah.[232] As previously stated, the prophetic corpus played a central role in establishing Pharisaic doctrines, such as resurrection of the body, the expected arrival of a Messiah, the last judgment, rewards and punishments in the afterlife, and proselyte baptism, to name a few.[233] Furthermore, it is important to note that Jesus is not alone in Second Temple Judaism in appealing to the prophetic tradition of water and Spirit and the necessity of spiritual rebirth. The Qumran community also assimilated similar traditions dealing with spiritual cleansing where water and spirit are combined as in the OT: "He will sprinkle over him the spirit of truth like lustral water (in order to cleanse him) from all the abhorrences of deceit and from the defilement of the unclean spirit" (1QS 4:21–22).[234] So, spiritual renewal, symbolized by water, which is Spirit, is attested in Second Temple Judaism. Put differently, spiritual rebirth symbolized by water and Spirit should have been recognizable as an eschatological concept to the teacher of Israel.

Eschatological Outpouring of the Spirit Anticipated in the Wilderness

All of the passages previously mentioned regarding the outpouring of the Spirit are originally grounded in the wilderness narratives of Numbers. As

---

230. Quoted in Murray, *Collected Writings*, 2:173–74. Italics added.

231. Bell, *Exploring the New Testament World*, 33.

232. On the importance of Scripture in Pharisaism, see Davies, *Introduction to Pharisaism*, 12–14.

233. Ferguson, *Backgrounds of Early Christianity*, 516; Bell, *Exploring the New Testament World*, 36. Abrahams, *Studies in Pharisaism and the Gospels*, 1:36–46, has amassed several scriptural proofs from the prophets such as Ezek 36:25–27, which may stand behind the practice of proselyte baptism as regeneration among the Pharisees. However, his methodology stems solely from later rabbinic sources, which he takes as substantially reflective of Pharisaic theology. This assumption has been challenged by Neusner, *From Politics to Piety*.

234. Moloney, *Belief in the Word*, 115. English translations of the Dead Sea Scrolls are taken from Martínez, *Dead Sea Scrolls Translated*.

previously demonstrated, the Spirit's influence is important for Nicodemus's faith. As a leader of the Jews, his ineptitude regarding the Spirit—both as the personal agent of faith as well as the poured out gift of God in the messianic era—stands as a hallmark of Johannine irony. What is more, my argument is that John's emphasis on the Spirit should be traced not only to the prophetic corpus, but even more so to the Pentateuch (e.g., Num 11), for it anticipates the later prophetic promises regarding the outpouring of the Spirit. John, therefore, magnifies the irony of Nicodemus's ignorance by showing his ineptitude regarding the outpouring of the Spirit in the Pentateuch, the very foundation of sacred Scripture for Pharisees. While the eschatological Spirit does not at first appear to be related to John's wilderness motif, in reality its embryonic inception occurs in the wilderness narratives of Numbers.

The Spirit's influence is significant for commissioning Israel's leaders in the wilderness, a common OT theme[235] that John subtly echoes in his portrait of Nicodemus. Numbers speaks of the Spirit (τό πνεῦμα) more than any other book in the Pentateuch, which helps to establish its significance in the wilderness tradition. Most important for the present purpose is the outpouring of the Spirit in Num 11:16–29 on the seventy elders as well as the recognition that Joshua, as Israel's leader, is "a man in whom is the Spirit" (27:18). John, therefore, contrasts Nicodemus lack of the Spirit with various leaders in the wilderness tradition, namely, Moses,[236] the seventy elders, Eldad and Medad, and Joshua. The Spirit rests on these leaders of Israel in order to empower them to lead the people.

The Seventy Elders

The first mention of the Spirit in the wilderness narratives of Numbers occurs in Num 11, a passage that has been described as the OT counterpart to the outpouring of the Spirit at Pentecost in Acts 2.[237] Numbers 11 recounts the narrative when the people, spurred on by the "rabble" (Num 11:4 ESV) among them, complain against Moses about the manna they have been forced to eat: "Oh that we had meat to eat! We remember the fish we ate in Egypt that cost nothing, the cucumbers, the melons, the leeks, the onions, and the garlic. But now our strength is dried up, and there is

235. Ladd, *Theology*, 331. Hildebrandt, *Theology*, 104–50, discusses the role of the Spirit on Israel's leadership throughout the OT, not only in the wilderness.

236. Moses will receive more attention in chapter 4 below. My concern at this stage is with the seventy elders, Eldad and Medad, and Joshua.

237. Cole, *Numbers*, 193; Cotton, "Pentecostal Significance," 3–10; Duguid, *Numbers*, 155. The textual tradition of Num 11 is beyond the scope of this study. For this, see Coats, *Rebellion in the Wilderness*, 96–115, 124–27.

nothing at all but this manna to look at" (11:4b–6 ESV). The manna is yet another example of God testing the people with a miraculous sign to see whose hearts were faithful (Deut 8:16). Feeling that God has placed an unfair burden on him, Moses feels the weight of ministering to the people: "Why have I not found favor in your sight, that you lay the burden of all this people on me? Did I conceive all this people? Did I give them birth?" (Num 11:11–12 ESV). He asks how he is going to supply all the people with meat implying that God has rashly promised something that Moses cannot deliver (11:13–15).[238] Moses, sensing the impossibility of the task at hand, asks God to end his wretchedness by killing not the people, but him: "If you will treat me like this, kill me at once, if I find favor in your sight, that I may not see my wretchedness" (11:15 ESV). God's solution to Moses' plight is to appoint seventy elders of the people (πρεσβύτεροι τοῦ λαοῦ) to shoulder the burden of ministry (11:16–17).[239] More important for the present study, these seventy elders must be endowed with God's Spirit, who currently rests only on Moses: ἀφελῶ ἀπὸ τοῦ πνεύματος τοῦ ἐπὶ σοὶ καὶ ἐπιθήσω ἐπ' αὐτούς ("I will take of the Spirit that is on you and will place it on them," 11:17). Scholars debate whether πνεῦμα should be taken here in a theological sense (i.e., God's Spirit) or in a psychological sense (i.e., Moses' spirit, or state of mind).[240] However, there can be little doubt that it is indeed God's Spirit that is referred to here as being "on" (ἐπί with a genitive direct object) Moses.[241] The text indicates that Moses clearly understands it as God's Spirit (11:29).[242] God's Spirit allows Moses and the seventy elders to minister to the people in a unified fashion that surpasses ordinary human effort. Ed-

---

238. Wilson, *Prophecy and Society*, 153.

239. Olson, *Numbers*, 67, points out that the notion of seventy elders continued in Judaism in the form of seventy members of the Sanhedrin. Milgrom, *Numbers*, 383, goes so far as to suggest that the assembly of seventy elders is the prototype for the seventy members of the Sanhedrin. He also proposes that the number seventy may be nothing more than symbolic of a large group rather than an exact figure (p. 86). If Nicodemus was indeed a member of the Sanhedrin, this makes for an interesting parallel with the leadership of Israel in the wilderness. I mention this here only as interesting parallel and not as a firm intertextual connection point between John 3 and Numbers.

240. Ashley, *Numbers*, 211.

241. Ibid.; Budd, *Numbers*, 128; Cole, *Numbers*, 189; Cotton, "Pentecostal Significance," 5; Duguid, *Numbers*, 154; Milgrom, *Numbers*, 87, 90–91; Olson, *Numbers*, 68; Wilson, *Prophecy and Society*, 153; Young, *My Servants*, 69. Against "spirit" as God's Spirit, see Gertel, "Transferred Spirit," 73–79. I agree that "spirit" can be used in Numbers in a psychological sense indicating a feeling or frame of mind, as in the case of Caleb (Num 14:24), as observed by Ashley, *Numbers*, 261, Budd, *Numbers*, 159, and Levine, *Numbers 1–20*, 324. Nevertheless, Gertel's view has not won the day among most commentators. For more on the Spirit in the OT, see Hildebrandt, *Theology*.

242. Ashley, *Numbers*, 211.

ward Young observes, "In order that the seventy might work with Moses in one spirit and purpose, they were equipped with the same Spirit which had filled him."[243] As the seventy elders are filled with the Spirit, they temporarily prophesy showing evidence of their divine commission: "And as soon as the Spirit rested on them, they prophesied. But they did not continue to do so" (11:25). Little is known about the exact nature of ἐμπροφήτευσαν ("they prophesied"). It may have been ecstatic tongues, but the term itself is unclear.[244] The more important point involves the empowering of the seventy elders by the Spirit. As Wilf Hildebrandt observes, "Whereas the act of prophesying served to publicly endorse the elders as newly appointed leaders, the *rûaḥ* served to enable them with the necessary resources for their task."[245]

Eldad and Medad

The Spirit is not limited to those elders who were assembled at the tabernacle (11:16), but is also poured out on two elders who remained in the camp: Eldad and Medad (11:26). Joshua, Moses' young aid (11:27–28), sees the ecstatic behavior of Eldad and Medad and immediately recognizes that the Spirit of God has come upon them too. Interpreting this as a potential threat against Moses' leadership,[246] he objects: "My lord Moses, stop them" (11:28 ESV). Hildebrandt notes "Moses assures him that Spirit possession/reception is a necessary endowment for leadership—it is a paradigmatic requirement for all who assume leadership duties."[247] Moses then corrects young Joshua by insisting that he wishes that God's Spirit would be placed on all the people: "Would that all the LORD's people were prophets, that the LORD would put his Spirit on them!" (11:29). This story does not have a happy ending for the people. In an obvious double entendre on the term πμεῦμα ("spirit," "wind") in vv. 29 and 31, God indeed gives them the meat they so desired by causing a "wind" (πνεῦμα) to rise up and bring quail into the camp:

> δῷ κύριος τὸ πνεῦμα αὐτοῦ ἐπ'αὐτούς (11:29)
> The Lord would give his Spirit to them

---

243. Young, *My Servants*, 69.

244. For more on this, see Ashley, *Numbers*, 213–14; Cole, *Numbers*, 193; Milgrom, *Numbers*, 380–83; Wilson, *Prophecy and Society*, 153; Young, *My Servants*, 69.

245. Hildebrandt, *Theology*, 111.

246. Cole, *Numbers*, 195; Wilson, *Prophecy and Society*, 154.

247. Hildebrandt, *Theology*, 110.

καὶ πνεῦμα ἐξῆλθεν παρὰ κυρίου (11:31)
And a wind went forth from the Lord

Interestingly, this is exactly the same wordplay as in John 3:8, where Jesus uses the wind to illustrate the comings and goings of those who are born from above through God's Spirit.[248] Granted, the contexts are different. John is concerned with the invigorating, yet unpredictable, activity of the Spirit on the human heart, while Num 11 is concerned with God's response to the people's desire to eat meat. The wind ultimately brings the judgment of God on the complaining people when it blows in so many quail that the people gorge themselves; they are then struck by a deadly plague (11:34). Nevertheless, because John implements a similar wordplay on spirit-wind, it cannot be ruled out that he is motivated by a similar literary technique as in Num 11 by building on the double entendre associated with πνεῦμα.

Joshua

Not only are the seventy elders and Eldad and Medad filled with the Spirit, Joshua, who is introduced as a rather immature[249] "young man," (11:28) eventually develops into a mature leader who bears the Spirit. When transferring leadership of Israel from Moses to Joshua, God gives his rationale for choosing Joshua as Moses' successor as the next leader of Israel: "Take Joshua the son of Nun, a man who has the Spirit, and lay your hands on him" (27:18). Again, as was the case with Moses in Num 11, πνεῦμα, while it lacks the definite article here (ἄνθρωπον ὃς ἔχει πνεῦμα), it should not be taken in a psychological sense,[250] but rather in a theological sense. It is unquestionably God's Spirit that is the prerequisite for choosing Joshua to succeed Moses, as Deut 34:9 makes clear: "And Joshua the son of Nun was full of the Spirit of understanding, for Moses had placed his hands on him."[251] Hildebrandt notes Joshua's endowment with the Spirit as the prerequisite for his being chosen as Moses' successor: "The ability to perform his duties is not attributed directly to a period of apprenticeship with Moses but to the recognition that Joshua was a man in whom was the *rûaḥ*."[252] Joshua

---

248. Ezekiel's valley of dry bones contains a similar double entendre between "breath" and "Spirit" (Ezek 37).

249. Ashley, *Numbers*, 216.

250. However, Milgrom *Numbers*, 235, sees a psychological reference here.

251. Budd, *Numbers*, 306–07, observes that that πνεῦμα should be taken as a reference to God's Spirit in Num 27:18. See also, Ashley, *Numbers*, 551–52; Cole, *Numbers*, 469.

252. Hildebrandt, *Theology*, 109.

is singled out as a leader of Israel who bears the Spirit of God as was the case with Moses, the seventy elders, and Eldad and Medad.[253] While Joshua already possesses the divine Spirit, Moses visibly transfers the Spirit of leadership in a climactic commissioning scene in Num 27.[254]

Obviously, the Spirit plays a crucial role in the wilderness narratives of Numbers. Whatever the intricacies of the prophetic activity of the seventy elders and Eldad and Medad in the context of Num 11, what is more central to this study is the general observation of the Spirit's outpouring on the leaders of Israel in the wilderness.[255] Two observations deserve comment in relation to John's portrait of the Spirit in Jesus' dialogue with Nicodemus: 1) Spiritual leadership and 2) the eschatological expectation of the Spirit. First, the Spirit and leadership/ministry are interconnected in Num 11,[256] and in the wilderness experience as a whole. Roger Cotton aptly expresses the situation in the wilderness, "God's active, wind-like presence which gives vitality to all to fulfill their God-given functions, especially providing wisdom to people placed in critical leadership positions."[257] Again, Cotton states the matter plainly: "A leader chosen by God was empowered and motivated by God's Spirit."[258] Divine empowerment is not optional for the leading of God's people; instead, it is a necessary resource.[259] If Moses and Joshua are to lead the people as God would have them, Spiritual empowerment is a requirement. Similarly, the seventy elders cannot shoulder the burden of ministry as mere men; instead, they also must experience divine empowerment from God's Spirit. In short, the endowment of God's Spirit is a prerequisite for leadership in Israel. God ordered the sharing of leadership responsibilities (11:26–30) but enabled and empowered his servants to do

---

253. The Spirit is also on Balaam as he prophesies his third oracle (Num 24:2), but he is not an Israelite leader. His endowment with the Spirit is only for the purpose of his oracle. For more on Balaam's endowment with the Spirit of God, see Hildebrandt, *Theology*, 162–66.

254. On the abiding Spirit in Joshua's life as well as its visible transfer from Moses to Joshua, see Cole, *Numbers*, 469. Russell, "Holy Spirit's Ministry," 237, also sees in the transfer scenes in Numbers a parallel in the Johannine account of Jesus breathing the Spirit onto his disciples in John 20:22.

255. Ladd, *Theology*, 333, notes that John attributes nothing of the ecstatic or marvelous to the coming of the Spirit.

256. Cotton, "Pentecostal Significance," 3.

257. Ibid., 6.

258. Ibid. I do not agree with Cotton that the ecstatic event in Num 11 is intended as a paradigm/prototype of what should be expected for all God-ordained leadership (ibid., 6–7). While the Spirit is required for leadership, ecstatic experiences are sufficiently rare in Scripture to call into question Cotton's expectation.

259. Budd, *Numbers*, 128.

so successfully. The possession of God's Spirit, therefore, plays an important role in authenticating Israelite leaders.

The intertextual echo[260] between Nicodemus, a leader of the Jews, the teacher of Israel, and the wilderness narratives is indeed ironic because John presents an Israelite leader who does not bear the Spirit of God. Moses, the seventy elders, Eldad and Medad, and Joshua all stand as testimonies against Nicodemus's lack of Spiritual influence and insight. He cannot shoulder the burden of ministering to the Jews any better than the seventy elders could apart from the Spirit. Without the experience of rebirth through the Spirit Nicodemus remains an inept and unqualified "leader" of the Jews. For John, it is unthinkable that a leader of God's people would be without God's Spirit. This is one reason why John records the Johannine Pentecost[261] in John 20:22: ἐνεφύσησεν καὶ λέγει αὐτοῖς· λάβετε πνεῦμα ἅγιον ("He breathed on them and said to them, 'Receive Holy Spirit'"). The disciples who will mature into the leaders of the messianic community must bear the Spirit as the empowering force in the eschatological era. In a classic instance of Johannine irony, John presents Nicodemus as a leader of the Jews who lacks the Spirit. Therefore, I argue for an intertextual connection point on the level of a thematic echo that contrasts Nicodemus with the leaders of Israel in the wilderness traditions of Numbers.

Secondly, there is a strong eschatological thrust to Moses' wish that God would give his Spirit to all his people (Num 11:29). This is reflected in the prophetic corpus as well as in John 3:3-8. Moses' wish turns into a fuller eschatological expectation in the prophetic writings, especially Isa 44:3-4, Ezek 36:25-27, and Joel 2:28-29 (LXX 3:1-2). Joel 2:28-29 is worth quoting

---

260. Several of Hays's criteria are met in John 3:5-8; Num 11; 27:18: Availability: John had access to the entire book of Numbers; Volume: wordplay on πνεῦμα; Recurrence: John appeals to wilderness imagery throughout his Gospel; Thematic Coherence: outpouring of the Spirit on the leaders of Israel; Historical Plausibility: first-century messianic expectations included the outpouring of the Spirit; Satisfaction: contributes to the larger context of the work of the Spirit in John 3.

261. For a thorough examination of the evidence to support a genuine Johannine Pentecost, see Burge, *Anointed Community*, 116-31. That John expects a climactic outpouring of the Spirit does not conflict with the later outpouring of the Spirit at Pentecost in Acts 2. John's expectation of the eschatological Spirit fits within his own economy and need not be seen as secondary to Acts 2. John 20:22 is clearly a determinative event for John; there is no room in his thought for a second anointing. In short, John records the commissioning of the disciples while Luke records their empowerment. As Burge notes, "John has compressed historically separate events into a theological unity: the death, resurrection, and ascension of Jesus as well as the gift of the Spirit all constitute a single movement in the Johannine economy" (ibid., 125). For a slightly different view, see Köstenberger, *Encountering John*, 186.

at length due to the striking similarities to Moses' hope that all the people would be prophets who bear God's Spirit:

> "I will pour out my Spirit on all flesh,
> > Your sons and your daughters shall prophesy,
> > Your old men shall dream dreams,
> > Your young men shall see visions.
> Even on the male and female servants,
> > In those days I will pour out my Spirit" (ESV).

Due to Joel's echoing of Moses' hope, promising that God's Spirit will be poured out on "all flesh" so that people may prophesy (2:28), commentators frequently see here an authoritative announcement of the eventual fulfillment of Moses' wish in the eschatological era.[262] Duane Garrett notes that "Joel apparently envisaged the coming of the Spirit as the fulfillment of Moses' prayer."[263] Moses' hope for the "democratization of prophecy"[264] later becomes Joel's promise of eschatological blessing. However, not only is this announcement made in Joel but also in Isa 44 and Ezek 36, as demonstrated earlier. These passages are interconnected given their emphasis on the presence of the Spirit in the eschatological era. Put differently, in each of these prophetic passages, as well as Moses' wish in Num 11:29, the major characteristic of the outpouring of the Spirit is its universality: all the people of God receive the Spirit.[265] To be sure, there are differing perspectives on the eschatological outpouring of the Spirit in the prophetic passages: Ezekiel promised that God would by his Spirit enable his people to obey from the heart; Isaiah foretold that God would pour out his Spirit in order to create a new community and a new people of God; Joel envisioned the outpouring of the Spirit as a promise that God's people will prophesy.[266] These differing perspectives are complimentary parts of the grand ministry of the Spirit in the eschatological era and reflect Moses' original hope in the wilderness:

---

262. Cole, *Numbers*, 195; Cotton, "Pentecostal Significance," 9; Garrett, *Hosea, Joel*, 368; Hildebrandt, *Theology*, 110; Hubbard, *Joel and Amos*, 69; Milgrom, *Numbers*, 91.

263. Garrett, *Hosea, Joel*, 368.

264. Gowan, *Eschatology*, 75; Hildebrandt, *Theology*, 109–10.

265. Garrett, *Hosea, Joel*, 369.

266. Ibid., 368.

Figure 1. Eschatological Spirit rooted in wilderness.

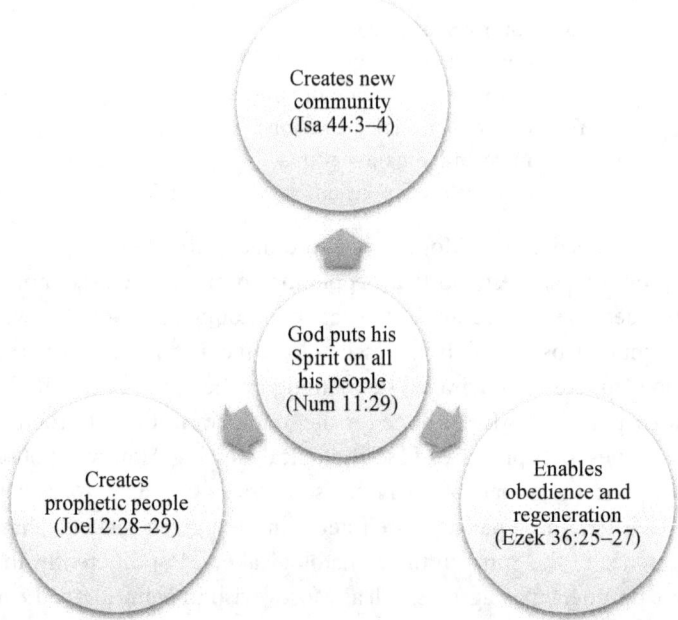

Therefore, the general point is the same in all of these passages: God will pour his Spirit onto his all people in the eschatological era. These texts evidence an interconnectedness that is rooted in descriptions of the Spirit in the eschatological era.

John's description of Spiritual rebirth as a prerequisite for entrance into the messianic kingdom is consistent with the message of the prophets. Further, given the proposed background referred to earlier for John 3:3–8, I believe it is safe to suggest an eschatological progression between Moses' hope in Num 11 and Jesus' description of birth from above in John 3. That is to say, where the prophets *promised* the fulfillment of Moses' hope that God would place his Spirit on his people, John announces its *arrival* in the ministry of Jesus who pours out the eschatological Spirit on the messianic community. Thus, there is a triad of expectations regarding the eschatological Spirit that is founded first on Moses' hope in the wilderness, develops into the prophetic promises, and finds fulfillment in Jesus and in the messianic community:

Figure 2. Triad of eschatological Spirit.

Jesus' Fulfillment	• John 3:3–5; cf. 20:22
Prophetic promises	• Isa 44:3–4 • Ezek 36:25–27 • Joel 2:28–29
Moses' hope	• Num 11:29

For John, Moses' hope in the wilderness has become a reality in Jesus Christ and in the messianic community; this is precisely Jesus' point to Nicodemus. Further, it serves as an instance of Johannine irony that Nicodemus could be so dull at understanding the foundational passage in the Torah that speaks of the outpouring of God's Spirit on his people. While the prophetic passages certainly stand behind John's description of "born from above" and "born of water and Spirit," the outpouring of the eschatological Spirit has earlier roots in the OT wilderness tradition of Num 11. It is myopic to suggest that John has only one passage in mind concerning the outpouring of the eschatological Spirit.[267] To be sure, Figure 2 above suggests that he uses several passages simultaneously for a cumulative effect regarding the eschatological Spirit. While this may at first seem inconsistent with the discipline of intertextuality which tends to emphasize a primary text's use of a single source text, a multiple text approach fits well with John's elusive use of the OT. As Gary T. Manning states, "Intertextual studies have often overemphasized one background text at the expense of others; analyzing the role of other passages can prevent such an overly narrow focus."[268] Simply put, John does not in this instance limit his intertextual use of the OT to a single text but appeals to multiple texts which he brings together to form a mosaic portrait of the eschatological Spirit expectation. Nevertheless, I believe that given the pervasiveness of wilderness imagery in John 3, and given the prominent role of Moses later in the pericope (3:14), not to mention in the Fourth Gospel as a whole, his wish for the eschatological Spirit in the wilderness forms the foundation of John's discussion here. The prophets

267. Manning, *Echoes of a Prophet*, 19 (cf. ibid., 199–200), makes this point regarding John's use of Ezek 15 and Jer 2 in John 15. For more on the use of multiple source texts in intertextuality, see Brunson, *Psalm 118*, 313n120.

268. Manning, *Echoes of a Prophet*, 19. Manning provides another example in John 10 where Jesus is the Good Shepherd; therefore, John simultaneously alludes to Num 27 and Ezek 34 (pp. 100–13, 199).

explain more details regarding the eschatological Spirit than does Moses; nevertheless, it remains Moses' hope first. Therefore, Moses' wish for the presence of the Spirit on the people of God in Num 11 forms an intertextual connection point to John's description of Spiritual rebirth in John 3:3–8.

The Inadequacy of Nicodemus's Signs-faith

Nicodemus originally approached Jesus as a representative of the many who "believed" in his name because of the miraculous signs he had performed in Jerusalem (2:23). While Nicodemus has been a confused character thus far in the dialogue, failing to grasp spiritual concepts such as rebirth, John illustrates the deficiency inherent in signs-faith in 3:11–12. At this point on, Nicodemus disappears from the dialogue that becomes a monologue; this is consistent with the author's style throughout the Gospel.[269] Most likely echoing Nicodemus's plural address earlier in 3:2 (οἴδαμεν, "we know"), Jesus replies in kind,[270] again with an authoritative declaration: ἀμὴν ἀμὴν λέγω σοι ὅτι ὃ οἴδαμεν λαλοῦμεν καὶ ὃ ἑωράκαμεν μαρτυροῦμεν ("Truly, truly, I say to you, we speak what we know, and we testify to what we have seen," 3:11). Jesus has first-hand knowledge of the spiritual realities discussed while Nicodemus has only second-hand knowledge, and even that is wholly deficient. In other words, Nicodemus has not plumbed the depths of his own acknowledgment that Jesus has come from God (3:2). Not only has Jesus come from God, he knows personally the spiritual reality (ὃ οἴδαμεν, 3:12) to which he testifies (ὃ μαρτυροῦμεν, 3:12), i.e., the activity of the Spirit.[271] Nicodemus is unfamiliar with Jesus' identity as well; but John's audience who knows the Prologue is better informed: The Word was with

---

269. Carson, *John*, 198; Dodd, *Interpretation*, 303. Debate surrounds the identity of the speaker, whether Jesus or John, esp. in vv. 13–21. Commentators generally see a shift from Jesus to John in v. 13 or v. 16. See Brown, *John*, 1:149, for a more detailed discussion. John's words are often impossible to distinguish from those of Jesus throughout the Gospel (Smith, *Theology*, 27). The stylistic unity (Keener, *John*, 1:252) of the Gospel also makes distinguishing John's from Jesus' voice problematic. Certainty is elusive in these matters. My own view reflects Brown's in that the speaker throughout the pericope is Jesus. This is not to dilute the role of the Evangelist. Brown notes that the Evangelist "has been at work in the discourse, but his work is not the type that begins at a particular verse" (*John*, 1:149). For more, see Ashton, *Understanding*, 279; Moloney, *John*, 100.

270. Much has been made of the plural language here. For good summaries of the various options, see Bryant and Krause, *John*, 94; Carson, *John*, 198–99; Michaels, *John*, 190–91.

271. Barrett, *John*, 211.

God in the beginning (1:1-2), was right beside the Father, and has uniquely revealed him (1:18). J. Ramsey Michaels states John's point with precision:

> Jesus, because of his preexistence, "speaks what he knows" and "testifies to what he has seen" in a way no human witness can do—not John (1:34), not the anonymous witness to the crucifixion (19:25), and not the Christian community (1 John 1:1-2). Their testimonies are all derivative, while his is the very fountainhead of Christian revelation.²⁷²

Nicodemus's failure to grasp the depths of Jesus' identity as well as the spiritual realities to which he testifies is more a crisis of faith than of understanding: καὶ τὴν μαρτυρίαν ἡμῶν οὐ λαμβάνετε ("Yet you all have not received our testimony," 3:11b).²⁷³ Put differently, not only has Nicodemus not understood Jesus' testimony, he has not received him in faith. As he represents those with signs-faith (2:23), he is also represents Jesus' own people who do not receive him (καὶ οἱ ἴδιοι αὐτὸν οὐ παρέλαβον, "Yet his own people did not receive him," 1:11).²⁷⁴ To receive (λαμβάνειν) Jesus is Johannine faith-language, as evidenced in the parallelism in the Prologue: ὅσοι δὲ ἔλαβον αὐτόν . . . τοῖς πιστεύουσιν εἰς τὸ ὄνομα αὐτοῦ ("But to whoever received him . . . to those believing in his name," 1:12). In contrast to Nicodemus, these believers are born of God (ἐκ θεοῦ ἐγεννήθεσαν, 1:13). John describes Nicodemus's unbelief with even stronger language in 3:12: εἰ τὰ ἐπίγεια εἶπον ὑμῖν καὶ οὐ πιστεύετε, πῶς ἐὰν εἴπω ὑμῖν τὰ ἐπουράνια πιστεύσετε;²⁷⁵ ("If I spoke earthly things to you and you do not believe, how can you believe if I should speak heavenly things to you?"). Here, perhaps as clearly as anywhere else in the Gospel, is proof that seeing miraculous signs does not always lead to firm faith. Nicodemus's failure was not a failure of intellect but a failure to believe Jesus' witness.²⁷⁶ Again, Michaels captures John's emphasis, "Ironically, even though Jesus is speaking to one who

---

272. Michaels, *John*, 192.

273. On the importance of testimony/witness (μαρτυρία) in John, see Bernard, *John*, 1:XC-XCIII; Köstenberger, *Theology*, 436-54; Lincoln, *Truth on Trial*; Morris, *Theology*, 238-42.

274. Michaels, *John*, 192.

275. While the present tense variant πιστεύετε at the end of v. 12 has early MS support in P75 (ca. CE 175-225), it is best seen as an assimilation to the πιστεύετε in the first part of the verse. A few MSS (Γ Δ Θ W *fam* 13) have an aorist subjunctive (πιστεύσητε) which aligns with the subjunctive εἴπω. However, the future tense πιστεύσετε best fits the context, as Jesus will elaborate on ἐπουράνια in the following verses.

276. Carson, *John*, 199.

presumably had 'believed in his name on seeing the signs he was doing' (2:23), the promise of that verse [1:12] is at this point unfulfilled."[277]

What is one to make of the knowledge of "earthly things" (τὰ ἐπίγεια, 3:12) and "heavenly things" (τὰ ἐπουράνια, 3:12) in the context of 3:1–21? In short, John leaves this undefined. However, "earthly things" probably refers to the content of the subject of the discourse—new birth.[278] While on the surface, "born from above" sounds more accurate as an example of "heavenly things," people experience new birth in *this* world. As Carson observes, "It is 'earthly' in that it takes place here on earth when people are born again."[279] Even more to the point, Nicodemus should have grasped the teaching on new birth because it is elementary[280] and basic to entrance into the kingdom of God; Jesus expected a more robust dialogue from the teacher of Israel. The discussion has been concerned with *entering* the kingdom of God, not with the kingdom of God per se. Therefore, if Nicodemus does not believe elementary teachings such as new birth, how will he believe the deeper, spiritual realities of the kingdom of God? Again, Carson observes, "If Nicodemus stumbles over this elementary point of entry, then what is the use of going on to explain more of the details of life in the kingdom?"[281] For John, this is a simple *qal wahomer* argument: If Nicodemus does not believe light teachings, neither will he believe heavier ones.[282]

Jesus will proceed to expound "heavenly things" in the remainder of the pericope (3:13–21). Much of his description hinges on the redemptive activity of God in the wilderness that serves as a paradigm for his redemptive activity in the kingdom. Chapter 4 will explore this redemptive activity of God; it also proposes the interpretive key to untangling the complex relationship of Johannine signs and faith.

---

277. Michaels, *John*, 193.

278. Carson, *John*, 199. For more options on the referents for earthly and heavenly things, see Michaels, *John*, 193–94; van der Watt, "Knowledge of Earthly Things," 289–310.

279. Carson, *John*, 199.

280. Ibid.

281. Ibid. Carson notes that Nicodemus may have apocalyptic leanings regarding the kingdom and wanted to know further about the new heavens and new earth (Isa 65:17). Brown, *John*, 1:132, cites a strikingly similar statement of Rabbi Gamaliel to the Emperor in the Babylonian Talmud: "You do not know that which is on earth; should you know what is in heaven?" (*b. Sanh*. 39a). Köstenberger, *John*, 126n38, quotes a similar verse from Wisdom of Solomon: "We can hardly guess at what is on the earth . . . but who has traced out what is in the heavens?" (Wis 9:16).

282. Keener, *John*, 1:559.

Chapter 4

EYES OF FAITH

THE PRIMARY CONCERN OF the previous chapter was to illustrate intertextual connections between John 2:23—3:12 and the wilderness traditions of Numbers. I set forth the issues of signs-faith and the need for spiritual rebirth as the main intertextual connection points between Jesus' dialogue with Nicodemus and wilderness narratives in Numbers. Chapter 4 has two primary objectives: 1) illustrate intertextual allusions and echoes which underscore the remainder of the pericope (vv. 13–21), and 2) propose faith-seeing the interpretive key for unlocking the complex relationship between Johannine signs and faith.

WHAT COMES DOWN MUST GO UP

Moses' Heavenly Ascents

The role of Moses in the Fourth Gospel cannot easily be overestimated. He is mentioned by name eleven times in John,[1] not to mention the plethora of images associated with him, which John takes from OT wilderness narratives (e.g., tabernacle, manna, signs, Torah, etc.). Moses is indeed the towering figure of Judaism in the first century.[2] He is also a key figure in John's Gospel, although John does not exalt him over Jesus. John presents Jesus not simply as a second Moses, but as one greater than Moses.[3] John has

---

1. Wayne Meeks, *Prophet-King*, 287.
2. Martyn, *History and Theology*, 101.
3. Glasson, *Moses*, 24–25n2; Keener, *John*, 1:278.

no antipathy toward Moses but he is concerned to place him in the proper perspective for those in the synagogue who would pledge loyalty to him while rejecting Jesus as the Messiah (ἡμεῖς δὲ τοῦ Μωϋσέως ἐσμὲν μαθηταί, "But we are the disciples of Moses," 9:28).[4] As John Pryor states, "John does not reject the place of Moses, but he does contest the claims of those who out of false loyalty to him, reject the person of Jesus."[5] J. Louis Martyn has pointed out that there is no opposition between Jesus and Moses in John. To be a disciple of Jesus is actually in continuity with the witness and writings of Moses; far from abandoning Moses, a disciple would simply attach himself to the one of whom Moses wrote.[6] Nevertheless, the exact relationship is quite complex and it involves a significant interplay between these two immense figures in John's Gospel.[7]

A key area of contrast between Moses and Jesus involves John's descent-ascent motif, especially as it regards the Johannine Son of Man: καὶ οὐδεὶς ἀναβέβηκεν εἰς τὸν οὐρανὸν εἰ μὴ ὁ ἐκ τοῦ οὐρανοῦ καταβάς, ὁ υἱὸς τοῦ ἀνθρώπου[8] ("And no one has ascended into heaven but the one who descended, the Son of Man," 3:13). While Moses is not named in 3:13, he is nevertheless included in the notable figures of Judaism such as Enoch, Elijah, Isaiah, and Ezekiel, who allegedly ascended into heaven for the purpose of receiving a direct revelation from God.[9] Moses receives a lot of reflection by later interpreters regarding his ascents into heaven. Wayne Meeks has

---

4. Pryor, *Covenant People*, 117. For more on this Moses-centered piety in John, see Meeks, *Prophet-King*, 298–301. Of course, this line of argument takes for granted that the background of John's Gospel involves some sort of first-century dialogue between Christians and Jews over the identity of the Messiah (20:31). Martyn's *History and Theology* has contributed greatly to this historical reconstruction, and while I do not subscribe to all the details of his reconstruction, or to his two-level drama reading strategy, I do agree with his basic historical reconstruction. For Martyn's two-level drama reconstruction, see Smith, introduction to *History and Theology*, by Martyn, 1–23.

5. Pryor, *Covenant People*, 118.

6. Martyn, *History and Theology*, 158.

7. Smith, *Theology*, 17.

8. Several Egyptian MSS (A (*) Θ Ψ 050 f 1.13, and others) add, ὁ ὤν ἐν τῷ οὐρανῷ. Scholars typically see this as a later interpretive gloss which tries to make sense of the perfect tense ἀναβέβηκεν and, therefore, not original. It reflects a post-ascension perspective because Jesus, as the Son of Man, is obviously not in heaven while speaking these words. However, ἀναβέβηκεν need not be taken in a historical sense (i.e., the Son of Man has *already* ascended), but rather in a gnomic sense as a general pronouncement. This latter view is that of Ridderbos, *John*, 136. For more on this, see Köstenberger, *John*, 132; Metzger, *Textual Commentary*, 174–75; Martyn, *History and Theology*, 135. Against this variant as a gloss, see Black, "The Text of John 3:13," 49–66.

9. As Köstenberger, *Theology*, 388n183, notes: Enoch: Gen 5:24; cf. Heb 11:5; Elijah: 2 Kgs 2:1–12; cf. 2 Chr 21:12–15; Moses: Exod 24:9–11; 34:29–30; Isaiah: Isa 6:1–3; Ezekiel: Ezek 1:10.

thoroughly probed this from a variety of early and late Jewish sources.[10] Later Jewish interpreters viewed Moses' ascent to the top of Mount Sinai (Exod 19:20, 23; 24:1-2, 9, 12-13, 18; 34:2-4) to be his ascent into heaven where he saw heavenly sights and received the revelation of God (i.e., Torah). It was *after* ascending into heaven that he then descended from the mountain in order to reveal Torah to the people of Israel. Multiple Jewish exegetes interpret Moses' Sinai experience as a heavenly one. For example, *4 Ezra* 14:4-5 (late first century CE) speaks of Moses' experience on the mountain where God revealed heavenly secrets to him: "And I led him [Moses] up on Mount Sinai, where I kept him with me many days; and I told him many wondrous things, and showed him the secrets of the times and declared to him the end of the times."[11] Philo also interprets Moses' ascent on Mount Sinai in Exod 20:21 as his entrance into heaven where he was in the very presence of God: "He [Moses] is said to have entered into the darkness where God was; that is to say, into the invisible, and shapeless, and incorporeal world" (*Moses* 1:158; cf. *QE* 2:40). Meeks rightly cautions that because the context of Philo's writings is far removed from John's, nevertheless, there are elements in Philo's portrait of Moses that may illuminate the background of John.[12] In addition to Philo, Josephus alludes to the belief among Jewish interpreters that Moses' Sinai ascent was thought to be his entrance into heaven: "Others said that he was departed and gone up (ἀνακεχωρηκέναι) to God" (*Ant.* 3:96; cf. 4:326). Examples of Mosaic ascent traditions can be multiplied, but these suffice to illustrate the prominent role that similar

---

10. Meeks, *Prophet-King*, 156-59, 205-11, 241-46. Meeks has also probed the Johannine descent-ascent of the Son of Man from a social-scientific perspective in his article, "Man from Heaven," 44-72. His basic point, which is beyond the scope of this study, is that the Gospel's language of Jesus' isolation, and his rejection by the Jews, reflects the situation of the Johannine community who has been expelled from the synagogue leading to its own sectarian identity. Meeks believes that this language reinforces the community's experiences of isolation and rejection.

11. Translated by B. M. Metzger.

12. Meeks, *Prophet-King*, 129. Meeks also states the importance of similar Mosaic ascent traditions for the Samaritans: "The Sinai ascension was the central, all-important event in Moses' life, so far as the Samaritan traditions are concerned. Upon this single event, to an even greater extent than on the Exodus itself and the crossing of the Sea, Moses' unique position is founded" (ibid., 241). He correctly cautions against the uncritical acceptance of Samaritan sources (ibid., 219-20). Samaritan sources are admittedly late, the fourth century CE being the earliest, and the twelfth and fourteenth centuries being the norm. Nevertheless, as with the use of rabbinic materials for NT studies, the traditions preserved in later sources probably stem from a much earlier period. For more on the Samaritans and their sources, see Anderson, "Samaritans," 5:75-80; Bowman, *Samaritan Documents*; Macdonald, *Theology of the Samaritans*; Williamson, "Samaritans," 724-28.

traditions held in the first century CE among Jewish exegetes.[13] Therefore, John's descent-ascent of the Son of Man should be interpreted against similar ascent traditions in Judaism.

Son of Man's Descent

The Johannine Son of Man[14] is among the most complex Christology in the NT. Its place in the Gospel of John has received much attention in terms of its OT background and messianic associations. The issues are immense and hotly debated.[15] An exhaustive analysis of the Johannine Son of Man is beyond the scope of this study. However, a few summary comments are in order to help shed light on the overall context of John's Son of Man saying in John 3:13–14. The most plausible background is the Danielic Son of Man figure in the OT:[16] ἐθεώρουν ἐν ὁράματι τῆς νυκτὸς καὶ ἰδοὺ ἐπὶ τῶν νεφελῶν τοῦ οὐρανοῦ ὡς υἱὸς ἀνθρώπου ἤρχετο καὶ ὡς παλαιὸς ἡμερῶν παρῆν καὶ οἱ παρεστηκότες παρῆσαν αὐτῷ ("I saw in a vision of the night,

---

13. Keener, *John*, 1:562. For more, see Kugel, *Traditions*, 636.

14. There is no difference of identity between the Son of Man and the Son of God in John's Gospel. For this, see Beasley-Murray, *Gospel of Life*, 28–29; Dodd, *Interpretation*, 244; Ridderbos, *John*, 134–35; Smith, *Theology*, 132. As with each of John's christological titles, there is a slight difference in function: only the Son of Man is "lifted up," while only the Son of God is "sent." Most important is that the place of origin is the same: both come from above. For more on christological titles, see Carson, *John*, 95–96; Cullmann, *Christology*; Culpepper, *Gospel and Letters*, 111; Kysar, *Maverick Gospel*, 35–40.

15. Ashton, *Understanding*, 240–76; Beasley-Murray, *Gospel of Life*, 28–29; Bernard, *John*, 1:CXXII–CXXXIII; Brown, *Introduction*, 257–59; Burkett, *Son of Man in the Gospel of John*; Carson, *John*, 164; Casey, *Solution*; Collins, "Son of Man," 5:341–48; Cullmann, *Christology*, 137–66; Dodd, *According to the Scriptures*, 116–18; Dodd, *Interpretation*, 241–49; Glasson, "Son of Man Imagery," 82–90; Ham, "The Title," *S-CJ* 1 (1998): 85–100; Horbury, "Messianic Associations," 34–53; Köstenberger, *Theology*, 386–89; Ladd, *Theology*, 280–82; Marshall, "Son of Man," 775–81; Martyn, *History and Theology*, 124–36; McGrath, "Going Up," 107–18; Moloney, *Text and Context*, 66–92; Moloney, "Johannine Son of Man," 177–89; Morris, *Theology*, 234–35; Morris, *John*, 150–52; Lincoln, *John*, 66–67; Pryor, *Covenant People*, 137–42; Pryor, "Descent-Ascent," 341–51; Ridderbos, *John*, 92–96, 133–37; Romanowsky, "Lifted Up," 100–16; Schmidl, *Jesus und Nikodemus*, 239–49; Smalley, "Son of Man Sayings," 278–301; Smith, *Theology*, 131–33; Witherington, *Christology of Jesus*, 233–62.

16. Dodd, *Interpretation*, 243 (cf. 31–32, 41–43), sees a Hermetic background to the Johannine Son of Man, while Bultmann, *John*, 150n1, sees the Gnostic Redeemer myth as the background. Both Hermetic and Gnostic sources are from the second century CE and therefore later than John's Gospel. Carson, *John*, 31–33, is on firm footing when he suggests the possibility that the Gospel may have influenced these later works rather than the other way around. For more, see Beasley-Murray, *John*, LV–LVII; Brown, *Introduction*, 116–26; Brown, *John*, 1:LII–LIX; Keener, *John*, 1:161–69, 375–76, 561; Ridderbos, *John*, 28–31.

and behold, coming on the clouds of heaven was one like a son of man, and he came to the Ancient of days, and was presented to him," Dan 7:13). I will interact more with John's Son of Man motif below when interacting with John 3:14; suffice it to say here that one central aspect of John's portrait is the heavenly origin of the Son of Man. Robert Kysar's summary of the Johannine understanding of the Son of Man is clear and concise: "The Son of Man originates in that heavenly home, descends into the human world, and will once again ascend after the completion of his task."[17] All of this is part and parcel of John's understanding of the Messiah as a pre-existent figure. As demonstrated in the previous chapter, John has so far described Jesus' messiahship in terms of the Mosaic prophet who performs signs (2:23), as well as the Davidic king (3:3, 5). Now he adds to these two figures the pre-existent Son of Man. While C. H. Dodd sees "little evidence" of Son of Man as a messianic title in pre-Christian Judaism,[18] many have challenged this assumption. As Ben Witherington notes, Messiah and Son of Man are frequently related and sometimes used interchangeably both before and during the first century CE.[19] To be sure, the messianic associations of the Son of Man title in the first century CE are debated.[20] Nevertheless, William Horbury has demonstrated that messianic exegesis of Dan 7:13 probably arose no later than the early first century CE, and possibly much earlier (e.g., Hasmonean period);[21] so much so that there was a tendency toward a titular use of "Son of Man."[22] The eschatological application of Dan 7:13 reflects a pronounced statement of majesty concerning the Son of Man, and this corresponds to the view found in *The Similitudes of Enoch* (*1 En.* 37–71).[23] The

---

17. Kysar, *Maverick Gospel*, 40.

18. Dodd, *Interpretation*, 241; Bauckham, *Testimony*, 237.

19. Witherington, *Christology*, 234. Bauckham also notes that in the late Second Temple period, the transcendent figure of Dan 7 was the Davidic Messiah himself (*Testimony*, 237).

20. For good treatments, see Glasson, "Son of Man Imagery"; Horbury, "Messianic Associations"; McGrath, "Going Up."

21. Horbury, "Jewish Messianism," 3–24.

22. Horbury, "Messianic Associations," 52. For a similar view, see Tuckett, "Early Christian Christologies," 164–90.

23. Cullmann, *Christology*, 155–56. While the dating of *1 Enoch* remains suspect according to Ferguson, *Backgrounds of Early Christianity*, 552, Witherington, *Christology*, 234, maintains that it was written about 105–64 BCE. This is simplistic because *1 Enoch* is a composite work. Collins, "Messiah, Jewish," 4:59–66, dates it in the early or mid first century CE. More problematic is the dating of *The Similitudes*, which is the only part of *1 Enoch* not found in the Dead Sea Scrolls. For a good discussion of the issues surrounding the date of *The Similitudes*, see Burkett, *Son of Man Debate*, 29–31, 70–72. See also, Collins, "Enoch, Books of," 313–18.

Messiah in *The Similitudes*, called the Righteous One and the Son of Man, is depicted as a pre-existent heavenly being.[24] *The Similitudes* evidence a group of Jews in which the messianic hope has an essentially different character from that of the majority of Judaism that hoped for an earthly Davidic king. The group represented by *The Similitudes*, however, did not expect a political Messiah who would defeat the enemies of Israel in an earthly battle and then establish a political kingdom, but rather the supernatural triumphant Son of Man who was a heavenly ruler and judge.[25] *First Enoch* 48:2-3 describes this pre-existent figure: "At that hour, that Son of Man was given a name, in the presence of the Lord of the Spirits, the Before-Time, even before the creation of the sun and moon, before the creation of the stars, he was given a name in the presence of the Lord of the Spirits."[26] Therefore, an eschatological Son of Man is not unheard of in a messianic sense around the first century CE. He is a pre-existent heavenly being who lives in heaven from the very beginning of time until he descends to earth on a mission from God.[27] John represents a similar pre-existent Son of Man in John 3:13 and contrasts his earthly descent with Moses' heavenly ascent.

Therefore, John 3:13 is probably a polemic against "Moses-centered piety" on the part of the synagogue that may have boasted stories of Moses' ascent into heaven.[28] John's primary point in 3:13 contrasts the Son of Man with Moses: only the former has ascended into heaven because he came from there in the first place.[29] The contrast hinges on how to translate the notori-

---

24. Isaac, Introduction to *1 Enoch* in *Old Testament Pseudepigrapha*, 1:9.

25. Cullmann, *Christology*, 142; Collins, "Son of Man," 5:343; Witherington, *Christology*, 236. Collins also notes that the messianic figure of *4 Ezra* 13 is modeled in part on the Son of Man of Dan 7 ("Son of Man," 343-44), thus offering an additional instance of a messianic reading of Dan 7 in the late first century CE. For more on *4 Ezra*, see deSilva, *Introducing the Apocrypha*, 323; Wright, "Esdras, Books of," 337-340. See also, Burkett, *Son of Man Debate*, 22.

26. Translation by Isaac. See also, *1 En.* 46:1-5; 48:10; 52:4; 62:5.

27. McGrath aptly notes that although there is evidence in Judaism prior to John's Gospel of a pre-existent and messianic Son of Man who descends from heaven, his later ascension back into heaven is a distinctive Johannine development ("Going Up," 111).

28. Borgen, "Exegetical Traditions," 243-58; Meeks, *Prophet-King*, 295-301; McGrath, "Going Up," 107-18; Moloney, *Text and Context*, 81. Against this, see Burkett, *Son of Man*, 76-92.

29. Moloney, *Text and Context*, 81-85, affirms the preexistence on the Son of Man, but not solely based on descent-ascent language of John 3:13. Moloney's position is quite nuanced; it is based on a diachronic reading of John's Son of Man passages that leads to the cumulative conclusion affirming the pre-existence of the Son of Man. Moloney argues that readers come to this conclusion in 3:13 because they already know the Prologue (1:1-18) and thus understand the bidirectional relationship of John's Son of Man motif (1:1-18; 3:13-14; 6:27, 53, 62; 8:28; 12:32-34).

ously difficult phrase, εἰ μὴ in 3:13, which the NIV and ESV translate as "except"; whereas, the KJV and NAS translate as a stronger contrastive "but," thus yielding the translation given here.[30] Francis Moloney's paraphrase helps to highlight John's intended contrast of ideas: "There is no one who has ascended, but, contrary to the fact of the protasis, one has descended, the Son of Man."[31] While OT figures are said to have entered heaven, only Jesus descended *from* heaven, because he was the heaven-sent Son of Man (1:51; 9:35).[32] He did not simply witness heaven; he is *from* heaven.[33] The contrast between Moses and Jesus could not be stronger in John's polemic: Moses ascended not into heaven, but rather a mountain where he spoke with God and received Torah; Jesus, however, pre-existed in heaven and has descended (καταβαίνω) to earth to reveal God to mankind. John's descending Son of Man language strongly emphasizes Jesus' pre-existence in much the same way as the Prologue's "In the beginning" (1:1–2). Jesus' heavenly home exalts him above every other messenger who has been sent from God in Jewish history. Pryor summarizes John's contrast of Moses and Jesus:

> Moses could never be thought of other than as a human prophet, commissioned by God to speak the revelation given to him—and as a mere human he could never know God as he is in himself. Jesus, on the other hand, reveals God as he is, for he has seen God, having himself descended from God in heaven (3:13; 5:19–20; 6:46); he has heard God (5:37; 8:26); and he has come from God (6:46; 7:29; 8:14; 17:27).[34]

This relates to the previous context of "heavenly things" (3:12) because what Jesus is saying is that he can speak of heavenly things, not because he has ascended (i.e., his glorification), which has not yet happened in the Johannine economy, but because he has descended (καταβάς, 3:13) from heaven. The descent from heaven precedes the ascent into heaven that will occur at a chronologically later time.[35] The descending Son of Man is therefore an-

30. For more on εἰ μὴ in 3:13, see Carson, *John*, 199–200; McGrath, "Going Up," 112n14; Moloney, *Text and Context*, 80.

31. Moloney, *Text and Context*, 80. Against this, see Ashton, *Understanding*, 350.

32. Köstenberger, *Theology*, 388.

33. Keener, *John*, 1:563. Keener also notes that this fits the overall context of rebirth because Jesus came from above to begin with and grants others a birth "from above" (3:3).

34. Pryor, *Covenant People*, 121.

35. Ridderbos, *John*, 95, 136. This verse should not be taken as an anachronistic reflection of the later church regarding Jesus' ascension into heaven. Per this view, the Evangelist is looking backward through history at Jesus' resurrection and ascension, and is anachronistically inserting that motif into the Nicodemus dialogue. For more on

other Johannine way of speaking about the incarnation.³⁶ As the incarnate Word came from heaven, so also the Son of Man.³⁷ Jesus' message to Nicodemus is that the divine Son of Man descends from heaven to earth in order to convey τὰ ἐπουράνια to mankind.³⁸ John makes an even more direct incarnational statement when he writes in 6:62 that the pre-existent Christ has descended from heaven into the world of mankind: ἐὰν οὖν θεωρῆτε τὸν υἱὸν τοῦ ἀνθρώπου ἀναβαίνοντα ὅπου ἦν τὸ πρότερον; ("Then what if you were to see the Son of Man ascending where he was before?"). Again as in 3:13, the descent of the Son of Man, which John captures by the use of "before" (τὸ πρότερον), precedes his ascent. Therefore, the claim of the Messiah's heavenly origin is characteristic of John's descent-ascent Christology and presents the truth of Jesus' identity in terms of his divine origin as Son of Man.³⁹ The Son of Man sayings which speak of his descent (3:13; 6:62) are strong indicators of the deity of Jesus in John's Gospel and convey the notion of Jesus' eternal nature. John suggests that the Son of Man descended from heaven because he was the Word who was with God in the beginning. Simply put, God's revelation has descended into the realm of mankind in the person of Jesus Christ. This may not appear to reflect a wilderness motif at first; however, I will now demonstrate that there is indeed a subtle, yet profound, connection to the wilderness traditions of Numbers.

The Descent of the Lord in Wilderness

The descent of the Son of Man is of immense importance for establishing the doctrine of the incarnation in John's Gospel. That Christ has descended from heaven where he was in the beginning with God (1:1) is axiomatic for John's portrait of the pre-existence of Christ. After all, the Word became flesh and "tabernacled" among mankind (1:14). This tabernacling of the Word is none other than the pre-existent Christ who was sent by the Father to speak the words of the Father (12:39) and to reveal the works of the Father (5:19). As Jesus proclaimed to the Jews who opposed him: "You are

---

this, see Borgen "Hellenism," 98–123. Moloney, *John*, 101, notes that Jesus did not say that he had ascended, but that no one (οὐδείς) had ascended. Thus, there is only one who can reveal God with ultimate authority—the Son of Man, who has descended in the incarnation.

36. Barrett, *John*, 212–13; Moloney, *Text and Context*, 70–71, makes this point but also emphasizes the suffering of the Son of Man which is followed by his vindication.

37. Ridderbos, *John*, 135.

38. Similarly, Barrett, *John*, 213.

39. Romanowsky, "Lifted Up," 109.

from below, I am from above; you are of this world, I am not of this world" (8:23).[40] One of the main missions of Christ as he descends into the realm of mankind in the Gospel of John is to proclaim the very words and works of God. Simply stated, the Word's mission is to reveal the unseen Father (1:18).

While the descent of the Son of Man motif primarily highlights Jesus' pre-existence in John's Gospel, this does not exhaust John's emphasis. Given the descent of the Son of Man in 3:13 (cf. 6:62), there is a subtle intertextual connection with the book of Numbers, which centers on the issue of divine descent. Numbers speaks of the "descent" (καταβαίνω) of God for the purpose of communicating with his people, especially Moses. When God speaks with his servants, he does so by descending in the form of a cloud at the entrance of the tabernacle/tent of testimony (Num 11:17, 25; 12:5).[41] The tabernacle succeeds Mount Sinai as the place of further divine revelation.[42] The tabernacle, then, is not only the place where God dwells in the midst of his people;[43] it is also the place where he reveals his will to his servants for the benefit of the people.

God's descents are not unusual in the OT. Jacob Milgrom cites ten examples where God enters the realm of humanity.[44] The Lord descends to earth to observe and to act, to empower certain individuals,[45] and to speak to his servants. "Descent" is the language of theophany in the OT.[46] In a theophany, God descends to earth and makes the divine-self known within the natural realm.[47] The tabernacle is the place of divine theophanies, or appearances, in Numbers. More specifically, the tabernacle is the

40. For more on Johannine dualism, see Ashton, *Understanding*, 387–417; Carter, *Storyteller*, 90–92; Charlesworth, "Dualism," 76–106, esp. 89–90; Keener, *John*, 1:743–44; Ladd, *Theology*, 252–53, 259–62, 265–72; Thompson, "John," 182–200, esp. 194–95.

41. God never descends upon the tabernacle per se, only the tent of meeting. However, I find no difference between the two and ascribe the difference in terminology to the complex composition history of Numbers. Ashley, *Numbers*, 46, adduces that the tent of meeting may have preceded the tabernacle (e.g., Exod 33:7, which refers to a time before the tabernacle was built). Ashley further concludes that the terms are interchangeable by the final stages of composition. For more on the tabernacle and tent of meeting traditions, see Milgrom, *Numbers*, 386–87; Von Rad, *Theology*, 1:234–39; Janzen, "Tabernacle," 5:447–58.

42. Janzen, "Tabernacle," 5:453.

43. As Vos, *Biblical Theology*, 148, so eloquently states, "It [tabernacle] embodies the eminently religious idea of the dwelling of God with His people."

44. Milgrom, *Numbers*, 87, 308n43: Gen 3:8; 11:5; 18:21; Exod 3:8; 19:20; Num 11:25 (cf. 11:17); 12:5; 2 Sam 22:10; Ezek 44:2; Zech 14:4. I will demonstrate that the examples from Numbers are especially important for John's descent-ascent motif below.

45. Cole, *Numbers*, 189n46.

46. Soll, "Descent, Descend," 2:102.

47. Farris, "Theophany in the NT," 5:565–66.

place of divine revelation where God speaks with his servants. While the name "tabernacle" conveys the notion of God's presence as he dwells in the midst of his people, "tent of testimony" (σκηνῆς τοῦ μαρτυρίου) conveys an additional function as the place of communication from God to man.[48] As Milgrom states, "The priestly Tent also served an oracular function, for it was the focus of God's revelation."[49] Numbers 11:17 records the Lord's announcement that he will descend to talk to Moses at the tent of meeting: καταβήσομαι καὶ λαλήσω ἐκεῖ μετὰ σοῦ ("I will descend and I will talk with you there"). In 11:25, the Lord does as he promises by descending in the visible form of a cloud to speak with Moses before placing his Spirit on the seventy elders: κατάβη κύριος ἐν νεφέλῃ ἐλάλησεν πρὸς αὐτόν ("The Lord descended in a cloud and spoke to him"). The descending cloud is the visible evidence of the presence of the Lord at the tent of meeting.[50] Whenever God wishes to communicate with Moses, and, conversely, whenever Moses wishes to inquire of God, Moses enters the tent while God's presence descends upon the tent.[51] The descending presence of God, then, serves a revelatory function as he communicates with Moses. Not only is Moses the recipient of divine revelation at the tent of meeting; God also confronts Aaron and Miriam for speaking against Moses for his Cushite wife. Once again, the descending cloud is the visible evidence of the presence[52] of God as he speaks to Aaron and Miriam: καὶ κατέβη κύριος ἐν στύλῳ νεφέλης καὶ ἔστη ἐπὶ τῆς θύρας τῆς σκηνῆς τοῦ μαρτυρίου ("The Lord descended in a pillar of cloud and stood at the door of the tent of testimony," 12:5). The language of theophany is clear as God descends at the tent of testimony to reveal his presence and to address his audience in speech.

God descended from above in order to communicate his will to Israel in the wilderness; this is not unlike John's Son of Man, who descends and, as the incarnate Word, functions as God's self-revelation.[53] On one hand,

---

48. Duguid, *Numbers*, 21. This is especially true in that the tent of testimony housed the Ten Words (Exod 25:16–22; 26:33–34; 40:3, 20). For more, see Cole, *Numbers*, 83.

49. Milgrom, *Numbers*, 386.

50. Cole, *Numbers*, 203. See also, Barrett, *John*, 165; Crew, "The Tabernacle and the Cloud," 84–86; House, *Theology*, 156–57; Milgrom, *Numbers*, 386; Von Rad, *Theology*, 1:236; Vos, *Biblical Theology*, 106–07.

51. Milgrom, *Numbers*, 365.

52. Cole, *Numbers*, 203. The cloud is also prominent in Exodus where it guides Israel through the wilderness and envelopes Moses on the mountain (Exod 13:21–22; 14:24). Exodus places little emphasis on the descent of the cloud on the tabernacle.

53. John's christological titles, while offering differing emphases, all converge on the one man, Jesus of Nazareth. These titles often overlap in function so I am justified in linking the Son of Man with the Word. For a similar view, see Brown, *Introduction*, 258–59; Moloney, *Text and Context*, 79–80, 92. On John's descending Word motif as

this underscores John's revelatory motif, which stresses the revelatory function of the Son who reveals the Father. However, on the other hand, this revelatory theme has a strong wilderness connection in the Prologue. The Prologue reaches its climax and goal at the proclamation that the Word became flesh and "tabernacled" among humanity (John 1:14).[54] That Jesus replaces the wilderness tabernacle as the place of God's presence among his people is also clear.[55] However, this does not exhaust John's tabernacle motif. There is a similarity between his Logos theology,[56] which stresses Christ's pre-existence and unity with the God of the OT (1:1; cf. Gen 1:1), and his Son of Man motif, which also stresses Christ's pre-existence and unity with Israel's God. Anthony Hanson asserts that John's Logos theology mirrors God's revelation to Moses on Mount Sinai, and even goes so far as to suggest that for John, "the Logos was Yahweh revealed on Sinai to Moses."[57] I believe a similar comparison is evident in the pre-existent Son of Man who descends and thus mirrors God's descending presence at the tent of testimony. John, by stressing the descending nature of the Son of Man, identifies him with the God who had appeared to Moses and Israel in the OT by descending in a cloud in the wilderness. This is not so different from Peder Borgen's observation that John associates the descending Son of Man with God's descent at Sinai: "The background ideas move from Moses' ascent to God's descent on Mt. Sinai. The latter thought model is then applied to Jesus."[58] If the Logos was revealed to Moses on Mount Sinai as Hanson suggests, I would argue that the descending Son of Man was similarly revealed at the tent of testimony.

Both John's Logos and Son of Man titles emphasize Christ's pre-existence and can be traced to the wilderness period. When John declares that the pre-existent Son of Man descended into the realm of humanity, he

---

analogous to the descent of wisdom in Judaism, see Achtemeier et al., *Introducing*, 181–83; Witherington, *John's Wisdom*, 47–59; Witherington, *Jesus the Sage*, 282–94, 368–80.

54. Hengel, "Prologue," 265–94.

55. Duguid, *Numbers*, 45; Köstenberger, *Theology*, 426.

56. On the Logos in John, see Anderson, "Word, The," 5:893–98, esp. 896; Beasley-Murray, *John*, 6–10; Bernard, *John*, 1:CXXXVIII–CXLVII; Cullmann, *Christology*, 249–69; Culpepper, *Gospel and Letters*, 93; Dodd, *Interpretation*, 263–85; Johnson, "Logos," 481–84, esp. 481–82; Keener, *John*, 1:350–63; Koester, *Word of Life*, 25–32; Köstenberger, *Encountering John*, 50–57; Ladd, *Theology*, 274–78; Kysar, *Maverick Gospel*, 29–34; Lincoln, *John*, 94–98; Morris, *Theology*, 225–28; O'Grady, "Prologue," 215–28, esp. 221–24; Ridderbos, *John*, 17–23; Smalley, *Evangelist and Interpreter*, 214–15; Thompson, "John," 186–88.

57. Hanson, *Prophetic Gospel*, 30.

58. Borgen, "Exegetical Traditions," 245.

echoes the descent of the Lord in the wilderness traditions of Numbers.[59] Put differently, the tent of testimony theophanies have their counterparts in the Johannine descent of the Son of Man (in addition to the tabernacling of the Word). As previously stated, God descends to earth and makes himself known within the natural realm in a theophany.[60] This is precisely the point behind the descent of the pre-existent Son of Man; this title highlights Christ's deity and pre-existence, and associates him with the revelation of God at the tent of testimony. What is more, the descent of the Son of Man in John's Gospel highlights the unity that exists between Christ and the God of the wilderness in much the same way as John's "I am" (ἐγώ εἰμι) sayings in their predicate (John 6:35, 48, 51; 8:12, 18; 10:7, 9, 11, 14; 11:25; 14:6; 15:1, 5), implied predicate (4:26; 6:20; 18:5–8), and absolute forms (8:24, 28, 58; 13:19).[61] These two motifs—descent and "I am"—come together in a unique wilderness reference in 6:51: ἐγώ εἰμι ὁ ἄρτος ὁ ζῶν ὁ ἐκ τοῦ οὐρανοῦ καταβάς ("I am the living bread that descended from heaven"). Similarly, after Jesus explains to the Jews that he is "from above," he merges the Son of Man and "I am" into one grand image of redemption: ὅταν ὑψώσητε τὸν υἱὸν τοῦ ἀνθρώπου, τότε γνώσεσθε ὅτι ἐγώ εἰμι ("When you have lifted up the Son of Man, then you will know that I am," 8:28). For John, the descending Son of Man and Jesus' "I am" statements point to his oneness with Israel's God in the OT.

The background to John's "I am" sayings is largely the refrain of Isaiah in which the Lord identifies himself as the redeemer of Israel, evoking the atmosphere and imagery of the Exodus tradition (Isa 41:4; 43:11, 13, 15, 25; 45:18; 47:10; 48:12; 51:12; cf. 46:4, 9; 48:17; Deut 32:39).[62] The phrase itself

---

59. I classify this as a probable allusion because it meets the following criteria: Availability: John had access to the whole books of Numbers, Isaiah, and Daniel; Volume: "Descent" (καταβαίνω) of God as the language of theophany; Recurrence: John appeals to wilderness imagery throughout his Gospel; Thematic Coherence: theophany, God descends into the realm of humanity; Historical Plausibility: John's audience was undoubtedly familiar with God's descent on the tent of meeting in the wilderness; messianic associations of Son of Man and Suffering Servant; History of Interpretation: Borgen on God's descent at Sinai as parallel with Son of Man's descent in John; Satisfaction: helps convey the pre-existence and descent of the Son of Man.

60. Farris, "Theophany in the NT," 5:565.

61. It is possible that ἐγώ εἰμι means nothing more than an emphatic "I." However, most scholars see this phrase as a reference to the divine name in the LXX. On John's "I am" sayings, see Achtemeier et al. *Introducing*, 186–87; Bauckham, "Monotheism," 148–66; Boismard, *Moses or Jesus*, 119–22; Bultmann, *John*, 226; Dodd, *Interpretation*, 248; Harner, *I-Am of the Fourth Gospel*; Kysar, *Maverick Gospel*, 45–49; Ladd, *Theology*, 286–87; Lincoln, *John*, 68; Morris, *Theology*, 235–38; Smith, *Theology*, 111–13; Thielman, *Theology*, 157–58; Thompson, "John," 189.

62. Smith, *Theology*, 113.

echoes the theophany at the burning bush where God reveals the divine name to Moses as ἐγώ εἰμι ὁ ὤν ("I am who I am," Exod 3:14).[63] It is a common assumption among many Johannine scholars that John's "I am" sayings demonstrate the unity Christ has with the God of the OT.[64] As George Eldon Ladd states, "The use of the absolute ἐγώ εἰμι, Jesus is in some real sense identifying himself with the God of the OT."[65] Andrew Lincoln states the matter even more provocatively: "Just as God in the Jewish Scriptures identifies Godself by this self-predication [ἐγώ εἰμι], now Jesus utters the same self-predication, indicating that Jesus and God are to be seen as sharing the same identity."[66] Lincoln clearly sees the "I am" language in John as the language of theophany.[67] Therefore, my assertion here is that the descending Son of Man sayings function analogously to John's "I am" sayings—as theophanies which associate Christ with Israel's God in the OT Scriptures. In summary, as the Lord revealed himself to Moses at the tabernacle by descending in a cloud, so also the Son of Man reveals God by descending from above.

UPLIFTED SON OF MAN

After discussing the descent of the pre-existent Son of Man, John now turns his attention to discussing his ascent (John 3:14). For John, Christ's ascension to heaven begins when he is lifted up on the cross. In fact, the crucifixion, far from being the tragic end to Jesus' life, is the beginning of his glorification—his return to the previous glory he shared with the Father in the beginning. John places the dynamic of the uplifting of the Son of Man in the context of spiritual rebirth that was introduced in 3:3. Simply stated, the possibility of spiritual rebirth is conditioned by the descent of the pre-existent Son of Man and his elevation.[68] Where 3:13 was likely a polemic against the proposed heavenly ascents of Moses and other OT figures, John now aligns his argument with Moses by way of a typological analogy.[69] In

---

63. Childs, *Isaiah*, 335.

64. This unity does not erase the essential difference between the Son and Father in John (Bauckham, "Monotheism," 164; Carter, *Storyteller*, 59–61).

65. Ladd, *Theology*, 287.

66. Lincoln, *John*, 68.

67. Ibid., 69. See also, Kysar, *Maverick Gospel*, 48.

68. Dodd, *Interpretation*, 307. I will interact with the elevation of the Son of Man in more detail below.

69. I will discuss the intricate details of John's typology below. It can be quite complex. My point in the following pages is to show the overall comparison. I will turn to the finer points when dealing specifically with John's typology in John 3:14 below.

order to illustrate the redemption brought about by the uplifting of the Son of Man, John provides a visual aid for his readers by alluding to the uplifted serpent of Num 21:4–9. For John, this intertextual allusion provides a powerful preview of the redemptive work of the Messiah. Before interacting with the complexities of John's argument that the Son of Man must be lifted up, I will summarize the narrative of the uplifted serpent in the wilderness.

The Uplifted Serpent of Num 21:4–9

Israel had grown quite accustomed to grumbling against Moses in the desert, and the situation leading up to the narrative of the uplifted serpent is no different. This is the last of the complaint stories in Numbers, and it is one of the worst.[70] For example, Dennis Olson notes that when the Israelites complain in the wilderness, they typically do so against Moses, and sometimes Aaron.[71] However, in this episode they speak against not only Moses, but also God: κατελάλει ὁ λαὸς πρὸς τὸν θεὸν καὶ κατὰ Μωυσῆ ("The people spoke against God and against Moses," Num 21:5).[72] Complaining as a whole is nothing new in the narratives of Numbers, for Israel's complaints deal with the same things: "The people drag out the same old laundry list of complaints about dying in the wilderness, yearning to go back to Egypt, the lack of food and water, and the monotony of the manna."[73] They also grumble about a military campaign against the Canaanites, fearing their size and strength (14:2, 27, 29, and 36). God often answers the people's complaints with his gracious provision. For example, after the Israelites grumble for lack of water, God miraculously provides water from the rock at Meribah (20:3–5, 11). Next, in a complaint-free episode, Israel gains a military victory as they defeat the Canaanite king of Arad (21:1–3). However, the enthusiasm that necessarily follows victory quickly wears off. The Edomites refuse the Israelites passage through their land, forcing Israel to travel another route. Moses finds himself in the midst of a complaining people once again (21:4–5). However, God's "provision" is not so gracious this time. He torments the people with deadly[74] serpents: καὶ ἀπέστειλεν

---

70. Olson, *Numbers*, 135.
71. Ibid.
72. Ibid.
73. Ibid.
74. The Hebrew describes the serpents as "fiery" (שרף), which is probably a description of the burning sensation of their bites upon human skin—an apt metaphor for the fiery anger of God (Num 11:1). For this view, see Ashley, *Numbers*, 404–05; Olson, *Numbers*, 135.

κύριος εἰς τὸν λαὸν τοὺς ὄφεις τοὺς θανατοῦντας καὶ ἔδακνον τὸν λαόν καὶ ἀπέθανεν λαὸς πολὺς τῶν υἱῶν Ισραηλ ("And the Lord sent unto the people deadly serpents, and they bit the people, and many people from the children of Israel died," 21:6). The people then repent of their sinful grumbling: ἡμάρτομεν ὅτι κατελαλήσαμεν κατὰ τοῦ κυρίου καὶ κατὰ σοῦ ("We sinned because we spoke against the Lord and against you," 21:7).[75] While the desperate circumstance of facing death by snakebite drives the Israelites to repent, they realize the seriousness of their sin and therefore express genuine regret.[76] They then entreat Moses to pray to the Lord on their behalf (εὖξαι οὖν πρὸς κύριον, 21:7); he obliges (21:8). God then commands Moses to make a replica serpent which is to be suspended aloft so that the people may look at it and be healed: ποίησον σεαυτῷ ὄφιν καὶ θὲς αὐτὸν ἐπὶ σημείου, καὶ ἔσται ἐὰν δάκῃ ὄφις ἄνθρωπον, πᾶς ὁ δεδηγμένος ἰδὼν αὐτὸν ζήσεται ("Make for yourself a serpent and place it on a standard, and it will be that when a serpent bites a person, everyone who is bitten, after looking at it, will live," 21:8).[77] Verse 9 concludes the narrative as Moses makes a copper serpent (ὄφιν χαλκοῦν)[78] and places it on a standard, or sign (σημείου), and whenever a serpent bit someone, that person would look (ἐπέβλεψεν) at the serpent and live (ἔζη). No one is spared from being bitten, but if one is bitten and obeys God by looking at the copper serpent, healing surely follows.[79] Ashley notes that both in the command (21:8) and its fulfillment

---

75. Olson, *Numbers*, 135–36, notes that Israel confessed sin after a rebellion only one other time in Numbers—the spy story of Num 13–14.

76. Cole, *Numbers*, 348.

77. Ibid., 349, notes that the LXX adds χαλκοῦν ("copper, bronze") to v. 8 to synchronize with v. 9. It is likely a gloss.

78. The issue has been raised as to why Moses made the serpent out of copper. There is no clear answer in the text, but there is a wordplay in the Hebrew between נחש ("serpent") and נחשת ("copper"). For more, see Milgrom, *Numbers*, 174; Wenham, *Numbers*, 177. Similarly, the JPS translation reads "copper" instead of "bronze." Milgrom, *Numbers*, 175, notes the usual practice of combining tin with copper to make the alloy bronze. A copper snake measuring five inches long was discovered at Timna, the copper mining and smelting region of the Arabah near the Red Sea, which dates 1200–900 BCE. The snake was found in the holy place of a tent shrine erected by a nomadic tribe. The place had been the site of a temple to the Egyptian god Hathor that had been abandoned by the Egyptians in about 1150 BCE. In other words, as Milgrom notes, we have a copper snake that is similar to the one fashioned by Moses and that originated in the same locale at approximately the same time (ibid., 459). Ashley, *Numbers*, 403, observes that such a material find at least confirms the possibility of such a metal snake at a time and place very near to that of this story in Numbers. I have followed Ashley, *Numbers*, 405, by using "copper" instead of "bronze" based on the finding at Timna. For more, see Cole, *Numbers*, 349–50; Wenham, *Numbers*, 156–57.

79. Ashley, *Numbers*, 403.

(21:9) healing must be accompanied by an act of obedience to God: looking at the image of the snake.[80]

The uplifted serpent narrative is full of interpretive cruxes. I can only summarize the main issues here and reserve further treatment for my analysis of John's typological use of the Numbers narrative. First, why would God command Moses to make a serpent at all?[81] Is not the biblical portrait of serpent symbolism profoundly negative? Gordon Wenham illustrates that in the Bible the serpent is unclean and even personifies sin (Gen 3; Lev 11:41–42).[82] However, this is far from conclusive, as James Charlesworth has recently illustrated in his book *The Good and Evil Serpent*. Charlesworth illustrates that the serpent is a polyvalent symbol in antiquity.[83] While some ancient cultures depict serpents negatively, symbolizing chaos, darkness, temptation, corrupt knowledge, fear, etc.,[84] this by no means exhausts serpent symbolism in antiquity. Nevertheless, I disagree with Charlesworth that serpent symbolism in the OT is positive throughout.[85] I think it is more accurate to suggest that serpent symbolism in the Bible is both positive and negative, and the best rule of thumb is to examine each instance on its own merits. Charlesworth acknowledges the same when he comments on the role of the serpent in Gen 3: "The narrative is definitive in ascertaining the meaning of the Nachash (serpent)."[86] Our Western culture has taken such symbolism to the extreme so much so that the serpent has become a pejorative symbol.[87] Charlesworth notes, "The conception of the snake as the embodiment of evil has permeated our Western culture."[88] The serpent can at times have a profoundly positive symbolic value, even symbolizing life, health, and healing.[89] These seem to be the dominant symbolism in Num 21.[90] In short, negative serpent symbolism need not prevail when exegeting Num 21:8–9. Charlesworth's reflection on Moses' activity regarding

80. Ibid., 405–06.
81. Wenham, *Numbers*, 176.
82. Ibid., 177.
83. Charlesworth, *Serpent*, 269.
84. Ibid., 197–218.
85. Ibid., 269–351. Charlesworth fails to mention that creatures that move on their bellies are unclean according to the law (Lev 11:42). Granted, unclean does not equate to evil, but it does produce defilement. I also find his positive spin on the role of the serpent in Gen 3 unconvincing (ibid., 269–324, esp. 311).
86. Ibid., 312.
87. Ibid., 2.
88. Ibid.
89. Ibid., 218–66.
90. Ibid., 251, 256.

the uplifted serpent is straightforward: "The image was none other than a serpent—the quintessential symbol of healing, health, and rejuvenation in the ancient Near East, including Palestine from ca. 1850 BCE to at least 135 CE."[91] If negative serpent symbolism is eisegeted into the text, it is more a symptom of presuppositions than exegesis.

A second interpretive crux, and more to the point for later Jewish and Christian interpreters, involves idolatry and the making of images. Are not idolatry and image-making violations of Mosaic Law? This action by Moses seems to contradict the first and second of the Ten Commandments, which forbids idolatry and making images, respectively (Exod 20:3–5).[92] Charlesworth's solution, which is unsatisfactory in my mind, portrays God as contradicting his own Torah: "The Ten Commandments were for the human, not for God."[93] I find this hard to reconcile given that the very issues at hand (i.e., idolatry and image making) threaten the heart of God's holy jealousy for his people. Further, the scriptural witness against idolatry and image-making is uniform and uncompromising. To be fair, Charlesworth notes the text does not say that the people worshiped the serpent; they simply looked at it.[94] Therefore, perhaps the technical charge of idolatry is misplaced at this stage in the copper serpent's history. The charge was eventually substantiated in the time of Hezekiah, as demonstrated below. Nevertheless, by commanding Moses to make the serpent, God seems to violate his own prohibition against image making, and this has not gone unnoticed by later interpreters.

A third interpretive crux involves the nature of "looking" at the copper serpent: if the people are simply looking at the serpent, what is the exact nature of looking? How can looking at the copper serpent effect healing? Speculations range from sympathetic magic, or homeopathic medicine,[95] to Jewish atonement practices. Regarding the first, Karen Joines defines sympathetic magic as "The belief that the fate of an object or person can be governed by the manipulation of its exact image."[96] Gazing upon the image of a poisonous animal was thought to heal or guard the person from further attack.[97] A form of sympathetic magic occurs elsewhere in the Bible when the Philistines capture the ark of the covenant, are then plagued by boils and mice, and then return the ark to Israel filled with gold votive offer-

---

91. Ibid., 336.
92. Similarly, Olson, *Numbers*, 136.
93. Charlesworth, *Serpent*, 333.
94. Ibid.
95. Milgrom, *Numbers*, 459.
96. Joines, "Copper Serpent," 245–56. See also, Charlesworth, *Serpent*, 334.
97. Olson, *Numbers*, 136.

ings in the form of the boils themselves and mice (1 Sam 5:6–6:18).[98] This magical practice was common among the Egyptians where the serpent was a symbol of evil power and chaos from the underworld, as well as a symbol of fertility, life, and healing.[99] Milgrom notes, "At the time of Moses, the belief prevailed in Egypt that images of serpents would repel serpents as well as heal wounds caused by them."[100] Similarly, serpents were well-known symbols of power and sovereignty in ancient Egypt, a fact illustrated by the image of a cobra on Pharaoh's headpiece.[101] Even so, such magical cures do not resonate with the biblical account against sorcery (Lev 19:26) and/or idolatry and image making (Exod 20:4). What is more, later Jewish interpreters often go to great lengths to clarify the exact nature of the healing in the Numbers narrative (see below). Egyptian magic is not the only way to address the issue of the healing from the snakebites. Wenham opts for a view that considers the purifcatory rites in the OT that convey the general principle of inversion:

> Blood which pollutes when it is spilled can be used to sanctify men and articles. The ashes of a dead heifer cleanse those who suffer from the impurity caused by death. In all these rituals there is an inversion: normally polluting substances or actions may in a ritual context have the opposite effect and serve to purify.[102]

The text is silent regarding both God's logic and the precise method of healing. The text begs more questions and presents more gaps than I have surveyed here. Later Jewish and Christian interpreters would fill in textual gaps like these. I will discuss some of these interpretive traditions later in this chapter. It is sufficient to note at this point that such a seemingly flagrant instance of sympathetic magic and image making, which the Law stands firmly against, raised questions in the minds of later interpreters. The fear of biblical support for magic, idolatry, and image making in Israel caused later interpreters to explain this story on many fronts. In fact, 2 Kgs 18:4 bears out this fear when Hezekiah later smashes the serpent made by Moses,

---

98. Cole, *Numbers*, 349n428; Milgrom, *Numbers*, 459.
99. Olson, *Numbers*, 136.
100. Milgrom, *Numbers*, 459.
101. Duguid, *Numbers*, 262. Duguid notes the irony of God's use of this Egyptian symbol of power as a means of judgment on Israel: repeatedly throughout Numbers, the Israelites have longed to return to Egypt.
102. Wenham, *Numbers*, 177.

named Nehushtan,[103] after the people turn to it in idolatry.[104] It seems that the concern expressed by later interpreters—that the serpent not be viewed as an idol—becomes an unfortunate reality in the monarchial period.

The Johannine Uplifted Son of Man

I have already discussed the Johannine understanding of the pre-existent Son of Man who descends from heaven. While this is certainly an aspect of the Johannine Son of Man, it is only one aspect of his identity. The Son of Man must also be lifted up (ὑψόω, John 3:14; 8:28; 12:32–34).[105] After emphasizing the descent of the Son of Man, John describes the necessity of his being lifted up in an analogous way to Moses' serpent in the wilderness: καὶ καθὼς Μωϋσῆς ὕψωσεν τὸν ὄφιν ἐν τῇ ἐρήμῳ, οὕτως ὑψωθῆναι δεῖ τὸν υἱὸν τοῦ ἀνθρώπου ("And as Moses lifted up the serpent in the wilderness, so also must the Son of Man be lifted up," 3:14). Before looking more closely at John's allusion to Num 21:8–9 in John 3:14, I must discuss the elevation of the Son of Man in his Gospel.

As stated earlier, the Son of Man not only descended from heaven, but must also be lifted up. I have also demonstrated that the descent of the Son of Man is rooted in OT texts such as Num 11:25, 12:5, and Dan 7:13. However, there is no clear OT text that speaks unambiguously of the elevation of the Son of Man. Nevertheless, for John, Jesus defines his mission precisely by a combination of these two motifs. While the OT does not reference the elevation of the Son of Man per se, it does reference the elevation of the Suffering Servant, and John combines these two OT figures into one—Jesus Christ.

In John, the idea that the Son of Man must be lifted up is critical for understanding his messianic task, especially regarding his atoning death. John appeals to a number of intertwined OT motifs to emphasize this. The

103. The name "Nehushtan" is a play on the two words נחש נחשת, and may be an onomatopoetic device (Charlesworth, *Serpent*, 348).

104. Various attempts have been made to explain the relationship between the serpent of Numbers and that of 2 Kings. The traditional view holds that over time, the Israelites idolized and worshiped the snake; therefore, Hezekiah destroyed it as part of his religious reform. Alternatively, the story in Numbers is a retrojection from the time of Hezekiah, and was invented to explain what happened in Hezekiah's time. However, as Milgrom, *Numbers*, 460, asks, could such a story have been written after Hezekiah's time—after the copper snake was declared an idolatrous object? For more on this, see Ashley, *Numbers*, 403; Budd, *Numbers*, 233–34; Charlesworth, *Serpent*, 326–29, 342–43; Cole, *Numbers*, 347–48; Milgrom, *Numbers*, 460; Rowley, "Nehushtan," 113–41.

105. I will demonstrate below the "lifting up" (ὑψόω) and the "glorification" (δοξάζω) of the Son of Man is the Johannine language of crucifixion/resurrection/ascension.

Servant of the Lord, or Suffering Servant, forms the heart of NT Christology.[106] The Suffering Servant motif is taken largely from Isa 52:13—53:12 (although it begins in Isa 49), a chapter, which Brevard Childs notes, "Is probably the most contested chapter in the Old Testament."[107] It should not be taken for granted that Isaiah's Servant refers to one historical individual. The referents from an Isaianic standpoint are Israel/Jacob (Isa 41:8-9; 42:1; 44:1-2, 21; 45:4; 48:20), Israel as faithful remnant (49:5-6), or an anonymous individual who will restore Israel from exile (44:24; 46:3; 49:1; 52:12-53:12).[108] While both the identity and function of the Servant are hotly debated, John axiomatically applies the suffering role to Jesus.[109] His emphasis in the Gospel lies on Christ being "lifted up" (ὑψόω) and "glorified" (δοξάζω),[110] an image he takes from Isa 52:13: ἰδοὺ συνήσει ὁ παῖς μου καὶ ὑψωθήσεται καὶ δοξασθήσεται σφόδρα ("Behold, my servant will discern, and he will be lifted up and greatly glorified").[111] This passage shows the two terms for glorification used in parallel.[112] The Servant of the Lord is to be exalted and glorified in consequence of his passion and death.[113] John's Son of Man sayings take the twin notions of "to lift up" and "to glorify" from Isaiah's Suffering Servant and applies them to Jesus. J. Ramsey Michaels stresses the centrality of Isaiah's Suffering Servant who is both "lifted up" and "glorified"; both verbs become decisively associated with Jesus as Son of Man.[114] These two verbs convey Jesus' crucifixion in John. I will speak more to the Johannine notion of "lifting up" the Son of Man below. Suffice it to say here that John captures the crucifixion not only with ὑψόω, but also with

---

106. Cullmann, *Christology*, 51. However, Morna Hooker, *Jesus and the Servant*, believes that the pervasiveness of the Servant motif in the NT has been "over-estimated." For more on the Suffering Servant in the NT generally, see Childs, *Isaiah*, 420–23; Cullmann, *Christology*, 51–82; VanGemeren, *Progress of Redemption*, 387–88.

107. Childs, *Isaiah*, 410.

108. Collins, "Servant of the Lord," 5:192–95; Dillard and Longman, *Introduction*, 278–79.

109. For more on Isaiah's Suffering Servant, see Childs, *Isaiah*, 420–23; Collins, "Servant of the Lord," 5:192–95; Dillard and Longman, *Introduction*, 278–79; France, "Servant of Yahweh," 744–47; Janowski and Stuhlmacher, eds. *Suffering Servant*. On John's application of the Isaianic Servant to Jesus, see Keener, *John*, 1:566; Reim, *Jochanan*, 135–36; Thielman, *Theology*, 188–89.

110. I.e., Christ's crucifixion, resurrections, and ascension (John 12:32–34).

111. Thielman, *Theology*, 188–89. Thielman notes that John does not develop the Servant theme as extensively as the Synoptics; he focuses on Jesus' rejection (John 12:37–38; cf. Isa 53:3) and exaltation (ibid., 188).

112. Wead, "Double Meaning," 106–20.

113. Dodd, *Interpretation*, 375.

114. Michaels, *John*, 198; Tuckett, *Son of Man*, 172.

δοξάζω. Therefore, when John says, δεῖ ὑψωθῆναι τὸν υἱὸν τοῦ ἀνθρώπου (John 3:14; 12:34), he means much the same as when he speaks of the Son of Man being glorified.[115] The cross is ultimately not Jesus' death but rather his glorification. When John writes about the cross, he says that the Son of Man is in fact "glorified" (12:23, 28; 13:31–32).[116] However, not only does John characterize the cross as Christ's glorification, but also his entire ministry is one of glory (1:14).[117] Nevertheless, his death on the cross is his most notable act of glorying God.[118] As John comments on the glorification of Christ, it is yet another example of a Johannine double meaning where δόξα/δοξάζω suggests that in Christ's death he glorifies God and gains glory himself by being restored to his pre-existent glory (cf. 1:14; 17:5).[119] As I will illustrate below with John's use of ὑψόω, his use of δοξάζω connotes his death, resurrection, and ascension in one grand redemptive event. Gail O'Day and Susan Hylen summarize the Johannine notion of Christ's glorification: "In John, Jesus' death, resurrection, and ascension are understood as one continuous event, which are regularly referred to together in John by the phrase 'glorified.'"[120] Dodd observes that Johannine double meaning is more accurately a "paradox" as John uses δοξάζω to connote both the death of Christ and his resurrection, which gives life to the world.[121]

Scholars debate the messianic associations of the Servant of Isaiah but it likely came to bear some kind of messianic significance in Judaism by the second century CE.[122] For example, *Tg. Isa.* 52:13, while later than the NT, may contain older traditions (i.e., first and second centuries CE).[123] It clearly equates the Servant with the Messiah: "Behold, my servant, *the Messiah,* shall prosper, he shall be exalted and *increase.*"[124] However, the vicarious suffering

---

115. Dodd, *Interpretation*, 247.

116. Morris, *Theology*, 234. Ridderbos, *John*, 52–52, notes John's additional use of δόξα that refers to the *kavōd* of God in the OT. For more on "glory" in John, see Ladd, *Theology*, 311–12; Smalley, *Evangelist and Interpreter*, 220–22.

117. Ladd, *Theology*, 312.

118. Ibid.

119. Similarly, Dodd, *Interpretation*, 208. Against this view, see Moloney, *Text and Context*, 86–90, who believes that δόξα refers only to the cross and not the exaltation/ascension in John.

120. O'Day and Hylen, *John*, 44.

121. Dodd, *Interpretation*, 374.

122. Cullmann, *Christology*, 58, holds that the Suffering Servant had messianic associations in the first century CE. Many scholars now hold this to be too early.

123. Collins, "Messiah, Jewish," 4:66; Evans, *Ancient Texts*, 195.

124. Targumic expansion italicized. I will interact more with the explanatory and expansionistic character of the Targumim later when commenting on the interpretation of Num 21 in *Pseudo-Jonathan*. Translation by Chilton, *Isaiah Targum*, 103. Cullmann,

of the Servant for the nation is difficult for the Targumist to accept, as the translation suggests (i.e., "prosper" and "increase"). It was difficult for later Rabbis to accept the idea of a suffering Messiah.[125] Oscar Cullmann observes that the thought that the Messiah has to suffer is foreign to the official expectation.[126] A Messiah who suffers for his people seems marginal in Judaism of the first century CE.[127] As Craig Keener notes, "It is unlikely that a specific suffering-Messiah view existed in the first century."[128] Nevertheless, the suffering of the Servant is clearly represented in the biblical text:

> "His appearance was so marred, beyond human semblance, and his form beyond that of the children of mankind;
> So shall he sprinkle many nations; kings shall shut their mouths because of him; for that which has not been told to them they see, and that which they have not heard they understand" (Isa 52:14–15 ESV).

Cullmann notes that the Targumist virtually eliminates everything that concerns the suffering of the Servant and interprets the text to mean the opposite:[129]

> *"Just as the house of Israel hoped for him many days—their* appearances *were so dark among the peoples,* and *their aspect beyond that of the sons of men, so he shall scatter many peoples;*

Christology, 56, notes that 1 *Enoch*, 4 *Ezra*, and 2 *Baruch* identify the Messiah indirectly with the Servant of the Lord. However, the Servant's essential task of vicarious suffering was not transferred to the Messiah. See also, Borgen, "Exegetical Traditions," 253. For more on *Targum Isaiah* and its messianic interpretation of the Servant, see Evans, *Ancient Texts*, 195.

125. Cullmann, *Christology*, 58.

126. Ibid. I cite Cullmann's observation here while taking into account his acknowledgment that the messianic expectations in first century CE are anything but monolithic (ibid., 116). It was once held by Robert Eisenman that the Dead Sea community knew of a suffering Messiah based on 4Q285, the so-called Pierced Messiah Text. Eisenman originally translated the commentary on Isa 11:3–4 as, "And they killed [or: will kill] the prince of the congregation, the branch of David." A later line was taken by Eisenman to refer to "his wounds" or "his piercings." Further research, however, bears out a more accurate translation: "And the prince of the congregation, the branch of David will kill [or: killed] him." Thus, the prince is likely doing the killing here. For more, see VanderKam, *Dead Sea Scrolls Today*, 179–80.

127. Cullmann, *Christology*, 60.

128. Keener, *John*, 1:288; Collins, "Messiah, Jewish," 4:66.

129. Cullmann, *Christology*, 59. Collins, "Messiah, Jewish," 4:66, notes the same targumic phenomenon where the Servant is not suffering but triumphant. Cullmann also notes that the Targum in its present form may be directed against the Christian identification of the Servant with Jesus. As Cullmann observes, however, there is no certain evidence of an anti-Christian polemic here.

kings shall *be silent* because of him, *they shall place their hands upon* their mouth; for *things* which *have* not been told to them they have seen, and that which they have not heard they have understood" (*Tg. Isa.* 52:14–15).[130]

Here, the Targumist applies the sufferings to the nation of Israel (e.g., "their") or to the representative remnant.[131] So, *Targum Isaiah* posits a two-pronged interpretive strategy to the Isaianic passage by applying Isa 52:13–53:12 to the Messiah but its sufferings to Israel.[132] It is clear, therefore, that the Targumist is uneasy with a suffering Messiah-king, yet this will be primary for John's understanding of Jesus' messiahship.

As previously noted, John combines both the Son of Man and the Suffering Servant into one figure—Jesus Christ. For John, the Son of Man is, in fact, the Servant of the Lord.[133] For John, when Jesus speaks of his person and mission, he thinks of the Son of Man who has descended from heaven (Dan 7:13; *4 Ezra* 13:3) and at the same time, the Suffering Servant who dies an atoning death (Isa 52:13). John's presentation of the Son of Man as the Suffering Servant is a unique blending of two seemingly disconnected figures. Granted, both figures may have carried messianic implications and therefore reflect the multiplicity of messianic understandings of various sects within first-century Judaism. However, they existed as disconnected figures from one another as well as from differing messianic expectations. Judaism knew not a Son of Man who was also a Suffering Servant. John, in contrast, shows that the mission of the Son of Man involves a central aspect of the mission of the Suffering Servant—he must be lifted up. Again, Cullmann's summary of the Johannine Son of Man is helpful:

> Both the Suffering Servant and the Son of Man already existed in Judaism. But Jesus' combination of precisely these two titles was something completely new. Son of Man represents the highest conceivable declaration of exaltation in Judaism; *eved Yahweh* is the expression of the deepest humiliation. Even if there was a concept of a suffering Messiah in Judaism, it cannot be proved that suffering was combined precisely with the idea of the Son of Man coming on the clouds of heaven. This is the unheard-of

---

130. Translation by Chilton.

131. Scholars debate the identity of the remnant. It has been interpreted both individually and corporately. For a discussion, see Cullmann, *Christology,* 54–55.

132. Keener, *John,* 1:566n315.

133. Sidebottom, *Christ of the Fourth Gospel,* 79–81.

new act of Jesus, that he united these two apparently contradictory tasks in his self-consciousness.[134]

John's method of combining the Son of Man with the Suffering Servant is both noteworthy and unique in the NT. His reference to the Son of Man who must "be lifted up" (ὑψωθῆναι, John 3:14) is a hybrid use of the Son of Man in Dan 7:13 and the Suffering Servant of Isa 52:13. John may be reflecting a Hebrew exegetical practice called "pearl stringing," which is the practice of bringing to bear on one point of an argument passages from various parts of the Bible in support of the argument and to demonstrate the unity of Scripture.[135] It is normally applied to specific texts to establish verbal parallels. However, John does not quote a text per se when he combines the Son of Man with the Suffering Servant; he simply alludes to several passages drawing out what he believes to be parallel ideas. John's use of Scripture here closely reflects Hillel's second rule of exegesis, *gezerah shawah*, where a verbal analogy from one verse is linked to another, where the same words are applied in two separate cases.[136] John clearly believes that the Son of Man is none other than the Suffering Servant who must be lifted up. His textual logic combines the roles of Suffering Servant and Son of Man into one figure, Jesus Messiah, and looks something like this:[137]

---

134. Cullmann, *Christology*, 161.
135. Longenecker, *Biblical Exegesis*, 99.
136. Ibid., 20.
137. While the diagram is my own, I have taken the process, phraseology, and biblical texts from Dodd, *Interpretation*, 246–47.

Figure 3. Interrelation of Suffering Servant, Son of Man, and Jesus Messiah.

This diagram illustrates the overlapping missions of the Servant and the Son of Man so that they become one figure—Jesus Christ. The Servant/Son glorifies God, gathers Israel, is a light in the darkness, shepherds Israel, and is lifted up and glorified. For John, Jesus is a combination of the Son of Man and Suffering Servant because their respective roles overlap in his person and mission. As Dodd suggests, "If this connection of thought be considered valid, we can see how easily the evangelist could connect the work of the suffering Servant, who is also the Son of Man, in gathering together the scattered children of God, with the death of Christ."[138]

John's Allusion to the Copper Serpent

Understanding the messianic mission of the Son of Man as that of being "lifted up" is crucial for perceiving the complexities of John's allusion to the copper serpent narrative.[139] Granted, there is no reference to the Son of Man

---

138. Dodd, *Interpretation*, 247.

139. That John 3:14 is an obvious allusion to Num 21:8–9 is hardly doubted by Johannine scholars today. However, see chapter 1 above for Enz's opposing view. Marrs,

in Num 21:8–9.[140] Nevertheless, for John, the lifting up of the copper serpent by Moses anticipates the lifting up of the Son of Man.[141] God commanded Moses to set the copper serpent on a standard, or a "sign" (σημεῖον, Num 21:8–9). The divine plan necessitated this specific action. In order for the Israelites to be healed from the poisonous bites of the fiery serpents, it was necessary for Moses to follow God's ordained plan. This is also true of the elevation of the Son of Man: he must (δεῖ, John 3:14) be lifted up. There is divine determination here.[142] As God stands behind the exaltation of the copper serpent, he also stands behind the elevation of the Son of Man. God is the responsible agent in both redemptive acts.

John's Son of Man must "be lifted up" (ὑψωθῆναι, 3:14), and as was the case with δοξάζω, this, too, is John's language of the crucifixion and

---

"Raised Serpent," 132, 139, refers to John's use of Num 21:8–9 as a "citation," but then also notes that John "alludes" to the OT event (p. 132). To be fair, Marrs's methodology is not intertextuality; therefore, his terminology should not be pressed. Nevertheless, it is not strictly speaking a citation for there is no introductory formula and no specific mention of ἡ γραφή. "Allusion" is probably the best intertextual descriptor of John's use of Num 21:8–9; it fits the following criteria: Availability: John had access to the entire book of Numbers; Volume: "Moses," "serpent," "wilderness" resonate loudly with the Numbers narrative; Recurrence: John appeals to wilderness imagery throughout his Gospel; Thematic Coherence: the lifting up of the Son of Man; Historical Plausibility: John's audience certainly knew the OT narrative along with its interpretive traditions (i.e., later Jewish and Christian interpreters interacted heavily with the narrative); History of Interpretation: Wisdom, Gospel of John, rabbinic works, and Apostolic Fathers repeatedly referred to the Numbers narrative with similar interpretive strategies; Satisfaction: fits well John's Moses/second exodus typology of the Gospel as a whole; it also completes the thought of John 3:14 and the lifting up in crucifixion and glory of the Suffering Servant and Son of Man. While not specifically works on intertextuality, those who classify John's use as an "allusion" include Burge, *Interpreting the Gospel of John*, 20; Carson, *John*, 91; Hanson, *Prophetic Gospel*, 46; Köstenberger, *John*, 128; Reim, *Jochanan*, 108.

140. Thielman, *Theology*, 187.

141. The anticipatory nature of the serpent narrative will emerge below in my discussion of John's typology. Thielman, *Theology*, 187, is mostly correct to point out that John's reference to the copper serpent is more an analogy to Jesus' atoning death than a prophecy of it. On one hand, this seems to be a very limited view of prophecy that sees it simply as prediction followed by fulfillment. True, this is not what John is doing. However, most Johannine scholars have viewed John's reference as typological, and typology has to do with the chronological development of redemptive history, as predictive prophecy does. Typology is not radically different from predictive prophecy, but it is not equated with it either. All typology is prophetic in that it depends on a chronological progression of redemptive-history, but not all prophecies exhibit typological relationships. Thus, the two are not autonomous, but they are not synonymous either.

142. Carson, *John*, 202; Charlesworth, *Serpent*, 380.

exaltation of Christ.¹⁴³ John applies a double meaning to ὑψόω (3:14; 8:28; 12:32–34) which combines the notions of being physically lifted up on the cross with the notion of exaltation to heaven.¹⁴⁴ John captures the "lifting up" of the Son of Man with ὑψόω, and 3:14 is the first, somewhat oblique, reference to Jesus' crucifixion in the Gospel; later developed in 8:28 and explicitly set forth in 13:32–33.¹⁴⁵ All of the Son of Man sayings point to the cross,¹⁴⁶ and 12:32–34 is a clear example: "'And when I am lifted up (ὑψωθῶ) from the earth, I will draw all people to myself.' He said this to indicate the kind of death he was to die. Then the crowd answered him, 'We have heard from the law that the Messiah remains forever. How can you say that the Son of Man must be lifted up (ὑψωθῆναι)? Who is the Son of Man?'" In typical Johannine fashion, the event of being lifted up has a veiled reference—the crucifixion is not presented as Jesus' humiliation, but as his exaltation and glorification.¹⁴⁷ Jesus dies a humiliating death by crucifixion, but at the same time begins to enter his exalted, eschatological glory. John, therefore, combines Jesus' crucifixion, resurrection, and exaltation into one theological concept encapsulated by ὑψόω. The "lifting up" of the Son of Man is therefore the comprehensive event of salvation in John.¹⁴⁸ Gary Burge explains the visible force of ὑψόω in the Johannine economy: "The movement up to the cross is a heavenward movement, which is the first step back to Jesus' former glory with God."¹⁴⁹

A comparison between John 3:14–15 and Num 21:8–9 makes it clear that John is not quoting the text per se but simply alluding to it. This fact does not weigh against an intertextual relationship between John 3:14–15

---

143. Ridderbos, *John*, 136. Scholars often debate whether John's language of ὑψόω refers also to the resurrection or ascension of Christ. Luke makes a distinction between the two events and emphasizes the "lifting up" as the ascension (Acts 1:3, 9). John does not make this distinction. The cross, resurrection, and ascension form one grand redemptive event for John. Though he does have one passage that speaks concretely of the ascension in distinction from the resurrection (John 20:17: "Do not hold on to me because I have not yet ascended (ἀναβέβηκα) to the Father"). However, this is the only unambiguous reference to the ascension in the Gospel and too much should not be made of this one verse. The other texts which mention Christ's exaltation envision the cross, resurrection, and ascension in a single all-inclusive salvific event in the Johannine economy. For more on this debate, see Kysar, *Maverick Gospel*, 42–43.

144. Carson, *John*, 201. See also, Kysar, *Maverick Gospel*, 41; Richard, "Double Meaning," 96–112, esp. 101; Romanowsky, "Lifted Up," 100–16; Wead, "Double Meaning,"108–11.

145. Köstenberger, *Theology*, 199.

146. Moloney, *Text and Context*, 69–92.

147. Ridderbos, *John*, 137.

148. Burge, *Anointed Community*, 132.

149. Ibid.

and Num 21:8–9 because John tends to lean away from verbal allusions toward more thematic uses of the OT precursor text. Therefore, verbal allusions and echoes need not weigh more than thematic ones in John. John 3:14–15 does not have many linguistic affinities with Num 21:8–9, but the chart below indicates that the ideas are much the same:

Table 4. Linguistic comparison between Num 21:8–9 and John 3:14–15.

Num 21:8–9	John 3:14–15
ἐποίησεν Μωυσῆς ὄφιν "Moses made a serpent"	καθὼς Μωϋσῆς ὕψωσεν τὸν ὄφιν "As Moses lifted up the serpent"
ἔστησεν αὐτὸν ἐπὶ σημείου "He set it on a sign"	ὑψωθῆναι δεῖ τὸν υἱὸν τοῦ ἀνθρώπου "The Son of Man must be lifted up"
πᾶς ὁ δεδηγμένος "Everyone who had been bitten"	πᾶς "Everyone"
ἰδὼν αὐτὸν "After seeing it"	ὁ πιστεύων ἐν αὐτῷ "Whoever believes"
ζήσεται "He will live"	ἔχῃ ζωὴν αἰώνιον "In him, may have eternal life"

Source: Slightly adapted from Anthony Hanson, *The Prophetic Gospel: A Study of John and the Old Testament* (Edinburgh: T&T Clark, 1991), 48.

D. A. Carson states that for John, the "deepest" point of connection between the copper serpent and the Son of Man is in the act of being lifted up.[150] This is a bit reductionistic because "lifted up" (ὑψόω) is not even mentioned in Num 21. As Günter Reim notes, it is striking that the concept "to lift up," which plays a large role in John, does not appear in Num 21:8–9.[151] Nevertheless, I will reserve my apprehensions regarding reductionistic typologies for later in this chapter. Even so, one can hardly argue against the lifting up as a point of comparison, especially given John's emphasis on ὑψόω in relation to the Son of Man saying in John 3:14 and elsewhere in the Gospel. As Moses set the copper serpent "on a sign" (ἔστησεν αὐτὸν ἐπὶ σημείου, Num 21:9), so also the Son of Man must be "lifted up" (ὑψωθῆναι, John 3:14). There is not an exact verbal parallel but the ideas are certainly parallel, and John clearly alludes to the Numbers narrative. It is regrettable that Charlesworth does not see John's use of Num 21:8–9 as a clear case of intertextuality

---

150. Carson, *John*, 201.
151. Reim, *Jochanan*, 135.

as I am arguing for in this study.¹⁵² Granted, John does not cite a specific OT precursor text, but even Charlesworth admits that John alludes to the copper serpent narrative of Numbers.¹⁵³ He also states that there is an "echo" of Num 21 in John's text. In spite of Charlesworth's reservation at seeing this as an instance of intertextuality, he has certainly used the language of intertextuality himself by referring to John's use of Numbers as "allusion" and "echo."¹⁵⁴ In contrast to Charlesworth, I am seeking to apply the intertextual method not only to John's uplifted serpent reference, but also to the larger pericope that encompasses that reference.

Serpent as Johannine Σημεῖον

It is significant for this study, which is focused in part on Johannine signs, that Moses places the copper serpent "on a sign" (ἐπὶ σημείου). I have previously demonstrated the importance of the term σημεῖον for John's Gospel as a descriptor for Jesus' miracles in chapter 2. The healing that occurs when the Israelites gaze upon the uplifted serpent is obviously a miraculous occurrence in the context of Num 21 because it is God's redemptive response to Moses' prayer on behalf of the people. When John refers to the miracle of Moses' uplifted serpent, he likely intends for his readers to see the uplifting of the Son of Man as a miraculous event. Put differently, the cross is a miraculous event by way of analogy, but with greater effects because Jesus is greater than Moses in John's Gospel. When describing the necessity of the cross, John may have been drawn to the serpent narrative of Num 21 because it was a "sign" which pointed to Jesus' atoning death and exaltation.¹⁵⁵ Somewhat surprisingly, John leaves this potential element of comparison largely unexplored.¹⁵⁶

The issue I am addressing here is whether John views the copper serpent as a miraculous sign and if so, its impact on Jesus' signs throughout the Fourth Gospel. Several scholars have seen a connection centering on

---

152. Charlesworth, *Serpent*, 393.

153. Ibid.

154. To be fair, Charlesworth's book is not about intertextuality; therefore, I am conscious of not overreacting to his imprecise terminology. I do find it odd, however, that he uses the term "intertextuality" as one of nine supporting proofs for one of the major theses of his book: Num 21:8–9 and John 3:14–15 are examples of positive serpent symbolism in the Bible (ibid., 373, 393–95).

155. Similarly, Charlesworth, *Serpent*, 394. As I will illustrate below, this is how many of the church fathers understood John's reference to the uplifted serpent.

156. Marrs, "Raised Serpent," 132–47.

the use of σημεῖον in Num 21 and John's Gospel as a whole.[157] The issue is not whether there is a connection, but rather the nature of that connection. When discussing signs in John's Gospel, Raymond E. Brown theorizes that the reference to the uplifted serpent might be an instance of a non-miraculous sign, especially because Moses set the serpent on a σημεῖον.[158] What Brown states as a non-miraculous sign, I want to state more affirmatively as a miraculous one. Given John's emphasis on Jesus' σημεῖα, the fact that the LXX refers to the standard or pole on which Moses placed the copper serpent as a σημεῖον suggests that John sees some special meaning in this incident.[159] For this reason, it is possible that John implies this particular point of comparison rather than overtly stating it, therefore leaving his audience to fill in the gap and find that special meaning based on the "hints and pointers" he has left in the text.[160] This is T. F. Glasson's logic who points to John's methodological use of Scripture in the Gospel as a whole: John does not mention the sign (σημεῖον) of Num 21:8–9 per se, but given his allusive use of the OT, he likely intends for his audience to make the necessary connection between being lifted up and placed on a σημεῖον.[161] Further, as Glasson notes, and as I have previously demonstrated, John is intensely interested in the "lifting up" of the Son of Man, an idea that he takes from the Servant passages of Isaiah. The verb translated as "lift up" (αἴρω) is repeated linked with σημεῖον throughout Isaiah (Isa 5:26; 11:12; 13:2; 18:3; 62:10),[162] and given John's interest in conflating the Son of Man with the Suffering Servant who must be "lifted up" (ὑψόω, Isa 52:13; John 3:14), he probably intends for his audience to connect ὑψόω and σημεῖον so that the Son of Man must be ὑψωθῆναι as a σημεῖον. To be clear, I have inferred this view based on Glasson's logic, but given John's allusive use of Scripture and his ambiguous use of terminology elsewhere in the Gospel, I believe the evidence substantiates my inference. After canvassing the evidence that sees a parallel between John's emphasis on Jesus' σημεῖα and the σημεῖον of the uplifted serpent, Glasson concludes: "The allusiveness of John would favour

---

157. Barrett, *John*, 213; Brown, *John*, 1:528; Charlier, "La notion de signe," 434–48; Charlesworth, *Serpent*, 325, 394; Glasson, *Moses*, 36, 38; Hanson, *Prophetic Gospel*, 46; Marrs, "Raised Serpent," 147; Thomas, "Healing," 23–39.

158. Brown, *John*, 1:528.

159. Hanson, *Prophetic Gospel*, 46.

160. Glasson, *Moses*, 36. Similarly, see Manning, *Echoes of a Prophet*, 198.

161. Glasson, *Moses*, 36.

162. The term used in these verses is αἴρω rather than ὑψόω. The terms are synonyms. Glasson posits that John may be relying on the Hebrew rather than the Greek (ibid.).

the view that he was not unaware of this further implication of the Brazen Serpent parallel."[163]

To further the proposal that John intends for his audience to see the uplifted serpent as a sign, several sources classify the event as a miracle. For example, C. K. Barrett illustrates that the miraculous nature of the event is inherent in the Hebrew word נס, the term for the "standard" or "pole" on which Moses placed the copper serpent. He illustrates that the Talmud understands נס as "miracle" in *b. Ber.* 4a: "The intention was to perform a miracle (נס) for Israel."[164] Granted, the Talmud is admittedly later than John's Gospel; nevertheless, it confirms that the term נס can at times be used to refer to a miracle. John likely implies the miraculous nature of the event based on the translation of נס as σημεῖον in LXX Num 21:8–9. Also, the midrash on Numbers states, "And Moses made a serpent of brass, and set it up by a miracle (נס). He cast it into the air and it stayed there" (*Num. Rab.* 19:23).[165] John does not corroborate the second statement; nevertheless, the miraculous nature of the episode is obvious in *Numbers Rabbah* and John similarly intends for his audience to recall it as such without necessarily referring to it as a σημεῖον. *Targum Onqelos,* the oldest and official Targum to the Pentateuch (ca. first century CE),[166] translates נס in Num 21:8–9 as את ("sign"). I noted previously in chapter 2 that the LXX typically translates את as σημεῖον, the usual Johannine term for "miracle."

As demonstrated in the above references to the "miracle" of the serpent in the Mishnah, John is not alone in seeing the serpent as a miraculous sign. I am conscious of not relying on the later passages in the Mishnah to corroborate John's interpretation. Therefore, Wisdom,[167] which likely predates John's Gospel, witnesses in its own way to the miraculous nature of the copper serpent by referring to it as a "symbol of salvation" (σύμβολον σωτηρίας, Wis 16:6), thus functioning as a "sign."[168] The terminology of symbol in Wis 16 is significant here: as the copper serpent is a visible σύμβολον σωτηρίας (16:6), so also the Son of Man must be lifted up as a visible symbol of God's salvation unto eternal life. John is fond of using symbols, and is even willing

---

163. Ibid., 38.

164. Barrett, *John,* 213. English translation of *b. Ber.* 4a taken from Epstein, ed., *Babylonian Talmud,* 12. See also, Kugel, *Traditions,* 797.

165. Glasson, *Moses,* 38. English translation of *Numbers Rabbah* by Slotki, *Midrash Rabbah: Numbers,* 772.

166. Evans, *Ancient Texts,* 187.

167. I will interact more with Wisdom below.

168. Keener, *John,* 1:565. Keener notes that the previous verses (John 3:12–13) resemble material from Wisdom (ibid., 562) and that an allusion to that work also makes sense in 3:14.

to interpret them for his audience.[169] Although John does not use exactly the same terminology as Wisdom's σύμβολον, preferring the term σημεῖον instead, the idea is the same: the miraculous nature of God's redemptive acts.[170] This is an example of John's allusiveness and ambiguity where he is often hesitant to draw concrete applications that he intends his audience to make on its own. As Leonard Goppelt states, "When Christ's being lifted up to the Father by the cross is compared with the snake's being set up on a pole in the wilderness, the significant thing is that in each instance a *symbol* of redemption was set up so that it could be seen by everyone and could help everyone."[171] In summary, I believe that John intends for his readers, who were familiar with the LXX, to see this signs-connection themselves and perceive Moses' uplifted serpent as a miraculous occurrence that points to the most miraculous event in John's Gospel—the cross. By alluding to the narrative that tells of the σημεῖον of the uplifted serpent, John intends to show that the greatest sign of all in his Gospel is the σημεῖον of the cross.[172]

JEWISH INTERPRETIVE TRADITION OF NUM 21:8-9

Aside from John's use of the copper serpent narrative, he also reflects the rich interpretive tradition surrounding the narrative. His analogy between the lifting up of the copper serpent in the wilderness and the lifting up of the Son of Man shares an interpretive milieu with various Jewish traditions from roughly the same period. What is more, John's similarity with the interpretive tradition provides a useful template for interpreting the complex relationship of seeing signs and believing in his Gospel. In short, John demonstrates an interpretive strategy that underscores the role of faithful hearts that "see" Jesus' miraculous signs and "believe" in his divine identity and messianic mission.

The interpretive tradition of Num 21:8-9 is quite strong; the narrative receives a lot of attention by later Jewish and Christian interpreters.[173] It is

---

169. Burge, *Anointed Community*, 153. Burge points to the possible anticipation of Peter's crucifixion in 21:18, the temple as the body of Jesus in 2:21, Spirit and water in 7:39, the copper serpent in 3:14, and the loaves/manna analogy in ch. 6.

170. Hanson, *Prophetic Gospel*, 47, cites Maneschg's view that Wisdom's use of σύμβολον is a rendering of σημεῖον in Num 21:8-9. For this, see Maneschg, *Die Erzählung von der ehernen Schlange*, 122, 127.

171. Goppelt, *Typos*, 183. Italics added.

172. Glasson, *Moses*, 38; Charlier, "La notion de signe," 444-45; Hanson, *Prophetic Gospel*, 46.

173. For good summaries, see Kugel, *Traditions*, 796-98; Marrs, "Raised Serpent," 132-47; Morris, *John*, 199n62; Turnage, "Serpent," 71-88.

attested in Wisdom, the Church Fathers (*Barnabas*, Justin Martyr, Irenaeus, and others), the Mishnah, and *Targum Pseudo-Jonathan*.[174] The Numbers narrative portrays the Israelites in a negative light because it was the people's grumbling that brings the divine punishment of the poisonous serpents in the first place. The people acknowledge this to Moses: "We have sinned by speaking against the Lord and against you" (Num 21:7). Therefore, the copper serpent that Moses makes becomes a visible reminder of God's forgiveness based on their confession and repentance. I emphasize the word "visible" because the Hebrew text may stress this aspect of the narrative more so than the LXX. The Israelites are to "look" (ראה, 21:8) at the mounted serpent, and whoever shall "look" (נבט, 21:9) will live. The idea behind the two words for "to look" may imply that something more than merely looking was required for healing.[175] Put differently, whoever looks at the serpent must also demonstrate a willingness to pay attention and believe.[176] There is more involved in the people's healing than a simple glance at the uplifted serpent; they must exercise faith in order to be healed. However, this is far from certain in the text itself. The notion of faith may be implied, as Ashley suggests, but the text leaves out this explanation. It is silent about the people's faith during the healing process. Granted, the people do ask Moses to "pray to the Lord" (εὖξαι οὖν πρὸς κύριον, 21:7) to take away the plague of poisonous serpents, but this is prior to them looking at the copper serpent. Neither the MT nor the LXX states unambiguously that the people had faith *while looking* at the copper serpent, and there is no explicit mention of God's agency in bringing about the healing process. To be sure, God commanded Moses to make the serpent but nothing more is said about God in the narrative. One is left to wonder if the copper serpent, or perhaps Moses, was responsible for the miracle cure. Therefore, I disagree with Charlesworth's observation that Numbers makes it "clear" that the serpent is not the source of healing, but rather, the combined actions of looking to the upraised serpent and believing in God who is the source of all healing.[177] Despite Charlesworth's observation, the text itself does not make this clear, and this is precisely the problem that later interpreters sought to solve.

174. This is not an exhaustive list, but simply serves to illustrate the long interpretive history associated with the narrative beginning in the first century BCE with Wisdom and continuing through the Middle Ages with *Pseudo-Jonathan*.

175. Ashley, *Numbers*, 406. Ashley cautions against seeing the two verbs as too distinct from each other in meaning. The author of Numbers may be simply using two different verbs for stylistic reasons. Nevertheless, Ashley believes the notions of contemplating and believing are implicit in the Hebrew text. Such a distinction is absent in the LXX which uses the synonyms ὁράω in v. 8 and ἐπιβλέπω in v. 9.

176. Ibid.

177. Charlesworth, *Serpent*, 334.

Wisdom of Solomon

Wisdom 11–19 is essentially a recasting of the exodus story in an eschatological light making it a timeless event of salvation.[178] The allusion to the serpent in the wilderness of Num 21 is particularly noteworthy. Wisdom draws a parallel between the plagues sent by God on the Egyptians and the poisonous serpents that he sent to torment the grumbling Israelites in the wilderness. However, the author shatters the parallel by illustrating the beneficent healing of God via the copper serpent, not the serpent itself. Wisdom emphasizes that God is the main actor in the drama, and only he receives credit for healing the people: "For the one who turned toward it was saved, not by the thing that was beheld, but by you, the Savior of all" (Wis 16:7 NRSV). Wisdom also clarifies that the serpent was only a "symbol of salvation" (σύμβολον σωτηρίας, 16:6); God was the real healer.[179] The author makes the same point again in 16:12: "For neither herb nor poultice cured them, but it was your word, O Lord, that heals all people" (NRSV). The author of Wisdom exegetes the serpent narrative of Num 21 so that God alone is the source of healing for his people. As Charlesworth helpfully summarizes, "God commands and Moses obeys. God tells those who are dying from snakebite to look up to the copper serpent on the pole. When they do, God is the source of acceptance, healing, and life."[180] Wisdom is the earliest extant reflection on Num 21:8–9, and it is evident that from the beginning of the history of exegesis on the copper serpent story that there is a tendency to shift the emphasis from the serpent itself to God's power that lay behind it.[181]

Targum Pseudo-Jonathan

Targum Pseudo-Jonathan exhibits a similar interpretative strategy as Wisdom. Targumim reflect the oral interpretation of Israel's Scriptures. They have a tendency to explain and expand certain narratives by filling in what they believe to be unresolved gaps in the biblical text. For example, the Numbers narrative potentially allows for the charge of idolatry and Egyptian magic, especially given that the text only narrates that the Israelites "looked" at the

---

178. Mack, *Hebrew Epic*, 186. The dating of Wisdom is extremely complicated; nevertheless, it may tentatively be dated between 220 BCE and 100 CE For more on the introductory issues of Wisdom, see Evans, *Ancient Texts*, 14–15; de Silva, *Apocrypha*, 127–52; Kolarcik, "Solomon, Wisdom of," 5:330–34.

179. Similarly, Charlesworth, *Serpent*, 337.

180. Ibid.

181. Hanson, *Prophetic Gospel*, 47–48.

Eyes of Faith 159

raised serpent. The biblical narrative says nothing about the people's faith. Jewish interpreters seek to resolve this tension and clarify what they believe the intent of the biblical text to be—the people believed in God, not the serpent.

An example of the expansionistic and explanatory character of the Targumim is clearly seen in *Tg. Ps.-J.* Num 21:8–9. *Targum Pseudo-Jonathan* was composed in the seventh to ninth centuries CE. This is admittedly much later than John's Gospel and I use *Pseudo-Jonathan* with caution to illustrate my point regarding the steady interpretive tradition surrounding the serpent narrative. I have previously commented in chapter 2 on the relevance of using rabbinic materials like the Targumim and Midrashim in the study of the NT, specifically Johannine studies. Again, I affirm the relevance of rabbinic materials in that they frequently preserve older traditions; yet, I use them cautiously here so as not to draw anachronistic conclusions. Nevertheless, because *Pseudo-Jonathan* contains some traditions also found in *Targum Onqelos*[182] and Wisdom (as illustrated below), it clearly preserves early traditions, making it relevant for portions of John's Gospel and the NT as a whole.[183] As previously stated, the Targumists believed that the biblical text allowed for charges of idolatry and sympathetic magic, both of which the law stands adamantly against. Joines notes that discussions of sympathetic magic likely emerged whenever this narrative was discussed in Israelite society.[184] Admittedly, the text lends itself to such explanations because there is no word about God's role in the miraculous healing or the faith of the Israelites. James Kugel asks pointedly about God's role in the narrative, "If He had wanted to heal the people, surely He could have done so directly."[185] The explicit notion of heart-felt faith in God is lacking in the OT text (MT and LXX) but is supported in *Tg. Ps.-J.* Num 21:8–9:

> Then the Lord said to Moses: "Make for yourself *a venomous bronze serpent* and put it in *a place, aloft*. Then it shall be [that] all whom *the serpent* bites, *when they look at it*, shall live, *if his heart pays attention to the Name of the Memra*[186] *of the Lord.*" So

---

182. Kaufman, "Targums," 4:471–73; Ronning, *Jewish Targums*, 11.

183. Evans, *Ancient Texts*, 188. For examples of parallels between *Pseudo-Jonathan* and John's Gospel, see ibid., 210–11. For more on *Targum Pseudo-Jonathan*, see ibid., 188–89; Kaufman, "Targums," 5:471–72; Maher, *Pseudo-Jonathan*, 9–14, 167–85; McNamara, "Interpretation," 167–97. On the Targums reflecting earlier traditions which extend to the first century CE and even earlier, see Alexander, "Targum, Targumim," 6:320–31; Charlesworth, *Serpent*, 334; Evans, *Ancient Texts*, 2; Glasson, *Moses*, 11.

184. Joines, "Bronze Serpent," 251.

185. Kugel, *Traditions*, 797.

186. *Memra* reflects the Targumic practice of avoiding making God the subject or object of an action. God is presented abstractly, avoiding any sense of anthropomorphic

> Moses made the bronze serpent and placed it in *a place, aloft.* And it was whenever the serpent bit a man and he was looking at the bronze serpent, *and his heart was paying attention to the Name of the Memra of the Lord,* then he lived.[187]

The Jewish understanding of this passage insists that God, not the serpent, brought deliverance.[188] *Pseudo-Jonathan* clarifies that in order for the people to live their hearts must look to God and believe in him. Therefore, belief in God is a missing element on the surface of the Numbers narrative that *Pseudo-Jonathan* explicitly stresses. In looking at the serpent, one is really looking to God by turning his heart in faith toward him. The idea is that the serpent has no healing power of its own, and to protect the biblical text from implications of idolatry and Egyptian magic, the Targumist, like the author of Wisdom, explains that God is the healing agent in the narrative. Therefore, the Targumist clarifies the meaning of the biblical text as it has been passed along the interpretive tradition: God, not the serpent, healed the Israelites when they looked to him with belief in their hearts.[189] John Ronning's summary of *Pseudo-Jonathan*'s expansion is helpful: "Numbers 21:8–9 does not mention any requirement of faith on the part of the Israelites who looked to the snake in order to live, and *Tg. Ps.-J.* apparently tried to make up for this perceived lack by adding that in order to live, the one who was bitten must direct his heart toward the name of the Word of the LORD."[190] As previously stated, although *Pseudo-Jonathan* is much later than John's Gospel, portions of it may reflect similar interpretive streams from the same period. Given that *Pseudo-Jonathan*'s emphasis regarding the serpent narrative (e.g., exercising faith in God rather than the serpent) is

---

activity. The word essentially means "word" from the root אמר ("to say"). *Memra* is characteristic among the Targums and not attested in other Jewish sources. McNamara, "Interpretation," 177–79, notes that over time, terms such as *Memra*, *Shekinah*, and *dibbera* may have become "buffer words" and used as synonyms to protect divine transcendence. For a recent discussion of *Memra* and John's Logos theology, see Ronning, *Jewish Targums.*

187. Targumic expansion italicized. Translation by Clarke, *Pseudo-Jonathan*, 247.

188. Morris, *John*, 199.

189. The Mishnah (ca. 200 CE) contains a similar idea in *Roš Haš.* 3.8: "But could the serpent slay or the serpent keep alive!—it is, rather, to teach thee that such time as the Israelites directed their thoughts on high and kept their hearts in subjection to their Father in heaven, they were healed." Translation by Danby, ed., *Mishnah*, 192. This is yet another example of the steady interpretive tradition of the Numbers narrative. A similar interpretive strategy is found in *Mekilta de-Rabbi Ishmael* (observed by Turnage, "Serpent," 80)

190. Ronning, *Jewish Targums*, 180.

very similar as that found in older traditions such as Wisdom, its comparatively late date adds to the consistency of the interpretive tradition.

A similar interpretive tradition lies behind both Wisdom and *Pseudo-Jonathan*. It is as though there is a real danger of misreading the Numbers narrative that imports notions of idolatry and Egyptian sympathetic magic into the biblical text. This reading of the biblical narrative profoundly troubled ancient interpreters.[191] The interpretive tradition finds itself attached to the story as it has been passed down through the Jewish sources from Wisdom to a Medieval Targum like *Pseudo-Jonathan*.

John's Resemblance to the Interpretive Tradition of Num 21

In his handling of the uplifted serpent, John demonstrates a similar interpretive strategy evidenced in Wisdom and *Pseudo-Jonathan*. I have already examined John's allusion to the copper serpent of Num 21 in John 3:14. However, to appreciate more fully the depth of his interaction with the narrative, vv. 14–15 must be taken together: καὶ καθὼς Μωϋσῆς ὕψωσεν τὸν ὄφιν ἐν τῇ ἐρήμῳ, οὕτως ὑψωθῆναι δεῖ τὸν υἱὸν τοῦ ἀνθρώπου, ἵνα πᾶς ὁ πιστεύων ἐν αὐτῷ[192] ἔχῃ ζωὴν αἰώνιον ("And as Moses lifted up the serpent in the wilderness, so also must the Son of Man be lifted up, so that everyone who believes in him may have eternal life"). John's allusion to the Numbers narrative expresses similar notions found in the interpretive tradition on several fronts. Though I do not hold that John is dependent upon either Wisdom or *Pseudo-Jonathan* for his interpretation, he nevertheless stands in a similar interpretive stream. "Everyone who believes" (πᾶς ὁ πιστεύων) in v. 15 is crucial to the analogy because it shares a similar sentiment as *Pseudo-Jonathan* and Wisdom: God heals when people believe. Andreas Köstenberger's comment reveals the primary role of God in the narrative as explained in the interpretive tradition: "As in the case of wilderness Israel, it is ultimately not a person's faith, but rather the God in whom the faith is placed, that is the source of salvation."[193] John virtually eliminates the role of the serpent in order to move toward belief in the uplifted Son of Man.[194]

---

191. Kugel, *Traditions*, 796.

192. P66 reads ἐπ αὐτῷ. Several MSS (א A Θ Ψ) read εἰς αὐτόν, which is the more usual Johannine construction, and is likely an assimilation to v. 16. Metzger gives the reading ἐν αὐτῷ a B rating because except for this passage, John always uses εἰς after πιστεύειν (34 times), never ἐν. For this discussion, see Köstenberger, *John*, 132; Metzger, *Textual Commentary*, 175. A few MSS (P63 A Θ Ψ *f*13) add μὴ ἀπόληται ἀλλ' in order to harmonize with v. 16.

193. Köstenberger, "John," 415–512.

194. Hanson, *Prophetic Gospel*, 46. Similarly, Charlier, "La notion de signe," 445.

While John says nothing about the people's hearts that are turned to God as in *Pseudo-Jonathan*, he expresses essentially the same sentiment by emphasizing the role of faith in the Son of Man. Due to the unity of the Father and the Son in John's Gospel (10:30; 17:21), and given John's christological conviction regarding Christ as the goal of Israel's Scriptures (5:39–40, 46), he stresses the role of faith in relation to the Son here in 3:15.[195] Put differently, faith in the Son is faith in the Father for John, and this leads to eternal life. Therefore, belief in God remains a critical link in the interpretive tradition. John's similarity to the interpretive tradition surrounding the serpent is a good example to show that he is not confined to Greek sources (e.g., Wisdom, LXX Numbers) but may also have access to Aramaic literature and tradition, which also highlights the role of faith in the Numbers narrative.[196] Martin Schmidl states the matter affirmatively in that John must know the OT wisdom tradition and the rabbinical interpretations in the Targums so that these traditions are in the background for John.[197] Similarly, I do not suggest direct dependence, but it illustrates that John, the author of Wisdom, and the Targumist partake of a similar interpretive environment that highlights the role of faith in the narrative. Nevertheless, John goes his own way by emphasizing that faith in the Son leads to eternal life.

Another possible link between John and the Aramaic tradition can be seen in John's use of "lift up." I have already demonstrated the close connection to Isaiah's Suffering Servant and that John's use consistently points to Jesus' crucifixion (3:14; 8:28; 12:32–34). *Pseudo-Jonathan* expresses the action of the serpent being placed on a standard as being "set aloft" (תלי, Num 21:8), which Marcus Jastrow defines as "to hang as in execution," i.e., "to crucify."[198] If John is familiar with similar Targumic traditions as that found in *Pseudo-Jonathan*, his use of "lift up" may very well carry with it the sense of "to crucify." This fits well with John's habit of using words with double meanings.

---

195. On John's christological use of Scripture, see Beutler, "The Use of Scripture," 147–62. On the christological convictions of the NT writers, see McCartney, "New Testament's Use of the Old Testament," 101–16.

196. Hanson, *Prophetic Gospel*, 49; Morris, *John*, 199n62. Of course, John may be relying on the two verbs ראה and נבט in the MT, which may imply that something more was involved than vision alone. I would argue, however, that John has more in common with the tradition's emphasis on belief than with the Hebrew text on this point.

197. Schmidl, *Jesus und Nikodemus*, 268.

198. Jastrow, "תלי, תלה," 1670–71. Even if it is not granted that John is familiar with a similar tradition as expressed in *Pseudo-Jonathan*, his discussion with Nicodemus may very well have been in Aramaic, where the corresponding term for the Greek ὑψόω would have been אזדקף, which has both conations of "to exalt" and "to crucify" (Brown, *John*, 1:146; Lincoln, *John*, 153; Marrs, "Raised Serpent," 141).

Faith-Seeing as Interpretive Key

The act of looking plays a key role in the copper serpent narrative in Numbers. Both Wisdom and *Pseudo-Jonathan* clarify that looking at the serpent was an expression of faith in God, not the serpent. This is an example of faith in action. This seeing-and-believing motif is prominent in John's Gospel as well. Vision, while not always equivalent to belief in John, is at times associated with faith: "This is indeed the will of my Father, that all who see the Son and believe in him may have eternal life" (6:40; cf. 20:8). Put differently, vision should lead to faith, but as I demonstrated in chapter 3, there are no guarantees. I believe the Targumic emphasis on seeing with eyes of faith forms the interpretive key for unlocking the complex relationship of seeing signs and believing in John's Gospel. For John, "seeing" must be properly defined as "faith-seeing."[199] People must see Jesus' miraculous signs with eyes of faith in order to interpret them rightly as pointers to his unity with God.[200] Only then will they move beyond signs-faith to heart-felt commitment and full-fledged discipleship. Ridderbos notes the overall contextual connection between seeing-believing and being born from above: "But to be able to see and to believe in the heaven-descended, cross-exalted Son of man—that takes a different set of eyes, and for that one must be born from above."[201] To suggest that those who "see" Jesus' signs must do so with faith in their hearts in order to understand his identity as the divine Son seems to be a matter of common sense. After all, faith is indispensable for seeing Jesus' signs rightly. However, John never states this explicitly, but his use of the copper serpent narrative, along with sharing similar characteristics with its interpretive tradition, strongly implies it. The table below shows a comparison between "looking" and "believing" in the two passages and illustrates John's reading of the text:

Table 5. Seeing is believing.

Num 21:9	John 3:15
ἰδὼν αὐτὸν ζήσεται "After seeing it he will live"	ὁ πιστεύων ἐν αὐτῷ ἔχῃ ζωὴν αἰώνιον "Whoever believes in him may have eternal life"

---

199. The terminology comes from Kysar, *Maverick Gospel*, 87.

200. Similarly, Keener, *John*, 2:883; Smalley, *Evangelist and Interpreter*, 217.

201. Ridderbos, *John*, 137. Similarly, Keener, *John*, 1:569, notes, "Faith in the crucified Jesus yields eternal life (3:15–16), life initiated at a birth from above (3:3–5)."

The connection between seeing and believing is not complete in either passage; only a conflation of the two unambiguously conveys the thought that eyes of faith are necessary to interpret miraculous signs rightly. This is essentially the same interpretive strategy exhibited in the tradition surrounding the Numbers narrative but with a christological appropriation (i.e., "in him"). Looking is incomplete in itself; faith completes the action. This logic runs consistently through John's Gospel. He portrays many who believe in Jesus because they see his miraculous signs. However, many of these same characters reject Jesus later in the Gospel (e.g., the Jerusalemites, the lame man at Bethesda, the crowd of 5,000, etc.). John's readers, therefore, must weigh for themselves which characters truly believe and which only have signs-faith. Therefore, John, without overtly stating it, affirms the same notion as the interpretive tradition of the copper serpent: seeing signs must be accompanied by heart-felt belief in God.

The emphasis on faith in God, which is all but absent on the surface of the Numbers narrative, continues in a steady stream of interpretive tradition, which includes Wisdom, rabbinic materials, John, and the Apostolic Fathers. The *Epistle of Barnabas* quotes Moses as exhorting the Israelites who had been bitten by the poisonous serpents to "hope and believe" as they look to the copper serpent: "When any one of you is bitten, let him come to the serpent placed on the pole (Gk. ἐπὶ τοῦ ξύλον, "on the tree/wood"); and let him hope and believe, that even though dead, it is able to give him life, and immediately he shall be restored" (*Barn.* 12:7). Similarly, Justin Martyr quotes Moses as saying to the people: "If ye look to this figure, and believe, ye shall be saved thereby" (*First Apology*, 60). This emphasis on belief is clearly lacking from the Numbers narrative; however, Justin fills in the gap in the same way as the Targumist regarding the role of faith in the healing process. Similarly, he aligns himself with the tradition in Wis 16:7 which clarifies that the copper serpent itself did not heal the people: "For the Spirit of prophecy by Moses did not teach us to believe in the serpent, since it shows us that he was cursed by God from the beginning" (*Dialogue*, 140). Granted, the idea is not quite the same as Wisdom that places the emphasis specifically on God as the source of healing. Nevertheless, Justin's sentiment is close in that he turns the attention away from the serpent. One could of course argue that he strongly implies that God is the real source of healing. There are additional aspects of the interpretive tradition reflected in the Apostolic Fathers, but the previously mentioned serve to highlight the remarkable consistency of the tradition.

There is more to say concerning the interpretive tradition surrounding the copper serpent narrative. John may also express additional interpretive tendencies similar to Wisdom.²⁰² One example involves John's Logos theology. John's Gospel gives the unique ὁ λόγος title to Jesus (1:1, 14). Jesus as the Word has been compared to the relation of the word "name" (שׁם) of God in the OT, in which the name of God sometimes stands alongside him as a separate power and yet, in fact, is not anything separate.²⁰³ The word of God describes him in his actions and especially as he reveals himself (Exod 23:21; Pss 9:2, 10; 33:6; Prov 8; and others).²⁰⁴ Thus, Jesus as the Word is God's clearest expression of his own revelation and creative and redemptive action to mankind. As Leon Morris notes, "It is a strong statement of the incarnation."²⁰⁵ For John, Jesus the Word is none other than God himself. When commenting on the copper serpent narrative, Wis 16:12 carefully points out the role of God's word in the curative process: "For neither herb nor poultice cured them, but it was your word (ὁ σός κύριε λόγος), O Lord, that heals all people" (NRSV). The point is essentially the same as above—God is the sole source of healing for the people. It was neither the copper serpent nor Moses that cured the people, but God alone, specifically his λόγος.²⁰⁶ John may have this passage in mind and may intend for his audience to think back and realize that it was none other than God's λόγος that healed the Israelites. For John, Jesus the incarnate Word and Son of Man must be lifted up in order to inaugurate eternal life. As was the case with *Pseudo-Jonathan*, John's interpretation of the serpent episode does not depend on Wisdom; nevertheless, he shows an awareness of a common interpretive tradition. Reim concludes that although John is not dependent on the book of Wisdom for his interpretation of the serpent episode, it is nevertheless evident that his usage shows an acquaintance with the tradition of Wisdom.²⁰⁷

Serpent Sign as Test of Faith

The end result of seeing and believing in both Num 21 and John is life (ζωή). John 3:15 indicates, "So that everyone who believes in him may have eternal life" (ἵνα πᾶς ὁ πιστεύων ἐν αὐτῷ ἔχῃ ζωὴν αἰώνιον). It should be noted that in Num 21, it is not said that everyone who looked at the serpent was healed, but when one looks he will live (ζήσεται, Num 21:8) . . . and when

202. For additional examples, see Reim, *Jochanan*, 198.
203. Bryant and Krause, *John*, 37.
204. Ibid.
205. Morris, *Theology*, 227.
206. Patrick Wilson, "Snake on a Stick," 223.
207. Reim, *Jochanan*, 198.

one looked he lived (ἔζη, 21:9). The implication is that not *everyone* had the faith to look and live but only those who demonstrated faith.²⁰⁸ It is along this same line that miraculous signs are tests of faith both in the wilderness and in John's Gospel. The miracle of the uplifted serpent illustrates this testing motif. The copper serpent ultimately pointed to God's healing; Wisdom and *Pseudo-Jonathan* make this point abundantly clear. The people were to believe in God upon seeing the miraculous serpent sign. However, as previously stated, not everyone looked and believed. Iain Duguid's perceives the testing function of the serpent sign:

> It is not coincidental that the Lord chose this means of healing the people, for faith is the key marker of those who would enter the Promised Land. The unbelieving generation of their parents, including Moses and Aaron, were excluded from the land because of their unbelief (Num 14:11; 20:12). The judgment by the fiery serpents would similarly eliminate any from the new generation who were lacking in faith, for those who refused to look to the Lord through the bronze serpent would die. Only those who believed could enter the land, for only those who believed would live.²⁰⁹

Thus, the miraculous serpent sign functions in part to divide the wilderness generations between those who exercise faith and those who do not. The serpent sign, therefore, functioned as a test of faith to see whose hearts were hard and whose were soft, and this is not unlike signs in John's Gospel. As T. David Gordon observes, "Like the signs of the Exodus period, they [Jesus' signs] demand a response of faith, and therefore divide the audience that does not singularly exhibit such faith."²¹⁰ Those who did not exercise faith died in the wilderness but those who believed lived (ἔζη, 21:9) in the Promised Land. Where the serpent narrative underscores life, (ζωή) this term is likewise a key word in the Fourth Gospel,²¹¹ and John stresses that believing in the Son of Man leads to eternal life (ζωὴν αἰώνιος, John 3:15–16).

---

208. Duguid, *Numbers*, 263; Olson, *Numbers*, 137, also notes the story of copper serpent stands in a strategic place in Numbers, between the old wilderness generation whose last remnants will die in the apostasy of Num 25, and the beginning of a new generation of hope who will be counted in the census before entering Canaan.

209. Duguid, *Numbers*, 263.

210. Gordon, "Final Wilderness," 32.

211. Glasson, *Moses*, 34; O'Day and Hylen, *John*, 45; Morris, *Theology*, 266–69.

JOHN'S TYPOLOGICAL INTERPRETATION OF NUM 21:8-9

One of John's favorite exegetical techniques is typology. Carson goes so far as to suggest that typology is John's "dominant approach" to the OT, where he illustrates patterns of continuity across the sweep of salvation history.[212] Examples of Johannine typology include Jesus as the true temple, the copper serpent, the true manna, the true water-giving rock, the true fiery pillar, the eschatological Moses, the new Torah, and the true Passover lamb.[213] John's use of the copper serpent in John 3:14 has been described as typological by many Johannine experts.[214] Even Reim, who believes that many Johannine scholars "overestimate" (*Überbewertung*) John's use of typology as an interpretive strategy, views the reference to the copper serpent as typological.[215] I agree with D. Moody Smith in viewing John's reference to the copper serpent as a "classic typology."[216] That is, it bears the hallmarks typological exegesis: it is redemptive-historical in character; the nature of the type lies in the main message (i.e., salvation), and the antitype (the fulfillment) is greater than the type.[217] Further, the grammar of 3:14 points to a typological comparison where John uses the technical formula καθώς ... οὕτως, which is characteristic of his Moses-Prophet/Messiah typology (e.g., 6:58).[218] Typology is part and parcel of John's christological hermeneutic where the OT finds its fulfillment in Christ. In John, Jesus emphasizes that Israel's Scriptures testify concerning him (5:39, 46), and he refers to various details contained in the Jewish "law" (νόμος) to justify his claims (8:17; 10:34) and to interpret the salvation he has brought (6:45; 7:38).[219] He often does this typologically by pointing out the prophetic anticipation of persons, events, festivals, etc., and his subsequent fulfillment.

"Typology" is a broad term, so scholars typically call for a refinement of terminology. John illustrates different types of typology: Davidic (2:17), Mosaic (1:17), festival (7:37-39), second exodus/wilderness (1:29, 36; 6:30-58), to name a few. I have indicated earlier in this study that John's Gospel

---

212. Carson, "John and the Johannine Epistles," 245-64.

213. Longenecker, *Biblical Exegesis*, 136-37.

214. Köstenberger, *Theology*, 199; Lincoln, *John*, 79; Longenecker, *Biblical Exegesis*, 136; Reim, *Jochanan*, 266; Schmidl, *Jesus und Nikodemus*, 277; Smith, *John*, 98.

215. Reim, *Jochanan*, 266.

216. Smith, *John*, 98.

217. McCartney and Clayton, *Reader*, 167.

218. Martyn, *History and Theology*, 115-16; Reim, *Jochanan*, 266. Charlesworth, *Serpent*, 377, demonstrates that καθώς modifies not only the verb ὕψωσεν, but also the noun τὸν ὄφιν. Therefore, the entire clause is typological.

219. Goppelt, *Typos*, 179.

evidences a great deal of wilderness typology.[220] The reference to the copper serpent in the wilderness is a notable example because "Moses," "wilderness," and "life" play key roles in the complex typological analogy. I only emphasize this to refine my typological terminology. John 3:14 is certainly not an instance of Davidic typology so to label it as "typology" is not specific enough to describe John's interpretive approach. Therefore, the context of new birth, which is so prominent in John 3, allows Goppelt to offer another typological category to the mix—creation typology. He draws attention to John's creation typology where he presents Jesus as making all things new.[221] The Prologue evidences John's creation typology where it calls attention to Jesus' role as the Word in creation. John's Gospel goes on to explain how this same Jesus makes all things new by inaugurating the age to come. As Goppelt states, "In Jesus the redemptive gifts of the former salvation time come in perfected form, and this signifies that the first creation is being perfected in a new one."[222] This creation motif proves relevant in Jesus' dialogue with Nicodemus: by being lifted up like the serpent in the wilderness, the Son of Man inaugurates new birth and a newer, fuller eternal life. As Dodd states, "The possibility of such rebirth is conditioned by the descent of the Son of Man and His ascent, or 'elevation.'"[223] Therefore, to label John's interpretive method simply as "typology" oversimplifies the matter.[224] My conviction is that John's use of the copper serpent narrative in Numbers is a conflation of wilderness and creation typologies.

Whatever typological relationships exist between John 3:14 and Num 21:8–9, they are not easy to pin down. John offers nothing in the text to give guidance.[225] The Numbers narrative does not mention "lift up" or "believe" as John does; John, on the other hand, does not mention "looking" as does the Numbers narrative.[226] Scholars debate, therefore, what exactly constitutes the type (OT precursor) and the antitype (NT fulfillment). Dorothy A. Lee has the typological comparison backwards when she suggests that the copper serpent is the antitype and Jesus the type.[227] This misses a basic

---

220. See chapter 2 above. As is often the case, Mosaic and wilderness typology overlap because Moses' mission in Numbers involved leading the Israelites through the wilderness.

221. Ibid., 182.

222. Ibid.

223. Dodd, *Interpretation*, 307.

224. Carson, "John and the Johannine Epistles," 249, is aware of oversimplifying John's typological approach.

225. Dodd, *Interpretation*, 306.

226. Michaels, *John*, 199.

227. Lee, *Symbolic Narratives*, 40.

characteristic of NT typology in which the antitype must be greater than the type.[228] Attempts to solve the precise relationship between the Numbers narrative and John's reference are often confusing. One obvious typological comparison is between the pole, or standard, and the cross. This is how the author of *Barnabas* understood it: "Moreover Moses, when he commanded, 'Ye shall not have any graven or molten [image] for you God,' did so that he might reveal a type (τύπον) of Jesus. Moses then makes a brazen serpent, and places it upon a beam" (*Barn.* 12:6)." What other typologies exists between the two passages? Is the serpent the type of the Son of Man?[229] Is Moses the type of the Son of Man?[230] Both are feasible, although Barrett suggests his uneasiness with such a seemingly odd correspondence between the serpent and Jesus: "The point of comparison is not the serpent but the lifting up."[231] Rudolf Bultmann expresses a similar sentiment, "John puts no emphasis on the identification of Jesus with the serpent."[232] Michaels concedes the comparison between the snake and Christ but calls it "grotesque."[233] Similar statements are made by several Johannine scholars who are reticent to see a comparison between the serpent and Christ beyond that of simply being "lifted up," which they believe to be the central element in the comparison.[234] Smith speaks for this general trend, "Of course, comparisons of Jesus with the serpent are misplaced; the analogy applies only to being lifted up."[235] However, John must be allowed to shock his audience with this kind of analogy, even if it seems odd to modern sensibilities. John Calvin acknowledged John's direct correlation between the serpent and Christ and concluded: "The metaphor is not inappropriate or far-fetched."[236] Charlesworth has gone to great lengths to demonstrate that a comparison between Christ and the serpent, in addition to being lifted up, is exactly what John intends: "The typology entails both Jesus' being lifted up *and* his portrayal as the serpent on the pole or cross."[237] He summarizes his work by positing a direct

228. McCartney and Clayton, *Reader*, 167.
229. Smith, "Exodus Typology," 329–42.
230. Ibid., 331.
231. Barrett, *John*, 214.
232. Bultmann, *John*, 152n1.
233. Michaels, *John*, 199.
234. Keener, *John*, 1:565; Smith, *John*, 98; Carson, *John*, 201. Charlesworth, *Serpent*, 402–04, lists five reasons why scholars tend to reject analogies between the serpent and Christ.
235. Smith, *John*, 98.
236. Calvin, *John*, 17:122.
237. Charlesworth, *Serpent*, 414. Charlesworth lists nine reasons to affirm that John intended a comparison between the serpent and Jesus (ibid., 372–402). For a similar

analogy between Moses' copper serpent and Jesus: "Moses' bronze serpent represented God's saving of those dying in the wilderness, so Jesus on the cross symbolized the saving of all humanity."[238] Nevertheless, perhaps there is no single typological relationship which John makes, but several. Merrill C. Tenney notes several points of contact between the serpent and Jesus:[239] 1) both were prepared by God's command, 2) both symbolized God's way of saving those under the condemnation of sin, 3) both made the curative power available on the basis of faith, 4) both were lifted up on a standard, 5) both were representations of God's judgment on sin, and 6) the destiny of the individual was determined by his response to God's invitation. This is not an exhaustive list, and drawing similar parallels can easily become exhausting. I believe it is more profitable to see both of the entire episodes as typologically related.[240] Thus, the *narrative* of Moses' lifting up the serpent in the wilderness is a type of the Son of Man being lifted up on the cross. The OT narrative is the type, the NT narrative the antitype.

It is important for typology that there be a *qal wahomer* quality to the typological comparison. As Dan McCartney and Charles Clayton state plainly, "The antitype (the fulfillment) must be greater than the type."[241] This highlights the redemptive-historical nature of the comparison where God's salvific event of the NT is greater than that of the OT. The life-typology that John presents follows a lesser to greater progression. The Israelites were healed *physically* from the poisonous bites of the serpents; those who experience birth from above are healed *spiritually* by the lifting up of the Son of Man. Whoever looked the serpent obtained natural life (ζάω, Num 21:9), while whoever believes in the Son of Man has eternal life (ζωὴ αἰώνιος, John 3:15, 16).[242] As B. F. Westcott notes, "As the wounded who looked on

---

direct comparison between the serpent and Jesus, see Marshall, "Serpent of Salvation," 385–93. Marshall discusses the view of Martin Luther who believed that the "offensive" comparison between the serpent and Christ corresponds to the offense of the cross in John's Gospel.

238. Charlesworth, *Serpent*, 414–15.

239. Tenney, *John*, 88. Incidentally, this is where Charlesworth has not gone far enough when he posits only a dual-pronged typological relationship between Jesus and the serpent (Charlesworth, *Serpent*, 414).

240. This is close to McCartney and Clayton, *Reader*, 167, who suggest that the nature of the type must lie in the main message of the material, not in some incidental detail. Keener also observes the absurdity of what can result when the details are pressed too far: "To press the analogy too far would link Jesus' enemies (8:28) with Moses, who lifted up the serpent" (*John*, 1:565n305, cf. 564).

241. McCartney and Clayton, *Reader*, 167.

242. Menken, "Observations," 125–43. Michaels, *John*, 199, notes that John 3:15 is first mention of "eternal life" in John's Gospel. On the eschatological implications

the brazen serpent were restored to temporal health, so in this case *eternal life* follows from the faith of the believer on the crucified and exalted Lord."[243]

Eternal Life

I drew attention in chapter 3 to John's eschatological portrait of the Kingdom of God that he introduced earlier in the dialogue with Nicodemus (3:3, 5). I also noted that John prefers to speak of "eternal life," or "life"[244] rather than "Kingdom of God" in terms of his eschatology but that he sees no difference between the two.[245] God's offer of eternal life is his offer of Kingdom life. Johannine scholars have perceived John's emphasis on eternal life as a present reality (3:15–16, 36; 4:14; 6:47, 53; 17:3), thus minimizing its futuristic aspect.[246] To suggest that John minimizes futurist eschatology is not to suggest that he negates it (5:28–29; 6:39–40, 44, 54; 12:25, 31–32, 47).[247] To be sure, eternal life is also a future promise to be fully realized at the resurrection. Nevertheless, John's emphasis lies in eternal life as being available for God's people here and now: ἐγὼ ἦλθον ἵνα ζωὴν ἔχωσιν καὶ περισσὸν ἔχωσιν ("I have come that they may have life, and have it abundantly," 10:10). Eternal life is both/and, not either/or regarding its present and future dimensions. The purpose of Jesus' mission was to bring people a present experience of the future life.[248]

To speak of the temporality of eternal life is one discussion; defining it is another. Barrett proposes 17:3 as John's definition of eternal life: αὕτη δέ ἐστιν ἡ αἰώνιος ζωὴ ἵνα γινώσκωσιν σὲ τὸν μόνον ἀληθινὸν θεὸν καὶ ὃν ἀπέστειλας Ἰησοῦν Χριστόν ("And this is eternal life, that they may know you the only true God, and Jesus Christ who you have sent").[249] To "know" (γινώσκω) God and Christ, then, is eternal life. Reflecting the Hebrew concept of knowledge (ידע) as a relational, fellowship-oriented experience (e.g.,

---

of eternal life in John, see Beasley-Murray, *Gospel of Life*, 1–14; Brown, *Introduction*, 238–48; Brown, *John*, 1:CXV–CXXI; Burge, "Life," 3:655–61, esp. 659; Dodd, *Interpretation*, 144–50; Keener, *John*, 1:328–29; Köstenberger, *Theology*, 284–87; 342–43; Kysar, *Maverick Gospel*, 97–105; Ladd, *Theology*, 290–95; Morris, *Theology*, 266–69; Smith, *Theology*, 149–51; Thielman, *Theology*, 171–79.

243. Westcott, *John*, 54.

244. "Eternal life" and "life" are synonymous in John's Gospel (Dodd, *Interpretation*, 144; Keener, *John*, 1:328; Köstenberger, *Theology*, 285; Thielman, *Theology*, 171).

245. Beasley-Murray, *Gospel of Life*, 2.

246. Ibid., 3; Brown, *Introduction*, 245; Ladd, *Theology*, 293.

247. Beasley-Murray, *Gospel of Life*, 5; Gordon, "Final Wilderness," 56.

248. Ladd, *Theology*, 293.

249. Barrett, *John*, 503.

Ps 1:6; 36:10; Jer 10:5; Isa 45:4–5),²⁵⁰ John describes eternal life in terms of an intimate relationship between the believer and God, through Christ. Edward W. Klink offers this helpful summary of eternal life in John: "Life in John is a living event, not an abstract concept. It is real and relational—rooted in the communion of God and humans. It is rooted in eternity; it is rooted in the one who is called 'the Way, the Truth and the Life.'"²⁵¹ Due to the emphasis on faith in Num 21:8–9 and John 3:14–15, it is important to note that faith in Christ is the means by which believers appropriate the eschatological blessing of eternal life (πᾶς ὁ πιστεύων ἐν αὐτῷ ἔχῃ ζωὴν αἰώνιον, 3:15; cf. 3:16; 6:40, 47).²⁵² John's audience should not miss the typology: those who *believed* in the wilderness received physical life; those who *believe* in the Son of Man receive eternal life. It is difficult to do better than Bultmann, "For John, as for Paul, faith is the way to salvation."²⁵³

Eternal life relates to the comprehensive typology of the two texts. A greater and more comprehensive life is offered by the antitype, Jesus, who far exceeds the type.²⁵⁴ However, the life-typology in the two texts is no more significant than any other aspect of typology in the overall comparison. It is simply another example of John's multifaceted typological approach to the OT. He is, therefore, not interested in simplistic one-to-one correspondence between type and antitype, whether it be in the act of "lifting up," the standard or the cross, the serpent and the Son of Man, or physical and eternal life. Rather, the entire complex of both narratives serves his typological exegesis. In summary, John's allusion to the serpent in the wilderness underscores the role of faith, which in turn leads to life. Jesus' message to Nicodemus is that eternal life is available now for those who not only look at the Son of Man's experience of cross, resurrection, and exaltation, but also do so in faith.

While John 3:16 is one of the most quoted verses from the NT, its context has not always been appreciated, especially regarding its relationship to the uplifting of the Son of Man in vv. 14–15. In addition to being a statement about the magnitude of God's love for the world (ὁ κόσμος),²⁵⁵ it

---

250. Ladd, *Theology*, 297–98. Ladd also notes that knowledge in Greek thought, as contemplative reflection, is likely not the background for John's concept of knowledge (ibid., 296–97). For more, see Dodd, *Interpretation*, 49, 151–69.

251. Klink, "Light of the World," 74–89.

252. Burge, "Life," 659. Burge also notes that belief in the present age is the key to attaining life.

253. Bultmann, *Theology*, 2:75.

254. Menken, "Observations," 140.

255. For the world (ὁ κόσμος) in John's Gospel, see Keener, *John*, 1:329–30; Koester, *Word of Life*, 80–81; Köstenberger, *Theology*, 281–82; Ladd, *Theology*, 261–63; Morris,

forms a summary for what John has previously stated in vv. 14–15, as well as a recapitulation of Jesus' entire dialogue with Nicodemus.²⁵⁶ The connection to the previous verse is clearly indicated by the conjunction γάρ ("For" ESV, NAS, NIV, NLT). There is considerable debate as to the precise nuance of the οὕτως . . . ὥστε construction. Does it indicate the magnitude of God's love for the world (i.e., "For this is how much God loved the world, that he gave . . ."),²⁵⁷ or does it indicate the manner in which God loved the world ("For in this way [i.e., crucifixion of the Son] God loved the world, that he gave . . .")?²⁵⁸ There is no compelling reason to reject either because both conceptually support John's Christology.²⁵⁹ The verse both refers back to the uplifting of the Son in vv. 14–15 and at the same time moves the reader's attention forward to the measure of God's love that underscores that lifting up.²⁶⁰ Nevertheless, taking it as the *manner* in which God loved the world best fits the context of the Son being lifted up in crucifixion. Ben Witherington's paraphrase helps illuminate John's intent in relation to the context: "In this way [i.e., by means of Jesus' being lifted up on the cross] God loved the world, that he gave the unique (or only) Son, in order that all the ones believing in him should not perish but have everlasting life."²⁶¹ The relation to the overall lifting up context is crucial for seeing v. 16 as the recapitulation of vv. 14–15. O'Day and Hylen note John's progression of thought: "In verse 15, the source of eternal life is Jesus' crucifixion [v. 14]; in verse 16, the source of eternal life is God's love, and the combination of these two verses helps us see how Jesus' death and God's love are related."²⁶² John 3:16, then, completes the thought of 3:14–15 which involves the lifting up of the Son of Man. Further, he links vv. 15–16 together with the repeated mention of "everyone who believes" (πᾶς ὁ πιστεύων) in the Son "may have eternal life" (ἔχῃ ζωὴν αἰώνιον).

Theology, 279–81; Smith, *Theology*, 80–85.

256. Similarly, Bernard, *John*, 1:117.

257. Brown, *John*, 1:129; Beasley-Murray, *John*, 44; Carson, *John*, 204; Köstenberger, *John*, 128–29n43.

258. Bryant and Krause, *John*, 98; Gundry and Howell, "Syntax," 24–39; Keener, *John*, 1:566; Ridderbos, *John*, 138; Witherington, *John's Wisdom*, 101.

259. Ridderbos, *John*, 138.

260. Ibid.

261. Witherington, *John's Wisdom*, 101. This rendering, while I believe to be most accurate, admittedly makes for more difficult memorization of this well-loved summary of the gospel.

262. O'Day and Hylen, *John*, 46.

Contrasting Choices: Unbelief or Belief

I noted previously in this chapter the role of the copper serpent of Num 21 as both a miraculous sign as well as a test of faith. Stated simply, it was a sign that called for faith to which people could look and be delivered from death.[263] Similarly, I drew attention to signs in general as tests of faithfulness in the wilderness in chapter 1. My goal here in this final section is to illustrate that by referring to the serpent sign that tested the faithfulness of the Israelites in the wilderness (as evidenced in the interpretive tradition of Wisdom and *Pseudo-Jonathan*), John intends for Jesus' miraculous signs to test the hearts of those who see them.[264] This is especially true of Nicodemus who has seen Jesus' signs and who is their primary witness in John 3. That miraculous signs are tests of faithfulness implies a response on the part of those who witness them, and this is the substance of the remainder of the pericope (John 3:18–21). I am proposing here very subtle intertextual echoes between the response of the wilderness community who saw miraculous signs and those who witness the miracles of Jesus in John. Put differently, I am proposing a simple analogy between the two parties which demonstrates dual responses to miraculous signs: unbelief, which John characterizes as "darkness" (τό σκότος, 3:19), and belief, which he illustrates as coming to the light (ἔρχεται πρὸς τὸ φῶς, 3:20–21) or doing the truth (ὁ ποιῶν τὴν ἀλήθειαν, 3:21).

Responding to the Serpent Sign

The narrative of the copper serpent stands at a strategic place in Numbers where it forms a bridge between the two wilderness generations.[265] It marks the beginning of the end of the old wilderness generation, whose last vestiges die of a plague after indulging in sexual immorality with Moabite women, and then bowing to their gods in Num 25.[266] It also marks the beginning of a new, more faithful generation who stands on the edge of the Promised

---

263. Duguid, *Numbers*, 264.

264. While my intent is to demonstrate the testing function of Jesus' signs, I do not want to do so at the expense of recognizing their function of "attesting" to Jesus' identity and mission (Keener, *John*, 1:665n16). Put differently, John presents an attesting function of signs where they declare Jesus' unity with God as well as a testing function where they test the hearts of those who witness them. While I am demonstrating continuity with Anderson's testing function of signs, I see no reason to discount their attesting function as he does (Anderson, *Christology*, 250).

265. Olson, *Numbers*, 137.

266. Ibid.

Land, ready to enter Canaan (cf. Num 26:63-65).[267] If anyone from this new generation inherits the faithlessness of his parents, the copper serpent exposes his unbelief. Lack of obedience to God's command to "look" to the serpent would eliminate all from the new generation who were lacking in faith,[268] while at the same time propelling toward the Promised Land all who exercised faith by looking. The narrative, then, forms a "weeding out" of sorts of the faithless from the faithful. The choice between life and death could not be more apparent than in the individual Israelite's decision to either look upon the uplifted serpent and live, or refuse to look and die in the desert. To be sure, the text does not state that everyone looked and lived, but only that he who looked lived (21:9).[269] The text is replete with individual repentance, confession, and faith as each individual Israelite needs to take the confession of sin (21:7) and the need for God's deliverance to heart.[270] The result in Numbers of the faithless first generation and the faithful second generation was death and life, respectively. The first generation died in the wilderness according to the decree of God (Num 14:22-23) while the second generation stood on the border of Canaan, full of life and confident of their eventual entry.

The new wilderness generation has a different character than the old generation; it respects the authority of Moses and its leaders, and it has a different spirit of obedience.[271] As Olson notes, the legacy left at the end of Numbers is not faithlessness and death, but rather faith, life, and hope.[272] The uplifted serpent sign anticipates the faithful hearts of the second wilderness generation. It serves a dual function of death and life. It reveals the faithless hearts of many of the first generation (and any of the second for that matter), while revealing the faithful hearts which characterize the second.[273] It is quite literally a sign and a test of faith that confirms the testing function of signs as remembered in Deuteronomy (Deut 4:34; 8:2, 16). As Duguid observes, "Faith is the key marker for those who would enter the Promised Land,"[274] and the copper serpent narrative illustrates the begin-

267. Ibid.
268. Duguid, *Numbers*, 263.
269. Ibid.; Olson, *Numbers*, 137.
270. Olson, *Numbers*, 136. Olson also notes the communal nature of confession of sin and forgiveness in the narrative.
271. Ibid., 193.
272. Ibid.
273. Not that every individual Israelite of the first generation proves faithless in the narrative; in fact, many repent and believe and continue to live until the final rebellion of Baal Peor (Num 25), which brings an end to last vestiges of the first generation.
274. Duguid, *Numbers*, 263.

ning of the transition between the two generations by contrasting the hearts of each. To summarize, the serpent sign functions in Numbers as a test of faith and yields two contrasting results: death for the faithless and life for the faithful.

Responding to Jesus' Signs

If signs are tests of faith, it necessarily follows that they require a response, as in the wilderness. Where John 3:14–17 introduced the visible sign of God's love for the world (i.e., the crucifixion of the Son), vv. 18–21 record the responses of the world to that sign: unbelief or belief. These two responses are also reminiscent of the first and second wilderness generations—the first generation proved unfaithful and died in the desert, and the second generation proved faithful and eventually entered the Promised Land. John calls his readers to make a decision not only to Jesus' signs but also ultimately to God's offer of salvation—a thought that John introduced in v. 15 and develops further in vv. 16–21.[275] Hence, the immediate context of the "lifting up" of the Son of Man still lingers strongly in this final section of the pericope.[276] Further, in this final section John continues his emphasis on faith as the hallmark of those who would inherit eternal life. Moloney observes that by using the familiar language of "life," "light," and "darkness," from the Prologue (1:4–8), John presents the importance of decision: a commitment to belief or unbelief, which leads to life or death (3:18).[277] Those who believe walk in the light, but those who do not believe walk in darkness.[278]

Wilderness Light

John's use of "light" in the Gospel often has strong wilderness overtones. John's audience has previously encountered Jesus as the Light (τὸ φῶς, 1:4–5), which enlightens (φωτίζει, 1:9) all of humanity in the Prologue. The themes of *Logos*, life, and light are introduced in the Prologue, and this "cluster" dominates the symbolic system of the remainder of John's narrative.[279] My argument here is that John's use of light as a metaphor for Christ's identity and mission is often soaked in wilderness imagery and in-

---

275. Moloney, *Belief in the Word*, 118.
276. Ibid.
277. Ibid., 119.
278. Köstenberger, *Theology*, 470.
279. Culpepper, *Anatomy*, 190.

forms its use in 3:19–21. On one hand, light is a common religious symbol[280] indicating among other things the morally upright path on which humanity should walk in contrast to that of darkness, shame, wickedness, ignorance, and lack of knowledge. However, John's reference to Jesus as the Light is strongly soteriological,[281] not only moralistic.[282] The Light entered the darkened world not only to demonstrate uprightness, but also to save it so that others might see by his saving light (8:12; 9:5; 11:9–10; 12:35–36, 46). While not every instance of τὸ φῶς in the Gospel carries wilderness implications (e.g., 11:9–10), many do. Given John's saturation with OT imagery and symbols, as well as the very Jewishness[283] of the Gospel, τὸ φῶς often has a wilderness hue in certain contexts. Again, the Prologue, which peaks at the "tabernacling" of the Word, the "glory" that filled the tabernacle, and the "grace and truth" that God announced at Sinai (1:14), is highly reminiscent of the wilderness period. Light is a dominant motif in the Prologue, and its placement there suggests that it too has wilderness associations.[284] These associations, in turn, contribute to the background of "light" elsewhere in the Gospel.

Wilderness imagery is especially evident in 8:12 where Jesus states at the Feast of Tabernacles, "I am the light of the world" (ἐγώ εἰμι τὸ φῶς τοῦ κόσμου). That Jesus applies the imagery from the torch-lighting ceremony of the feast (*m. Sukkah* 5:1–4) to himself is obvious. Koester observes, "Jesus was the one in whom the hopes of the Festival of Booths were realized. He was the light that manifested the presence of God."[285] The lighting ceremony of the feast, while post-Mosaic in origin, recalls the fire cloud that led the Israelites through the wilderness and which conveyed the *shekinah* presence

---

280. Barrett, *John*, 335–38; Bultmann, *John*, 40–44, 342–43; Carson, *John*, 338; Charlesworth, "Critical Comparison," 76–106; Culpepper, *Anatomy*, 190–92; Dodd, *Interpretation*, 201–12; Keener, *John*, 1:382–85; Koester, *Symbolism*, 141–73; Köstenberger, *Encountering John*, 113–15; Lewis, "Light and Darkness," 3:662–64.

281. Charlesworth, "Critical Comparison," 91. Barton observes, like Charlesworth, that John's light and darkness dualism is one of soteriological movement: the penetration of a world in darkness—ignorant of God, blind to the truth—disobedient to God's law—by the life-giving light of the divine Logos now incarnate in Jesus. See Barton, "Johannine Dualism," 3–18.

282. The moral dimension of John's light and darkness symbolism is discussed by Koester, *Symbolism*, 143–44, 159–60; Köstenberger: *Encountering John*, 114; Köstenberger, *John*, 30; Köstenberger, *Theology*, 166.

283. Carson, *John*, 338, makes a similar observation in that he sees John's light imagery as representative of the OT over against other religious works.

284. Similarly, Koester, *Symbolism*, 142–43.

285. Ibid., 159.

of God among his people (Num 9:15–23; cf. Neh 9:12, 19).[286] This is a common observation by Johannine scholars regarding John's reference to light in John 8:12 at the feast. Even so, given the fact that the lighting ceremony involved the lighting of a giant lampstand in the outer court of the temple that illuminated courtyards throughout Jerusalem,[287] I believe that there is another wilderness context that also illuminates John's use of light as a metaphor for Christ that has not received as much attention as the fire cloud. Numbers 8:1–4 records the lighting of the lampstand, or menorah,[288] in the tabernacle that shines (φωτίζω, 8:2; cf. John 1:9) light forward on the table of showbread.[289] It is not difficult to imagine that the lighting ceremony of the Feast of Tabernacles recalls the lighting of the golden lampstand in the Tabernacle, and that Jesus recalls this with his declaration, "I am the light of the world" in the context of the feast.[290] Whereas the light from the lampstand shined on the table of showbread, which had on it twelve loaves representing the twelve tribes of Israel,[291] Jesus shines upon not only Israel, but also the whole world. It is reasonable to conclude that John's use of light as a metaphor for Christ's identity and mission is soaked in wilderness imagery at other places in the Gospel besides John 8:12. Given John's use of "light" throughout the Gospel and the wilderness implications often associated with it, John appeals for a faithful response to God's light in 3:19–21. Light represents God's presence in the wilderness, both in the fire cloud and in the golden lampstand. If Israel were to be blessed by God in the wilderness, the people had to follow the light of the fire cloud and they were to be constantly cognizant of the illuminating presence of God among them, symbolized by the light of the lampstand. In a similar fashion in John, Christ is the Light and mankind's proper response is to follow that Light and to walk in it. Duguid notes that God's blessing in the wilderness "is not automatic; it has not only

---

286. Carson, *John,* 338; Glasson, *Moses,* 61; Keener, *John,* 1:739; Koester, *Symbolism,* 157; Longenecker, *Biblical Exegesis,* 136. The lighting ceremony also had an eschatological function in that it anticipated Zech 14:7, which says that when God comes to reign as King over all the earth, there will be continuous day; the text indicates that the people at that time will celebrate the Feast of Tabernacles (14:16). For this, see Carson, *John,* 338; Koester, *Symbolism,* 158.

287. For descriptions of the lighting ceremony, see Carson, *John,* 337; Koester, *Symbolism,* 157–58.

288. Milgrom, *Numbers,* 367.

289. Cole, *Numbers,* 145–46; Duguid, *Numbers,* 108–9; Wenham, *Numbers,* 106–7.

290. Duguid, *Numbers,* 109. Duguid makes the explicit connection between Jesus' statement at Tabernacles and the lighting of the lampstand in Numbers. See also, Gane, *Leviticus, Numbers,* 558.

291. Duguid, *Numbers,* 109; Wenham, *Numbers,* 107.

to be given, it also has to be received."[292] There is, therefore, a *response* to the Light in John that resembles Israel's choice to follow the fire cloud in the wilderness and to recognize the presence of God among them. In short, as light represents God's presence in the wilderness as displayed in the tabernacle and the fire cloud, it also represents his presence in John's Gospel where it enters a darkened world. In summary, John's light language in 8:12 reflects the fire cloud that led Israel in the wilderness (Num 9:15–23), as well as the light of the lampstand in the tabernacle (8:1–4), both symbolizing God's presence among his people. John intends light to be a polyvalent[293] symbol throughout the Gospel and as such, when considered as a whole, it has wilderness, soteriological, and moralistic implications. Because light is a polyvalent symbol, John shows that every instance of light imagery illuminates the others so that they become pregnant with multiple associations. There is not necessarily a clear intertextual connection between light in 3:19–21 and the wilderness narratives of Numbers, at least not as clear a connection as in 8:12. Nevertheless, there is an *intratextual* dynamic—an interplay within the work itself—between John's light references where every instance of τό φῶς carries multiple connotations and becomes a complex metaphor for Christ's identity and mission; these are indirectly related to the wilderness given John's polyvalent use of "light."[294]

Whatever wilderness imagery John associates with "light" in John 3:19–21, he places it in the context of responding in faith to God's love that is supremely evidenced in the sign of the uplifted Son of Man. Whether one receives God's saving love or rejects it is directly related to his faith, or lack thereof. Therefore, John's plea for a faithful response to Jesus' signs runs throughout the pericope: Nicodemus "believes" in a sense, though inadequately because his belief is signs-based. Jesus clarifies that one must be born from above through God's Spirit which enables mature belief. One must not only see but also believe in the sign of the uplifted Son of Man, which yields eternal life. Those who refuse to believe are condemned; whereas, believers work the works of God, of which faith is central (6:29). The flow of the dialogue focuses on signs and the need for a faithful response to them. Such faith hinges on the new birth and whether one has experienced it.

This final section circles back to Jesus' introductory remarks in John 3 about being born from above: people demonstrate their character, either

292. Duguid, *Numbers*, 110.

293. "Polyvalence" refers to the multiplicity of connections, associations, and meanings that accompany—both preceding and following—any theme or its significance in a given text." For this definition and a discussion of polyvalence in John's Gospel, see Anderson, "Johannine Polyvalence," 93–119.

294. For more on intratextuality in John, see Zumstein, "Intratextuality," 121–35.

as part of the world or as those born anew from above, by their "works" (τὰ ἔργα, 3:21).²⁹⁵ This concluding section focuses not only on faith and its eternal benefits, and not only in whom faith is placed (i.e., ὁ μονογενὴς υἱός τοῦ θεοῦ, "the unique Son of God," 3:16, 18), but also on what it produces in the life of the believer—works that are worked in God (τὰ ἔργα ὅτι ἐν θεῷ ἐστιν εἰργασμένα, 3:21). Therefore, the proper response to Jesus' signs is not only faith but also faith that produces fruit as a result of having received eternal life. Additionally, the believer's works, like Jesus' signs, reveal God's presence with the believer because those works are worked in God. That the believer's works function analogously to Jesus' signs is yet another way that John rounds out the entire pericope that began with Nicodemus's acknowledgment that Jesus' signs demonstrated that God was with him. Similarly, "works," a term that John sometimes substitutes for Jesus' "signs" (7:3, 21; 9:3–4; 10:25, 32–33, 37–38; 14:10–12; 15:24),²⁹⁶ demonstrate that God is present with the believer. This also relates to the overall context of being born from above through God's Spirit: birth from God's Spirit is necessary for genuinely good works.²⁹⁷ In summary, John calls for not only mature faith on the part of those who see Jesus' signs but also mature works that evidence the presence of God.

NICODEMUS'S FAITH JOURNEY

Nicodemus was last heard uttering words of bewilderment at Jesus' teaching in 3:9: "How can these things be?" He has been silent ever since as Jesus describes life in the kingdom. John clearly introduced Nicodemus as one who saw the miraculous signs of Jesus but displayed signs-faith. For John, only those who have been born from above exhibit mature faith. John referenced the uplifted serpent in the wilderness as a miraculous sign that was meant to test the faith of the Israelites who looked upon it. Similarly, the miraculous sign of the uplifted Son of Man on the cross is meant to test the faith of Nicodemus to see whether he grows beyond signs-faith.

Nicodemus exhibits no signs of mature faith at this point in the narrative.²⁹⁸ His last words were words of confusion. However, this is not the last word on Nicodemus in the Gospel. He re-emerges in a Pharisaical debate regarding the origins of Jesus, at which point he defends him against an unfair trial: "Does our law judge a man without first hearing from him and

---

295. Keener, *John*, 1:574.
296. Ibid.
297. Ibid.
298. Köstenberger, *Theology*, 199n61; Moloney, *Belief in the Word*, 121.

knowing what he does?" (7:51).²⁹⁹ He is sympathetic to Jesus' plight, but does he exhibit mature faith? Nicodemus re-emerges for the final time in the Gospel after Jesus' crucifixion where he, along with Joseph of Arimathea—a secret disciple of Jesus on account of fear of the Jews (ὢν μαθητὴς τοῦ Ἰησοῦ κεκρυμμένος δὲ διὰ τὸν φόβον τῶν Ἰουδαίων, 19:38)—receive the body of Jesus to give him a proper Jewish burial. Nicodemus comes well equipped with about 100 pounds of spices for the occasion (19:39). He who first came to Jesus at night (3:1, 39) steps into the light of day out of respect for Jesus, the teacher from God. Do these instances convey a progressive journey of faith for Nicodemus? Does he in fact become a believer who exhibits a mature, working faith? Scholarly reviews on Nicodemus's faith are mixed and there is no consensus. On one hand, his journey seems to progress from a fumbling Pharisee to a bold believer who has been born from above and demonstrates through his last actions in the Gospel that his faith is genuine.³⁰⁰ On the other hand, Nicodemus's journey has been viewed negatively as falling far short of mature faith.³⁰¹ He lives in constant fear of being thrown out of the synagogue along with Joseph of Arimathea.³⁰² Granted, he defends Jesus' right to a fair trial, but he never confesses his faith in the public forum.³⁰³ Does this not fall short of full-fledged faith? What is more, the fact that he takes such care to bury Jesus' body shows he does not understand that Jesus is to be raised. Does this not indicate within Nicodemus the "inability to see beyond the grave, a ludicrous attempt to preserve from decay the body of the one who is in life and death the resurrection and the life"?³⁰⁴ In short, there is no final word on the figure of Nicodemus in the Fourth Gospel.³⁰⁵ He remains at best ambiguous in his commitment when compared to other characters, such as the Samaritan woman or the man born blind. Such ambiguity is not good enough for this Gospel.³⁰⁶

---

299. That the question expects a negative answer is expressed by μή with the indicative κρίνει.

300. Cotterell, "Nicodemus Conversation," 237–42; King, "Nicodemus and the Pharisees," 45; Martyn, *History and Theology*, 88–89, 112–14; Moloney, *Belief in the Word*, 120.

301. Bassler, "Mixed Signals," 635–46; Culpepper, *Anatomy*, 136; de Jonge, "Nicodemus and Jesus," 337–59; Pazden, "Nicodemus and the Samaritan Woman," 145–48.

302. On seeing both Joseph of Arimathea and Nicodemus as "secret believers" who fear being thrown out of the synagogue by the Jews, see Culpepper, *Anatomy*, 136; Martyn, *History and Theology*, 88.

303. Culpepper, *Anatomy*, 136.

304. Bassler, "Mixed Signals," 642.

305. Ibid., 643.

306. Ibid., 646.

Ambiguity, while not boding well for Nicodemus's faith, serves a useful end for John and his communicative strategy to his audience. Specifically in John 3, Nicodemus's silent response to the sign of the uplifted Son of Man serves to stimulate John's audience not to remain silent, but to believe and exhibit genuine faith that works the works of God. God tested the faith of the wilderness generations with his miraculous signs. The copper serpent is a paramount example of this testing function of signs. Tests of faith call for a response. Those who looked on the serpent with belief in God's healing power lived. Similarly, the uplifted Son of Man, the miracle of the crucifixion/exaltation, is a test of faith for Nicodemus. John portrays Nicodemus as a wilderness traveler who has also been tested by Jesus' signs. John shades Nicodemus's response to Jesus' signs in an effort to spur his audience to reflect on their own wilderness journey, and to reflect on their own response to Jesus' signs, especially the greatest sign of all in the Fourth Gospel—the cross.[307] While faith in John's Gospel is not merely a decisional response to the cross, but rather a heart-felt commitment to the Son stemming from a relationship with the Father, Nicodemus's journey does challenge the reader of the Gospel that a decision must be made.[308] As Moloney notes, "One is called to a decision to accept or refuse the saving revelation of the Father who sent the Son."[309] Johannine signs are tests of faith and are meant to provoke a response on the part of those who see and read about them (20:29–31).

---

307. Charlier, "La notion de signe," 444–45.
308. Moloney, *Belief in the Word*, 119.
309. Ibid.

CONCLUSIONS

I HAVE DRAWN ATTENTION to the wilderness motif that underlies John 2:23—3:21 in this study; this motif extends well beyond John's allusion to the uplifted serpent in the wilderness (3:14) and permeates the pericope. Kenneth Pomykala notes that the wilderness experience of ancient Israel became a "treasure trove" for reflection by later interpreters.[1] John's Gospel is a good case in point where wilderness images saturate various narratives and discourses. I have applied a "wilderness reading" to John 2:23—3:21 in an effort to demonstrate that Jesus' dialogue with Nicodemus is best understood against the background of Israel's wilderness experience, especially as recorded in Numbers. John's reference to the uplifted serpent of Num 21:8–9 is an invitation to read the dialogue against the wider context of Numbers. I have therefore proposed a fresh reading of the dialogue that brings to the surface of the text underlying wilderness motifs.

Paul Anderson observes that the OT wilderness experience was not only a time of God's provision for Israel but it was also their "testing," designed to teach them humility and covenant faithfulness.[2] I have shared this driving assumption throughout this study and have demonstrated that miraculous signs were means by which God tested his people in the wilderness. God's tests require a response from those who experience them. People are at times captivated at the sight of miraculous signs (i.e., signs-faith), at other times they exhibit a heart-felt belief in the source of signs—God, still at other times they refuse to believe and die in the wilderness. Humanity is therefore "tested" regarding their response to signs.[3] John alludes to the copper serpent of Num 21:8–9 that serves as a prime example of a miraculous

---

1. Pomykala, ed., *Israel in the Wilderness*, IX.
2. Anderson, *Christology*, 204.
3. Ibid., 106.

sign that tested the hearts of the Israelites, to see whether they would believe in God. My working hypothesis has been to demonstrate that this testing function of signs in the wilderness is a useful lens for viewing the varied responses of Johannine characters to Jesus' signs, using Nicodemus as a test case. Anderson maintains that this testing theme occurs throughout the Gospel but he does not explore it beyond John 6.[4] In response to Anderson's proposition, I have attempted to demonstrate that the testing function of signs occurs in John 2:23—3:21 and is underscored by an intertextual reading between John's text and LXX Numbers. I have also proposed faith-seeing as the interpretive key for unlocking the relationship between seeing signs and believing in John's Gospel. Only those people who see with eyes of faith "see" Jesus' signs rightly as indicators of his unity with the Father and as descriptors of his messianic mission.

I have also accepted the challenge of Richard Hays that calls for exploring the lines of intertextual linkage between the gospel stories and their OT precursors.[5] I have applied the intertextual method and his criteria to the study of John's Gospel that is saturated with OT symbols pointing to Christ, thus making it ripe for intertextual connections.[6] Specifically, I have used an intertextual method to highlight wilderness images and themes that run consistently through John 2:23—3:21, not simply 3:14 (i.e., the uplifted serpent in the wilderness). An intertextual approach reveals multiple allusions and echoes of the wilderness narratives of Numbers in Jesus' dialogue with Nicodemus.

AREAS FOR FUTURE RESEARCH

Wilderness Motif in John 3–4

This study opens the door to future investigations of wilderness imagery in John's narratives and discourses. While T. David's Gordon's "Israel's Final Wilderness" has probed wilderness imagery in the Book of Signs (John 1–12), smaller pericopes like 2:23—3:21 are nonetheless replete with wilderness imagery. In another example, the story of the Samaritan woman at the well of Sychar (4:1–42) contains wilderness imagery from God's miraculous provision of water in the wilderness (4:14; cf. Num 21:16–18). It is probably not coincidental, given that the "song of the well" follows the copper serpent narrative in Numbers, thereby making it a structural parallel

---

4. Ibid., 193.
5. Hays, "Canonical Matrix," 53–75.
6. Ibid., 72.

to Jesus' encounter with the woman at the well, which follows his dialogue with Nicodemus. There is, then, a wilderness structure to John 3–4 that begs for further investigation. Upon encountering an OT allusion or image in a Johannine narrative or discourse, readers should ask if there is additional imagery in the pericope stemming from the wider literary context of the precursor text. This may be performed once an allusion has been identified.

Johannine Intertextuality

Intertextuality is a relatively recent method in Johannine studies as compared with Pauline studies, which was made most popular by Hays's *Echoes of Scripture in the Letters of Paul* in 1989. Nevertheless, John's Gospel is fertile ground for intertextual analyses given its sheer saturation with OT imagery. One can hardly read a chapter of John without coming face to face with the OT. I have applied Richard Hays's criteria for identifying intertextual echoes in this study. I am not the only one to do so given that his criteria dominate the landscape of many intertextual studies. I am justified in using Haysian criteria to the extent that other Johannine scholars do the same. They are helpful for maintaining methodological constraint in a potentially personal reading exercise. What is more, I believe they have helped me avoid rampant speculation in this study; John's wilderness motif can become so vast and expansive that the creative exegete can explore it without end. I am under no illusion that my readers will hear every echo that I hear in this study. Nevertheless, I have attempted to offer a reasonable explanation for the intertextual connections I propose.

With that said, I believe there is a methodological caution that deserves attention. The Fourth Gospel's use of the OT is mostly thematic and contains far fewer citations and specific allusions than Paul's letters.[7] As C. K. Barrett noted, John is more concerned with the sense and whole of the OT than with proof texts,[8] and I believe this lack of specificity regarding OT precursor texts may prove challenging for the application of Haysian criteria in Johannine studies in the future. For example, Hays places a great deal of weight on the "volume" of a particular echo.[9] Volume is either enhanced or diminished based on the degree of verbatim repetition of words

---

7. Note that there are two methodological issues involved: 1) authorial use of the OT (i.e., John's use vs. Paul's), and 2) generic use of the OT (i.e., Gospel intertextuality vs. epistolary intertextuality).

8. Barrett, "Old Testament," 155–69; Childs, *Biblical Theology*, 285.

9. Hays, *Conversion of the Imagination*, 34–37.

and syntactical patterns.[10] However, these are surprisingly muted in John where thematic echoes dominate, thereby making the criterion of thematic coherence louder than volume.[11] This is not unlike the influence of the OT upon Colossians that has no formal quotations. Christopher Beetham has demonstrated in *Echoes of Scripture in the Letter of Paul to the Colossians* that "though scholars have concluded that there are no quotations of Scripture in Colossians, this is not to say that scholars therefore have not seen *any* influence of the OT upon the letter."[12] Therefore, if intertextuality is to thrive in Johannine studies, there is a need to develop criteria for identifying allusions and echoes for John's Gospel that are distinct (though not without some overlap) from those applied to Paul's letters. Not only is there is a difference in how the two authors use the OT,[13] there is also a difference of genre (e.g., Gospel vs. epistle). The issue, then, is not whether there are allusions and echoes in John's Gospel; it is one of methodology: developing criteria specifically tailored for the Gospel's genre and for the author's elusive use of the OT.

---

10. Ibid., 35.

11. For the criterion of thematic coherence, see ibid., 38–41.

12. Beetham, *Echoes of Scripture in Colossians*, 3.

13. For discussions of John's and Paul's use of the OT, see Carson, "John and the Johannine Epistles," 245–64; Smith, "Pauline Literature," 265–91; Longenecker, *Biblical Exegesis*, 88–116, 135–39.

Appendix 1

ΕΡΗΜΟΣ IN THE NEW TESTAMENT

	Arid, solitary, desolate place	Israel's sojourn	John the Baptist /new exodus eschatology
Matthew			
3:1	x		
3:3			x
4:1–2		x	
11:7	x		
12:25	x		
14:13	x		
14:15		x	
15:33		x	
23:38	x		
24:15	x		
24:26			x
Mark			
1:3			x
1:4			x
1:12		x	
1:13		x	

Appendix 1

	Arid, solitary, desolate place	Israel's sojourn	John the Baptist /new exodus eschatology
1:35	x		
1:45	x		
6:31		x	
6:32		x	
6:35		x	
8:4		x	
13:14	x		
Luke			
1:80	x		
3:2	x		
3:4			x
4:1–2		x	
4:42	x		
5:16	x		
7:24	x		
8:29	x		
9:12		x	
11:17	x		
15:4	x		
21:20	x		
John			
1:23			x
3:14		x	
6:31		x	
6:49		x	
11:54	x		
Acts			
1:20	x		
7:30		x	
7:36		x	
7:38		x	

Ερημος in the New Testament 189

	Arid, solitary, desolate place	Israel's sojourn	John the Baptist /new exodus eschatology
7:42		x	
7:44		x	
8:26	x		
21:38	x		
1 Corinthians			
10:5		x	
2 Corinthians			
11:26	x		
Galatians			
4:27	x		
Hebrews			
3:8		x	
3:17		x	
11:38	x		
Revelation			
12:6		x	
12:14		x	
17:3	x		

Appendix 2

BAPTISM AND "WATER AND SPIRIT" IN JOHN 3:5

IT IS BEYOND THE scope of this study to plunge into the details of the baptism debate of John 3:5, but a few cursory comments are in order given that 3:5 falls within the pericope covered in this study (2:23—3:21) and because baptismal interpretations play a significant role in the history of interpretation of this passage. What is more, there are baptismal undercurrents associated with Israel's exodus/wilderness experience. For example, the crossing of the Red Sea was viewed by later Christian interpreters as a type of baptism (e.g., 1 Cor 10:2).[1] John may intend for his audience to think of similar interpretive traditions when reflecting on the "rebirth" of Israel at the exodus. In short, my view regarding a baptismal interpretation of "water and Spirit" in John 3:5 is consistent with Xavier Léon Defour who states, "It is necessary to perceive of two times of revelation: that of Jesus to Nicodemus and that of the Spirit to me, the reader of the Gospel."[2] I do not believe that Jesus is telling Nicodemus to be baptized with John's baptism, for it is not directly associated with the outpouring of the Spirit (cf. Matt 4:11; Mark 1:8; Luke 3:16; Acts

---

1. For the crossing of the Sea as a type of baptism, see Bandstra, "Interpretation," 5–21; Longenecker, *Biblical Exegesis*, 102.

2. Dufour, "Symbolic Reading," 439–56, esp. 450.

2:38; 19:1–7),³ nor Christian baptism for this is surely anachronistic.⁴ However, John's Gospel was written later to a Christian community where the combination of "water and Spirit" would have developed a baptismal undercurrent. After all, a similar construction occurs in Paul where he refers to Christian baptism as the "washing of regeneration and renewal of the Holy Spirit" (λουτροῦ παλινγγενεσίας καὶ ἀνακαινώσεως πνεύματος ἁγίου, Titus 3:5). This is not to suggest that Paul is dependent upon John for his baptismal terminology, but it does highlight their use of similar terminology connecting water and spiritual rebirth. Therefore, a sacramental application in the *Sitz im Leben Kirche* need not be excluded on grammatical-historical exegesis of the *Sitz im Leben Jesu*.⁵ In short, I agree with Robert Kysar that a sacramental interpretation is part and parcel to John's double meaning and ambiguity; therefore, the phrase "born of water and Spirit" may call to mind baptism while it need not refer directly to the later Christian rite.⁶

---

3. Further, seeing "water" as a reference to John's baptism assumes his baptism was so influential that the mere mention of water would conjure up his rite. If so, Nicodemus's oblivious response seems out of place (Carson, *John*, 193). Such a monolithic use of "water" does not do justice to this multifaceted symbol in John's Gospel.

4. Schmidl, *Jesus und Nikodemus*, 155.

5. This is essentially in line with Bernard, *John*, 1:CLXV; Brown, *John*, 1:141–44; Brown, *Introduction*, 234; Burge, *Anointed Community*, 170; Culpepper, *Gospel and Letters*, 135; Koester, *Symbolism*, 185; Koester, *The Word of Life*, 141; Smith, *Theology*, 26; Schnackenburg, *John*, 1:369; Westcott, *John*, 50. As Schmidl, *Jesus und Nikodemus*, 154, states, "Only the point of view of the Christian reader causes this perception." In short, being born of water and spirit does not refer to baptism but it points to it.

6. Kysar, *Voyages with John*, 249.

Appendix 3

NICODEMUS'S CONFUSION AT BEING BORN FROM ABOVE

WHAT ACCOUNTS FOR NICODEMUS's question in John 3:9 regarding the divine rebirth: πῶς δύναται ταῦτα γενέσθαι; ("How can these things be?")? More problematic for Nicodemus than the concept of rebirth may be the precise role of the Holy Spirit in the life of an individual Israelite. It has long been acknowledged that there was the belief in Second Temple Judaism that prophetic revelation had ceased, and that the Spirit of prophecy was no longer available in its OT fullness (*Soṭa* 48b).[1] The implication was that if the Spirit of prophecy had ceased, then the direct activity of the Holy Spirit in the individual had ceased as well.[2] As Craig Keener notes, "Palestinian authorities did not even claim to possess the Spirit."[3] Nevertheless, Israel Abrahams distinguishes between the Spirit proper and specific manifestations of the Spirit such as prophetic revelation: "In all ages he imparts of his grace to man, but not in all ages by the same means."[4] The belief that prophecy ceased does not suggest that the Holy Spirit ceased operating in the lives of individuals.[5] Again,

---

1. Keener, *John*, 1:203. See also, Abrahams, *Studies in Pharisaism*, 2:120–28; Greenspahn, "Why Prophecy Ceased," 37–49; Hawthorne, "Prophets, Prophecy," 636–42, esp. 637.

2. On equating the Spirit of prophecy with the Holy Spirit, especially in the Targumim, see Greenspahn, "Why Prophecy Ceased," 37.

3. Keener, *John*, 1:203.

4. Abrahams, *Studies in Pharisaism*, 2:128.

5. On rejecting the notion of a withdrawal of the Spirit from Israel, see Levison,

Abrahams, after surveying the rabbinic materials concludes: "The Holy Spirit has never ceased, can never cease, to operate in the lives of men."[6] All of this suggests that even if Nicodemus believed as other Jewish authorities believed that the Spirit of prophecy had been removed from Israel, this does not amount to a complete withdrawal of the Spirit in the lives of individual Israelites. Further, the Gospel of John's already-not-yet eschatology makes any perceived absence of the Spirit a moot point when considering the eschatological outpouring of the Spirit in the messianic era. Put differently, for John the ministry of Jesus announces the inauguration of the prophetic promises of the outpouring of the Spirit for the renewal of mankind (cf. John 7:37–39). If Nicodemus believed in the withdrawal of the Spirit from Israel, and if this belief led to his confusion regarding spiritual rebirth, Jesus announces the arrival of the much anticipated eschatological Spirit. Therefore, I conclude the following as possible reasons for Nicodemus's confusion regarding matters of the Spirit: 1) the metaphorical and non-scriptural terminology of γεννηθῇ ἄνωθεν, and 2) the belief in the withdrawal of the Spirit from Israel.

"Holy Spirit," 507–15, esp. 508–09.

6. Abrahams, *Studies in Pharisaism*, 2:127. Similarly, Schechter, *Rabbinic Theology*, 217, illustrates from rabbinic materials the work of the Holy Spirit in the individual at cultivating holiness.

BIBLIOGRAPHY

Abrahams, Israel. *Studies in Pharisaism and the Gospels.* First and second series. New York: Ktav, 1967.
Achtemeier, Paul. et al. *Introducing the New Testament: Its Literature and Theology.* Grand Rapids: Eerdmans, 2001.
Adams, Marilyn McCord. "Healing Judgment: Numbers 21:4-9 and John 3:14-21." *Expository Times* 117 (2006) 196-97.
Alexander, Philip. "Targum, Targumim." In *ABD* 6:320-31.
———. "The Jewish Translations of Hebrew Scriptures." Pages 217-53 in *Mikra: Text, Translation, Reading and Interpretation of the Hebrew Bible in Ancient Judaism and Early Christianity.* Edited by Martin Jan Mulder. Peabody: Hendrickson, 2004.
Alexander, T. D. *From Paradise to the Promised Land: An Introduction to the Pentateuch.* 2d ed. Grand Rapids: Baker Academic, 2002.
Alkier, Stefan. "Intertextuality and the Semiotics of Biblical Texts." Pages 3-21 in *Reading the Bible Intertextually.* Edited by Richard B. Hays, Stefan Alkier, and Leroy A. Huizenga. Waco: Baylor University Press, 2009.
Anderson, Lynn. "Born to Better Living (John 3:1-8)." *Restoration Quarterly* 31 (1989) 165-69.
Anderson, Paul N. "From One Dialogue to Another: Johannine Polyvalence from Origins to Receptions." Pages 93-119 in *Anatomies of Narrative Criticism: The Past, Present, and Futures of the Fourth Gospel as Literature.* Edited by Tom Thatcher and Stephen D. Moore. Atlanta: Society of Biblical Literature, 2008.
———. *The Christology of the Fourth Gospel: Its Unity and Disunity in the Light of John 6.* Eugene, OR: Cascade, 2010.
———. "The Johannine Conception of Authentic Faith as a Response to the Divine Initiative." Pages 257-60 in *What We Have Heard from the Beginning: The Past, Present, and Future of Johannine Studies.* Edited by Tom Thatcher; Waco: Baylor University Press, 2007.
———. "The Word." In *NIDB* 5:893-98.
Anderson, Robert T. "Samaritans." In *NIDB* 5:75-80.
Ashley, Timothy. *The Book of Numbers.* The New International Commentary on the Old Testament. Grand Rapids: Eerdmans, 1993.
Ashton, John. *Understanding the Fourth Gospel.* 2d ed. New York: Oxford University Press, 2007.

Bakhtin, Mikhail M. *The Dialogic Imagination.* Edited by Michael Holquist. Translated by Caryl Emerson and Michael Holquist. Austin: University of Texas Press, 1981; Russian original, 1975.

Bandstra, A. J. "Interpretation in 1 Corinthians 10:1–11." *Calvin Theological Journal* 6 (1971) 5–21.

Barrett, C. K. *The Gospel According to St. John.* 2d ed. Philadelphia: Westminster Press, 1978.

———. "The Holy Spirit in the Fourth Gospel." *Journal of Theological Studies* 1 (1950) 1–15.

———. "The Old Testament in the Fourth Gospel." *Journal for Theological Studies* 48 (1947) 155–69.

Barstad, Hans M. *A Way in the Wilderness: The "Second Exodus" in the Message of Second Isaiah.* Manchester: University of Manchester, 1989.

Barton, John. *Reading the Old Testament: Method in Biblical Study.* Rev. and enl. ed. Louisville: Westminster John Knox, 1996.

Barton, Stephen C. "Johannine Dualism and Contemporary Pluralism." Pages 3–18 in *The Gospel of John and Christian Theology.* Edited by Richard Bauckham and Carl Mosser. Grand Rapids: Eerdmans, 2008.

Bassler, Jouette M. "Mixed Signals: Nicodemus in the Fourth Gospel." *Journal of Biblical Literature* 108 (1989) 635–46.

Bauckham, Richard. *Jesus and the Eyewitnesses: The Gospels as Eyewitness Testimony.* Grand Rapids: Eerdmans, 2006.

———. "Monotheism and Christology in the Gospel of John." Pages 148–66 in *Contours of Christology in the New Testament.* Edited by Richard N. Longenecker. Grand Rapids: Eerdmans, 2005.

———. "The Relevance of Extra-Canonical Jewish Texts to New Testament Study." Pages 90–108 in *Hearing the New Testament: Strategies for Interpretation.* Edited by Joel Green. Grand Rapids: Eerdmans, 1995.

———. *The Testimony of the Beloved Disciple: Narrative, History and Theology in the Gospel of John.* Grand Rapids: Baker Academic, 2007.

Beale, G. K. *The Book of Revelation: A Commentary on the Greek Text.* The New International Greek Testament Commentary. Grand Rapids: Eerdmans, 1999.

———. *We Become What We Worship: A Biblical Theology of Idolatry.* Downers Grove: IVP Academic, 2008.

Beare, F. W. "Spirit of Life and Truth: The Doctrine of the Holy Spirit in the Fourth Gospel." *Toronto Journal of Theology* 3 (1987) 110–25.

Beasley-Murray, George R. *Baptism in the New Testament.* New York: St. Martin's, 1963.

———. *Gospel of Life: Theology in the Fourth Gospel.* Peabody: Hendrickson, 1991.

———. *Jesus and the Kingdom of God.* Grand Rapids: Eerdmans, 1986.

———. *John.* Word Biblical Commentary 36. 2d ed. Nashville: Thomas Nelson, 1999.

Becker, Jürgen. "Wunder und Christologie. Zum literarkritischen und christologischen Problem der Wunder im Johannesevangelium." *New Testament Studies* 16 (1969/70) 130–48.

Beckwith, Roger T. "Formation of the Hebrew Bible." Pages 39–86 in *Mikra: Text, Translation, Reading & Interpretation of the Hebrew Bible in Ancient Judaism & Early Christianity.* Edited by Martin Jan Mulder. Peabody: Eerdmans, 2004.

Beetham, Christopher A. *Echoes of Scripture in the Letter of Paul to the Colossians.* Biblical Interpretation Series 96. Atlanta: Society of Biblical Literature, 2008.

Bell, Albert A. Jr. *Exploring the New Testament World: An Illustrated Guide to the World of Jesus and the First Christians.* Nashville: Thomas Nelson, 1998.

Belleville, Linda. "'Born of Water and Spirit:' John 3:5." *Trinity Journal* 1 (1980) 125–41.

Berding, Kenneth, and Jonathan Lunde, eds. *Three Views on the New Testament Use of the Old Testament.* Grand Rapids: Zondervan, 2007.

Bernard, J. H. *A Critical and Exegetical Commentary on the Gospel According to St. John.* 2 vols. International Critical Commentary. Edinburgh: T&T Clark, 1928.

Beutler, Johannes. "The Use of 'Scripture' in the Gospel of John." Pages 147–62 in *Exploring the Gospel of John. In Honor of D. Moody Smith.* Edited by R. Alan Culpepper and C. Clifton Black. Louisville: Westminster John Knox, 1996.

Black, David Alan. "The Text of John 3:13." *Grace Theological Journal* 6 (1985) 49–66.

Black, Mark. *Luke.* The College Press NIV Commentary. Joplin, MO: College Press, 1996.

Blomberg, Craig. *The Historical Reliability of John's Gospel: Issues and Commentary.* Downers Grove: InterVarsity, 2001.

Boismard, Marie-Emile. *Moses or Jesus: An Essay in Johannine Christology.* Minneapolis: Fortress, 1993.

Borgen, Peder. "Some Jewish Exegetical Traditions as Background for Son of Man Sayings in John's Gospel (John 3:13–14 in Context)." Pages 243–58 in *L'Évangile de Jean: Sources, redaction, théologie.* Bibliotheca Ephemeridum Theologicarum Lovaniensium 44. Edited by M. de Jonge. Leuven: Leuven University Press, 1975.

———. "The Gospel of John and Hellenism: Some Observations." Pages 98–123 in *Exploring the Gospel of John: In Honor of D. Moody Smith.* Edited by R. Alan Culpepper and C. Clifton Black. Louisville: Westminster John Knox, 1996.

Born, Bryan. "Literary Features in the Gospel of John: An Analysis on John 3:1–21." *Direction Journal* 17 (1988) 3–17.

Bowen, John. "Coming to Faith in the Gospel of John." *Anvil* 19 (2002) 277–83.

Bowman, John. *Samaritan Documents Relating to Their History, Religion and Life.* Pittsburgh: Pickwick, 1977.

Boyarin, Daniel. *Intertextuality and the Reading of Midrash.* Bloomington: Indiana University Press, 1990.

Brawley, Robert. "An Absent Complement and Intertextuality in John 19:28–29." *Journal of Biblical Literature* 113 (1993) 427–43.

Brettler, Marc. "How the Books of the Hebrew Bible Were Chosen." Pages 108–12 in *Approaches to the Bible. Vol. 1: Composition, Transmission, and Language.* Edited by Harvey Minkoff. Washington DC: Biblical Archeological Society, 1994.

Brodie, Thomas. *The Gospel According to John: A Literary and Theological Commentary.* New York: Oxford University Press, 1993.

Brooke, George J. "Thematic Commentaries on Prophetic Scriptures." Pages 134–57 in *Biblical Interpretation at Qumran.* Edited by Matthias Henze. Grand Rapids: Eerdmans, 2005.

Brooks, Pat. "Alexander Campbell, the Holy Spirit, and the New Birth." *Restoration Quarterly* 31 (1989) 149–64.

Brown, Raymond. *An Introduction to the Gospel of John.* Edited by Francis J. Moloney. New York: Doubleday, 2003.

———. *The Death of the Messiah: From Gethsemane to the Grave.* London: Chapman, 1994.

———. *The Gospel According to John*. 2 vols. The Anchor Bible 29–29a. New York: Doubleday, 1966–1970.

———. "The Paraclete in the Fourth Gospel." *New Testament Studies* 13 (1967) 113–32.

Bruce, F. F. *The Gospel of John: Introduction, Exposition, and Notes*. Grand Rapids: Eerdmans, 1983.

Brueggemann, Walter. *The Book of Exodus: Introduction, Commentary, and Reflections*. The New Interpreter's Bible 1. Nashville: Abingdon, 1994.

———. *The Land: Place as Gift, Promise, and Challenge in Biblical Faith*. Philadelphia: Fortress, 1977.

Brunson, Andrew C. *Psalm 118 in the Gospel of John: An Intertextual Study on the New Exodus Pattern in the Theology of John*. Wissenschaftliche Untersuchungen Zum Neuen Testament 158. Tübingen: Mohr Siebeck, 2003.

Bryant, Beauford H. and Mark S. Krause. *John*. College Press New International Version Commentary. Joplin, MO: College Press, 1998.

Budd, Philip J. *Numbers*. Word Biblical Commentary 5. Waco: Word Books, 1984.

Bultmann, Rudolf. *The Gospel of John: A Commentary*. Translated by George R. Beasley-Murray. Philadelphia: Westminster, 1971.

———. *Theology of the New Testament*. 2 vols. Translated by Kendrick Groebel. New York: Charles Scribner's Sons, 1951–1955.

Burden, Terry L. *The Kerygma of the Wilderness Traditions in the Hebrew Bible*. New York: Peter Lang, 1994.

Burkett, Delbert. *The Son of Man Debate: A History and Evaluation*. Cambridge: Cambridge University Press, 1999.

———. *The Son of Man in the Gospel of John*. Journal for the Study of New Testament Supplement Series 56. Sheffield: Sheffield Academic Press, 1991.

Burge, Gary M. *Jesus and the Land: The New Testament Challenge to "Holy Land" Theology*. Grand Rapids: Baker Academic, 2010.

———. *John*. The New International Version Application Commentary. Grand Rapids: Zondervan, 2000.

———. *Interpreting the Gospel of John*. Grand Rapids: Baker Books, 1992.

———. "Life." In *NIDB* 3:655–61.

———. *The Anointed Community: The Holy Spirit in the Johannine Tradition*. Grand Rapids: Eerdmans, 1987.

Callaway, Mary C. "Canonical Criticism." Pages 142–55 in *To Each Its Own Meaning*. Edited by Steven L. McKenzie and Stephen R. Haynes. Louisville: Westminster John Knox, 1999.

Calvin, John. *The Gospel According to John*. Vol. 17 in Calvin's Commentaries. 22 Vols. Edited by William Pringle. Edinburgh: Calvin Translation Society. Repr. Grand Rapids: Baker, 1979.

Caragounis, C. C. "Kingdom of God/Heaven." In *DJG* 417–30.

Carson, D. A. *Divine Sovereignty and Human Responsibility: Biblical Perspectives in Tension*. Atlanta: John Knox, 1981.

———. *The Gospel According to John*. The Pillar New Testament Commentary. Grand Rapids: Eerdmans, 1991.

———. "John and the Johannine Epistles." Pages 245–64 in *It is Written: Scripture Citing Scripture: Essays in Honour of Barnabas Lindars*. Edited by D. A. Carson and H. G. M. Williamson. Cambridge: Cambridge University Press, 1988.

———. "The Purpose of Signs and Wonders in the New Testament." Pages 89–118 in *Power Religion: The Selling Out of the Evangelical Church?* Edited by Michael Scott Horton. Chicago: Moody Press, 1992.

———. "Understanding Misunderstandings in the Fourth Gospel." *Tyndale Bulletin* 33 (1982) 61–91.

Carter, Philippa A. "Signs in the New Testament." In *NIDB* 5:252–54.

Carter, Warren. *John: Storyteller, Interpreter, Evangelist*. Peabody: Hendrickson, 2006.

Casey, Maurice. *The Solution to the "Son of Man" Problem*. Library of New Testament Studies 343. London: T&T Clark, 2007.

Cathcart, Kevin. "Numbers 24:17 in Ancient Translations and Interpretations." Pages 511–20 in *Interpretation of the Bible*. Sheffield: Sheffield Academic Press, 1998.

Cathcart, Kevin, Michael Maher, and Martin McNamara. *The Aramaic Bible: Targum Pseudo-Jonathan: Numbers*. Translated by Ernest G. Clarke. Collegeville, MN: Liturgical Press, 1995.

Cerfaux, L. "Les miracles, signes messianiques de Jésus et œuvres de Dieu, selon L'Évangile de saint Jean." Pages 41–50 in *L'Attente du Messie*. Bruges: Mélanges J. Coppens, 1954.

Charlesworth, James H. "A Critical Comparison of the Dualism in 1QS 3:13–4:26 and The 'Dualism' Contained in the Gospel of John." Pages 76–106 in *John and the Dead Sea Scrolls*. Edited by James H. Charlesworth. New York: Crossroad, 1990.

———. *The Good and Evil Serpent: How a Universal Symbol Became Christianized*. New Haven: Yale University Press, 2010.

———. "The Interpretation of the Tanak in the Jewish Apocrypha and Pseudepigrapha." Pages 253–82 in *A History of Biblical Interpretation. Vol. 1: The Ancient Period*. Edited by Alan J. Hauser and Duane F. Watson. Grand Rapids: Eerdmans, 2003.

———., ed. *The Old Testament Pseudepigrapha*. 2 vols. New York: Doubleday, 1985.

Charlier, J.-P. "La notion de signe (ΣΗΜΕΙΟΝ) dans le Quatrième Évangile." *Revue des Sciences philosophiques et théologiques* 43 (1959) 434–48.

Childs, Brevard S. *Biblical Theology of the Old and New Testaments: Theological Reflections on the Christian Bible*. Minneapolis: Fortress, 1992.

———. *Introduction to the Old Testament as Scripture*. Philadelphia: Fortress, 1979.

———. *Isaiah*. Louisville: Westminster John Knox, 2001.

———. *The New Testament as Canon: An Introduction*. Valley Forge, PA: Trinity International, 1994.

Chilton, Bruce. "From Aramaic Paraphrase to Greek Testament." Pages 23–43 in *From Prophecy to Testament: The Function of the Old Testament in the New*. Edited by Craig Evans. Grand Rapids: Baker Academic, 2004.

———. "Rabbinic Traditions and Writings." In *DJG* 651–60.

———. "Targums." In *DJG* 800–04.

———. *The Isaiah Targum*. The Aramaic Bible 11. Wilmington, DE: Michael Glazer, 1987.

Clark, Douglas K. "Signs in Wisdom and John." *Catholic Biblical Quarterly* 45 (1983) 201–09.

Clarke, Ernest G. *Targum Pseudo-Jonathan*. The Aramaic Bible 4. Collegeville, MN: Liturgical Press, 1995.

Coats, George W. *Rebellion in the Wilderness: The Murmuring Motif in the Wilderness Traditions of the Old Testament*. Nashville: Abingdon, 1968.

Cole, R. Dennis. *Numbers*. New American Commentary 3B. Nashville: Broadman & Holman, 2000.

Collins, Adela Yarbro. "Son of Man." In *NIDB* 5:341–48.

Collins, John J. "Enoch, Books of." In *DNTB* 313–18.

———. "Messiah, Jewish." In *NIDB* 4:59–66.

———. *The Scepter and the Star: The Messiahs of the Dead Sea Scrolls and Other Ancient Literature*. New York: Doubleday, 1995.

Collins, Raymond E. "Servant of the Lord." In *NIDB* 5:192–95.

Cotterell, F. P. "The Nicodemus Conversation: A Fresh Appraisal." *Expository Times* 96 (1985) 237–42.

Cotton, Roger. "The Pentecostal Significance of Numbers 11." *Journal of Pentecostal Theology* 10 (2001) 3–10.

Craigie, Peter. *The Book of Deuteronomy*. The New International Commentary on the Old Testament. Grand Rapids: Eerdmans, 1976.

Crew, Roy P. "The Tabernacle and the Cloud." *Expository Times* 99 (1987) 84–86.

Cullmann, Oscar. *The Christology of the New Testament*. Rev. ed. Translated by Shirley Guthrie and Charles Hall. Philadelphia: Westminster, 1963.

Culpepper, R. Alan. *Anatomy of the Fourth Gospel: A Study in Literary Design*. Philadelphia: Fortress, 1983.

———. *John, the Son of Zebedee: The Life of a Legend*. Minneapolis: Fortress, 2000.

———. "Reading Johannine Irony." Pages 193–207 in *Exploring the Gospel of John: In Honor of D. Moody Smith*. Edited by R. Alan Culpepper and C. Clifton Black. Louisville: Westminster John Knox, 1996.

———. *The Gospel and Letters of John*. Interpreting Biblical Texts. Nashville: Abingdon, 1998.

Daniélou, Jean. "La Typologie de l'Exode dans l'Ancien et le Nouveau Testament." Pages 131–43 in *Sacramentum Futuri: Etudes sur les Origines de la Typologie Biblique*. Paris: Beauchesne, 1950.

Daly-Denton, Margaret. *David in the Fourth Gospel: The Johannine Reception of the Psalms*. Boston: Brill, 2000.

Danby, Herbert., ed. *The Mishnah*. Oxford: Oxford University Press, 1933.

Daube, David. *The New Testament and Rabbinic Judaism*. London: University of London, Athlone, 1956.

Davies, W. D. *Introduction to Pharisaism*. Philadelphia: Fortress, 1967.

———. *Invitation to the New Testament*. New York: Doubleday, 1969.

Day, Bill. *The Moses Connection in John's Gospel*. Piedmont, OK: Mariner Books, 1997.

De Jonge, Martinus. *Jesus: Stranger from Heaven and Son of God: Jesus Christ and the Christians in Johannine Perspective*. Edited and translated by John E. Steely. Missoula, MT: Scholars, 1977.

———. "Nicodemus and Jesus: Some Observations on Understanding and Misunderstanding in the Fourth Gospel." *Bulletin of the John Rylands Library* 53 (1971) 337–59.

Derrett, J. Duncan M. "Correcting Nicodemus (John 3:2, 21)." *Expository Times* 112 (2001) 126.

———. "The Bronze Serpent." *Estudios Biblicos* 49 (1991) 311–29.

———. "Not Seeing and Later Seeing (John 16:16)." *Expository Times* 109 (1997–1998) 208–09.

DeSilva, David. *Introducing the Apocrypha: Message, Contexts, and Significance*. Grand Rapids: Baker Academic, 2002.
Dillard, Raymond B., and Tremper Longman III. *An Introduction to the Old Testament*. Grand Rapids: Zondervan, 1994.
Dodd, C. H. *According to the Scriptures: The Substructure of New Testament Theology*. UK: Harper Collins Ltd., 1953. Repr., Eugene, OR: Wipf & Stock, 2006.
———. *The Interpretation of the Fourth Gospel*. Cambridge: Cambridge University Press, 1968.
Dozeman, Thomas. *The Book of Numbers: Introduction, Commentary, and Reflections*. The New Interpreter's Bible 2. Nashville: Abingdon, 1998.
Duke, Paul. *Irony in the Fourth Gospel*. Atlanta: John Knox, 1985.
Dufour, Xavier Léon. "Towards a Symbolic Reading of the Fourth Gospel." *New Testament Studies* 27 (1981) 439–56.
Duguid, Iain M. *Numbers: God's Presence in the Wilderness*. Wheaton, IL: Good News, 2006.
Edersheim, Alfred. *Bible History Old Testament*. Peabody: Hendrickson, 1995.
———. *The Life and Times of Jesus the Messiah*. New York: Herrick, 1886. Repr., Peabody: Hendrickson, 1993.
———. *The Temple: Its Ministry and Services*. Rev. ed. Peabody: Hendrickson, 1994.
Elliott, Mark W. "Typology." In *NIDB* 5:692.
Ellis, E. Earle. "Biblical Interpretation in the New Testament Church." Pages 691–725 In *Mikra: Text, Translation, Reading and Interpretation of the Hebrew Bible in Ancient Judaism and Christianity*. Edited by Martin Jan Mulder. Peabody: Hendrickson, 2004.
Elowsky, Joel C., ed. *John 1–10*. Ancient Christian Commentary on Scripture: New Testament 4A. Downers Grove: InterVarsity, 2006.
Enns, Peter. *Exodus*. New International Version Application Commentary. Grand Rapids: Zondervan, 2000.
———. *Exodus Retold: Ancient Exegesis of the Departure from Egypt in Wis 10:15–21 and 19:1–9*. Harvard Semitic Museum Monographs 57. Atlanta: Scholars, 1997.
Enz, Jacob J. "The Book of Exodus as a Literary Type for the Gospel of John." *Journal of Biblical Literature* 76 (1957) 208–15.
Epstein, I., ed. *The Babylonian Talmud: Berakoth*. Translated by Maurice Simon. London: Soncino, 1948.
Esler, Philip F., and Ronald Piper. *Lazarus, Mary, and Martha: Social-Scientific Approaches to the Gospel of John*. Minneapolis: Fortress, 2006.
Evans, Craig A., ed. *Ancient Texts for New Testament Studies*. Peabody: Hendrickson, 2005.
———. "Typology." In *DJG* 862–66.
Evans, Craig A., and James A. Sanders, eds. *Paul and the Scriptures of Israel*. Journal for the Study of the New Testament Supplement Series 83. Sheffield: Sheffield Academic Press, 1993.
Farris, Stephen. "Theophany in the NT." In *NIDB* 5:565–66.
Ferguson, Everett. *Backgrounds of Early Christianity*. 3d ed. Grand Rapids: Eerdmans, 2003.
Fish, Stanley. *Is There a Text in This Class?: The Authority of Interpretive Communities*. Cambridge: Harvard University Press, 1980.
Fishbane, Michael A. *Biblical Interpretation in Ancient Israel*. Oxford: Clarendon, 1985.

———. "Inner-Biblical Exegesis: Types and Strategies of Interpretation in Ancient Israel." Pages 3–21 in *The Garments of Torah: Essays in Biblical Hermeneutics.* Edited by Michael A. Fishbane; Bloomington: Indiana University Press, 1989.

Fletcher, Daniel H. "The Wilderness Motif in John3:1–21 and Its Impact on Johannine Signs and Faith: An Intertextual Case Study." Ph.D. diss., Westminster Theological Seminary, 2012.

Fortna, Robert. "The Gospel of John and the Signs Gospel." Pages 149–58 in *What We Have Heard from the Beginning: The Past, Present, and Future of Johannine Studies.* Edited by Tom Thatcher. Waco: Baylor University Press, 2007.

———. *The Fourth Gospel and its Predecessor: From Narrative Source to Present Gospel.* Philadelphia: Fortress, 1988.

———. *The Gospel of Signs: A Reconstruction of the Narrative Source Underlying The Fourth Gospel.* Cambridge: Cambridge University Press, 1970.

France, R. T. "Servant of Yahweh." In *DJG* 744–47.

Freed, Edwin. *Old Testament Quotations in the Gospel of John.* Leiden: Brill, 1965.

Fry, J. D. "Reformation Perspective: Past and Present: A Wilderness Faith." *Communio Viatorum* 12 (1969) 43–50.

Funk, Robert W. "The Wilderness." *Journal of Biblical Literature* 78 (1959) 205–14.

Gaffney, James. "Believing and Knowing in the Fourth Gospel." *Theological Studies* 26 (1965) 215–41.

Gane, Roy. *Leviticus, Numbers.* New International Version Application Commentary. Grand Rapids: Zondervan, 2004.

Garrett, Duane A. *Hosea, Joel.* New American Commentary 19A. Nashville: Broadman & Holman, 1997.

Gertel, Elliot B. "Moses, Elisha and Transferred Spirit: The Height of Biblical Prophecy? Part 1." *Jewish Bible Quarterly* 30 (2002) 73–79.

———. "Moses, Elisha and Transferred Spirit: The Height of Biblical Prophecy? Part 2." *Jewish Bible Quarterly* 30 (2002) 171–77.

Gibbons, Debbie. "Nicodemus: Character Development, Irony, and Repetition in the Fourth Gospel." *Proceedings: Eastern Great Lakes and Midwest Biblical Societies* (1991) 116–28.

Glasson, T. Francis. *Moses in the Fourth Gospel.* SBT 40. Naperville, IL: SCM, 1963.

———. "The Son of Man Imagery in Enoch 14 and Daniel 7." *New Testament Studies* 23 (1977) 82–90.

Goppelt, Leonhard. *Typos: Typological Interpretation of the Old Testament in the New.* Translated by Donald H. Madvig. Grand Rapids: Eerdmans, 1982.

Gordley, Matthew. "Seeing Stars at Qumran: The Interpretation of Balaam and His Oracle in the Damascus Document and Other Qumran Texts." *Proceedings: Eastern Great Lakes and Midwest Biblical Societies* 25 (2005) 107–19.

Gordon, T. David. "John 1–12: Israel's Final Wilderness." ThM Thesis. Westminster Theological Seminary. 1980.

Gowan, Donald. *Eschatology in the Old Testament.* 2d ed. Edinburgh: T&T Clark, 2000.

Greenspahn, Frederick E. "Why Prophecy Ceased." *Journal of Biblical Literature* 108 (1989) 37–49.

Greenspoon, Leonard. "Hebrew into Greek: Interpretation In, By, and Of the Septuagint." Pages 81–113 in *A History of Biblical Interpretation, Vol. 1: The Ancient Period.* Edited by Alan J. Hauser and Duane F. Watson; Grand Rapids: Eerdmans, 2003.

Grenz, Stanley J. *Theology for the Community of God.* Nashville: Broadman & Holman, 1994.

Grudem, Wayne. *Systematic Theology: An Introduction to Biblical Doctrine.* Grand Rapids: InterVarsity, Zondervan, 1994.

Guillet, Jacques. "Le Thème de la marche au desert dans l'Ancien et le Nouveau Testament." *Recherches de science religieuse* 36 (1949) 161–81.

Gundry, Robert H. and Russell Howell. "The Sense and Syntax of John 3:14–17 with Special Reference to the Use of ὉΥΤΩΣ ... ὭΣΤΕ in John 3:16." *Novum Testamentum* 41 (1999) 24–39.

Guthrie, Donald. "The Importance of Signs in the Fourth Gospel." *Vox Evangelica* 5 (1967) 72–83.

Hägerland, Tobias. "The Power of Prophecy: A Septuagintal Echo in John 20:19–23." *Catholic Biblical Quarterly* 71 (2009) 84–103.

Ham, Clay. "The Title 'Son of Man' in the Gospel of John." *Stone-Campbell Journal* 1(1998) 85–100.

Hanson, Anthony. *The Prophetic Gospel.* Edinburgh: T&T Clark, 1991.

Harner, Philip B. *The I-Am of the Fourth Gospel: A Study in Johannine Usage and Thought.* Philadelphia: Fortress, 1970.

Harrison, R. K. *Introduction to the Old Testament.* Peabody: Prince, 1999.

Harstine, Stan. *Moses as a Character in the Fourth Gospel.* JSNT Supp. 229. Sheffield: Sheffield Academic Press, 2002.

Hays, Richard, and Joel Green. "The Use of the Old Testament by New Testament Writers." Pages 222–38 in *Hearing the New Testament: Strategies for Interpretation.* Edited by Joel Green. Grand Rapids: Eerdmans, 1995.

Hays, Richard B. *Echoes of Scripture in the Letters of Paul.* New Haven: Yale University Press, 1989.

———. "The Canonical Matrix of the Gospels." Pages 55–73 in *The Cambridge Companion to the Gospels.* Edited by Stephen C. Barton. Cambridge: Cambridge University Press, 2006.

———. *The Conversion of the Imagination: Paul as Interpreter of Israel's Scripture.* Grand Rapids: Eerdmans, 2005.

Hazelton, Roger. "Believing is Seeing: Vision as Metaphor." *Theology Today* 35 (1979) 405–12.

Hengel, Martin. "The Prologue of the Gospel of John as the Gateway to Christological Truth." Pages 265–94 in *The Gospel of John and Christian Theology.* Edited by Richard Bauckham and Carl Mosser. Grand Rapids: Eerdmans, 2008.

Hilderbrandt, Wilf. *An Old Testament Theology of the Spirit of God.* Peabody: Hendrickson, 1995.

Hill, Charles E. *The Johannine Corpus in the Early Church.* Oxford: Oxford University Press, 2004.

Hodges, Zane. "Coming to the Light–John 3:20–21." *Bibliotheca Sacra* 135 (1978) 314–22.

Hirsch, E. D. Jr. *Validity in Interpretation.* New Haven: Yale University Press, 1967.

Hollander, John. *The Figure of Echo: A Mode of Allusion in Milton and After.* Berkeley: University of California Press, 1981.

Hooker, Morna D. *Jesus and the Servant: The Influence of the Servant Concept of Deutero-Isaiah in the New Testament.* London: S.P.C.K., 1959.

Horbury, William. "Jewish Messianism and Early Christology." Pages 3–24 in *Contours of Christology in the New Testament*. Edited by Richard Longenecker. Grand Rapids: Eerdmans, 2005.

———. "The Messianic Associations of 'The Son of Man.'" *Journal of Theological Studies* 36 (1985) 34–53.

Hoskyns, Edwyn Clement. *The Fourth Gospel*. 2 vols. Edited by Francis Noel Davey. London: Faber and Faber, 1940.

House, Paul R. *Old Testament Theology*. Downers Grove: InterVarsity, 1998.

Hubbard, David Allen. *Joel and Amos*. Tyndale Old Testament Commentaries. Downers Grove, IL: InterVarsity, 1989.

Hunt, B. P. W. Stather. *Some Johannine Problems*. London: Skeffington, 1958.

Hylen, Susan. "Nicodemus." In *NIDB* 4:69–70.

Janowski, Bernd, and Peter Stuhlmacher, eds. *The Suffering Servant: Isaiah 53 in Jewish and Christian Sources*. Translated by Daniel P. Bailey. Grand Rapids: Eerdmans, 2004.

Janzen, Waldemar. "Tabernacle." In *NIDB* 5:447–58.

Jastrow, Marcus. "תלי ,תלה." Pages 1670–71 in *A Dictionary of the Targumim, The Talmud Babli and Yerushalmi, and the Midrashic Literature*. New York: Jastrow, 1967.

Jenson, Robert W. "Bronze Serpent." *Dialog* 17 (1978) 251–86.

Jobes, Karen H. and Moisés Silva. *Invitation to the Septuagint*. Grand Rapids: Baker Academic, 2000.

Johnson, Brian D. "'Salvation is from the Jews': Judaism in the Gospel of John." Pages 83–99 in *New Currents Through John: A Global Perspective*. Edited by Francisco Lozada Jr. and Tom Thatcher. Atlanta: Society of Biblical Literature, 2006.

Johnson, D. H. "Logos." In *DJG* 481–84.

Joines, Karen Randolph. "The Bronze Serpent in the Israelite Cult." *Journal of Biblical Literature* 87 (1968) 245–56.

Jones, Brian C. "Wilderness." In *NIDB* 5:848–52.

Juel, Donald H. "Interpreting Israel's Scriptures in the New Testament." Pages 283–303 In *A History of Biblical Interpretation, Vol. 1: The Ancient Period*. Edited by Alan J. Hauser and Duane F. Watson. Grand Rapids: Eerdmans, 2003.

Kaufman, Stephen A. "Targums." In *NIDB* 5:471–73.

Keener, Craig. *Gift and Giver: The Holy Spirit for Today*. Grand Rapids: Baker, 2001.

———. *The Gospel of John*. 2 vols. Peabody: Hendrickson, 2003.

———. *The IVP Bible Background Commentary: The New Testament*. Downers Grove: InterVarsity, 1993.

King, J. S. "Nicodemus and the Pharisees." *Expository Times* 98 (1986) 45.

Kittel, G., and G. Friedrich, eds. *Theological Dictionary of the New Testament*. Translated by G. W. Bromiley. 10 vols. Grand Rapids, Eerdmans, 1964–1976.

Kline, Meredith G. *The Structure of Biblical Authority*. 2d ed. Eugene, OR: Wipf & Stock, 1989.

Klink, Edward W. "Light of the World: Cosmology and the Johannine Literature." Pages 74–89 in *Cosmology and New Testament Theology*. Library of New Testament Studies. Edited by Jonathan T. Pennington and Sean M McDonough. London: T&T Clark, 2008.

Koester, Craig. "Hearing, Seeing, and Believing in the Gospel of John." *Biblica* 70 (1989) 327–48.

———. *Symbolism in the Fourth Gospel: Meaning, Mystery, Community.* 2d ed. Minneapolis: Fortress, 2003.
———. *The Word of Life: A Theology of John's Gospel.* Grand Rapids: Eerdmans, 2008.
Kolarcik, Michael. "Solomon, Wisdom of." In *NIDB* 5:330–34.
Köstenberger, Andreas. *A Theology of John's Gospel and Letters.* Grand Rapids: Zondervan, 2009.
———. "John." Pages 415–512 in *Commentary on the New Testament Use of the Old Testament.* Edited by G. K. Beale and D. A. Carson. Grand Rapids: Baker Academic, 2007.
———. *Encountering John: The Gospel in Historical, Literary, and Theological Perspective.* Grand Rapids: Baker Academic, 1999.
———. *John.* Baker Exegetical Commentary on the New Testament. Grand Rapids: Baker Academic, 2004.
———. "The Seventh Johannine Sign: A Study in John's Christology." *Bulletin for Biblical Research* 5 (1995) 87–103.
Kristeva, Julia. "From Symbol to Sign." Pages 62–73 in *The Kristeva Reader.* Edited By Toril Moi. New York: Columbia University Press, 1986.
———. "Semiotics: A Critical Science and/or a Critique of Science." Pages 74–88 in *The Kristeva Reader.* Edited by Toril Moi. New York: Columbia University Press, 1986.
———. "The System and the Speaking Subject." Pages 24–33 in *The Kristeva Reader.* Edited by Toril Moi. New York: Columbia University Press, 1986.
———. "Word, Dialog, and Novel." Pages 34–61 in *The Kristeva Reader.* Edited by Toril Moi. New York: Columbia University Press, 1986.
Kugel, James L. *Traditions of the Bible: A Guide to the Bible As It Was at the Start of The Common Era.* Cambridge: Harvard University Press, 1998.
Kurtz, J. H. *Offerings, Sacrifices, and Worship in the Old Testament.* Translated by James Martin. Peabody: Hendrickson, 1998.
Kysar, Robert. *John, The Maverick Gospel.* Rev. ed. Louisville: Westminster John Knox, 1993.
———. "The Making of Metaphor: Another Reading of John 3:1–15." Pages 21–41 In *What is John: Readers and Readings of the Fourth Gospel.* Edited by Fernando Segovia. Atlanta: Scholars, 1996.
———. *Voyages with John: Charting the Fourth Gospel.* Louisville: Westminster John Knox, 2005.
Labahn, Michael. "Deuteronomy in John's Gospel." Pages 82–98 in *Deuteronomy in the New Testament.* Edited by Maarten J. J. Menken and Steve Moyise. New York: T&T Clark, 2007.
Ladd, George E. *A Theology of the New Testament.* Rev. ed. Edited by Donald A. Hagner. Grand Rapids: Eerdmans, 1993.
La Vaulx, Jacques de. *Les Nombres.* Paris: J. Gabalda, 1972.
Leal, Robert Barry. *Wilderness in the Bible: Toward a Theology of Wilderness.* New York: Peter Lang, 2004.
Lee, Dorothy. *The Symbolic Narratives of the Fourth Gospel: The Interplay of Form And Meaning.* Sheffield: Sheffield Academic Press, 1994.
Leung, Mavis. *The Kingship-Cross Interplay in the Gospel of John.* Eugene, OR: Wipf And Stock, 2011.
Levine, Baruch A. *Numbers 1–20.* Anchor Bible 4. New York: Doubleday, 1993.

Lewis, Arthur S. "The New Birth Under the Old Covenant." *Evangelical Quarterly* 56(1984) 35–44.

Lewis, Scott M. "Light and Darkness." In *NIDB* 3:662–64.

Lightfoot, John. *A Commentary on the New Testament from the Talmud and Hebraica*. 4 vols. N.P.: Oxford, 1959. Repr., Grand Rapids: Baker Book House, 1979.

Lieu, Judith. "Narrative Analysis and Scripture in John." Pages 144–63 in *The Old Testament in the New: Essays in Honour of J. L. North*. Edited by Steve Moyise. Sheffield: Sheffield Academic Press, 2000.

Lincoln, Andrew. *The Gospel According to St. John*. Black's New Testament Commentaries. New York: Continuum, 2005.

———. *Truth on Trial: The Lawsuit Motif in the Fourth Gospel*. Peabody: Hendrickson, 2000.

Lindars, Barnabas. *New Testament Apologetic*. London: SCM, 1961.

———. "The Place of the Old Testament in the Formation of New Testament Theology." *New Testament Studies* 23 (1976) 59–66.

Lohse, Eduard. "Miracles in the Fourth Gospel." Pages 64–75 in *What about the New Testament?: Essays in Honour of Christopher Evans*. Edited by Morna Hooker and Colin Hickling. London: SCM, 1975.

Loiseau, Anne-Françoise. "Traditions évangéliques et herméneutique juive: Le serpent D'airain de Jean ne-repose-t-il pas sur une guématrie?" *Ephemerides Theologicae Lovanienses* 83 (2007) 155–63.

Longenecker, Richard N. *Biblical Exegesis in the Apostolic Period*. 2d ed. Grand Rapids: Eerdmans, 1999.

Lust, Johan. "The Greek Version of Balaam's Third and Fourth Oracles: The Anthrōpos in Num 24:7 and 17: Messianism and Lexicography." Pages 233–57 in *VIII Congress of the International Organization for Septuagint and Cognate Studies, Paris, 1992*. Atlanta: Scholars, 1995.

Maccoby H. "Rabbinic Literature: Talmud," Pages 897–902 in *Dictionary of New Testament Background*. Edited by Craig Evans and Stanley Porter. Downers Grove: InterVarsity, 2000.

Macdonald, John. *The Theology of the Samaritans*. Philadelphia: Westminster, 1964.

Machen, J. Gresham. *New Testament Greek for Beginners*. 2d ed. Rev. by Dan G. McCartney. Upper Saddle River, NJ: Pearson, 2004.

Mack, Burton. *Wisdom and the Hebrew Epic: Ben Sirah's Hymn in Praise of the Fathers*. Chicago: University of Chicago Press, 1985.

Magri, Annarita. "Le serpent guérisseur et l'origine de la gnose ophite." *Revue de l'historie des religions* 224 (2007) 395–434.

Maher, Michael. *Targum Pseudo-Jonathan: Genesis*. The Aramaic Bible 1B. Collegeville, Minn.: Liturgical Press, 1992.

Maneschg, H. *Die Erzählung von der ehernen Schlange (Num 21:4–9) in der Auslegung der frühen jüdischen—eine traditiongeschichteliche Studie*. Frankfurt: Bern, 1981.

Manning, Gary T. *Echoes of a Prophet: The Use of Ezekiel in the Gospel of John and In Literature of the Second Temple Period*. Journal for the Study of the New Testament Supplement Series 270. London: T&T Clark, 2004.

Marrs, Rick R. "John 3:14–15: The Raised Serpent in the Wilderness: The Johannine Use of an Old Testament Account." Pages 132–47 in *Johannine Studies: Essays in Honor of Frank Pack*. Edited by James E. Priest. Malibu: Pepperdine University Press, 1989.

Marsh, John. *The Fulness of Time*. New York: Harper & Brothers, 1952.
Marshall, I. Howard. "An Assessment of Recent Developments." Pages 1–21 in *It is Written: Scripture Citing Scripture: Essays in Honour of Barnabas Lindars*. Edited by D. A. Carson and H. G. M. Williamson. Cambridge: Cambridge University Press, 1988.
———. "Son of Man." In *DJG* 775–81.
Marshall, Ronald F. "Our Serpent of Salvation: The Offense of Jesus in John's Gospel." *Word and World* 21 (2001) 385–93.
Martínez, Florentino García. *The Dead Sea Scrolls Translated: The Qumran Texts in English*. 2d ed. Leiden: Brill, 1996.
Martyn, J. Louis. *History and Theology in the Fourth Gospel*. 3d ed. Louisville: Westminster John Knox, 2003.
Mauser, Ulrich W. *Christ in the Wilderness: The Wilderness Theme in the Second Gospel and its Basis in the Biblical Tradition*. Studies in Biblical Theology 39. London: SCM, 1963.
McCabe, Robert V. "The Meaning of 'Born of Water and the Spirit' in John 3:5." *Detroit Baptist Seminary Journal* 4 (1999) 85–107.
McCartney, Dan, and Charles Clayton. *Let the Reader Understand: A Guide to Interpreting and Applying the New Testament*. 2d ed. Phillipsburg, NJ: P&R, 2002.
———. "The New Testament's Use of the Old Testament." Pages 101–16 in *Inerrancy and Hermeneutic*. Edited by Harvey Conn. Grand Rapids: Baker Book House, 1988.
McCasland, S. V. "Signs and Wonders." *Journal of Biblical Literature* 76 (1957) 149–52.
McNamara, Martin. "Interpretation of Scripture in the Targumim." Pages 167–97 in *A History of Biblical Interpretation Vol. 1: The Ancient Period*. Edited by Alan Hauser and Duane Watson. Grand Rapids: Eerdmans, 2003.
———. "*Logos* of the Fourth Gospel and *Memra* of the Palestinian Targum (Exod 12:42)." *Expository Times* 79 (1968) 115–17.
———. *Targum and Testament*. Grand Rapids: Eerdmans, 1972.
Meeks, Wayne A. "Man from Heaven in Johannine Sectarianism." *Journal of Biblical Literature* 91 (1972) 44–72.
———. *The Prophet-King: Moses Traditions and the Johannine Christology*. Leiden: Brill, 1967.
Mendner, Sigfried. "Nikodemus." *Journal of Biblical Literature* 77 (1958) 293–323.
Menken, Maarten J. J. "Observations on the Significance of the Old Testament in The Fourth Gospel." *Neotestamentica* 33 (1999) 125–43.
———. *Old Testament Quotations in the Fourth Gospel: Studies in Textual Form*. Kampen, the Netherlands: Pharos, 1996.
Metzger, Bruce M. *A Textual Commentary on the Greek New Testament*. 2d ed. Stuttgart: Deutsche Bibelgesellschaft, 1994.
Michaels, J. Ramsey. *The Gospel of John*. New International Commentary on the New Testament. Grand Rapids: Eerdmans, 2010.
Milgrom, Jacob. *Numbers*. The Jewish Publication Society Torah Commentary. Philadelphia: The Jewish Publication Society, 1990.
———. "Numbers, Book of." In *ABD* 4:1146–55.
Miller, Donald G. "John 3:1–21." *Interpretation* 35 (1981) 174–79.
Miller, Patrick D. *Deuteronomy*. Interpretation; A Bible Commentary for Teaching and Preaching. Louisville: John Knox, 1990.

Moessner, David. "Good News for the 'Wilderness Generation': The Death of the Prophet Like Moses According to Luke." Pages 1–34 in *Good News in History: Essays in Honor of Bo Reicke*. Edited by Ed. L. Miller. Atlanta: Scholars, 1993.

Moloney, Francis J. *Belief in the Word: Reading the Fourth Gospel: John 1–4*. Eugene, OR: Wipf & Stock, 1993.

———. *Glory Not Dishonor: Reading John 13–21*. Eugene, OR: Wipf & Stock, 1998.

———. *Literary Criticism and the Gospels: The Theoretical Challenge*. New Haven: Yale University Press, 1989.

———. *Signs and Shadows: Reading John 5–12*. Eugene, OR: Wipf & Stock, 1996.

———. *The Gospel of John*. Sacra pagina 4. Collegeville: MN: Liturgical Press, 1998.

———. *The Gospel of John: Text and Context*. Biblical Interpretation Series 72. Boston: Brill, 2005.

———. "The Johannine Son of Man." *Biblical Theology Bulletin* 6 (1976) 177–89.

Moran, Richard. "Seeing and Believing: Metaphor, Image, and Force." *Critical Inquiry* 16 (1989) 87–112.

Morgen, Michèle. "Le Fils de l'homme éléve en vue de la vie éternelle (John 3:14–15 Éclairé par diverses traditions juives)." *Revue des sciences religieuses* 68 (1994) 5–17.

Morris, Leon. *New Testament Theology*. Grand Rapids: Zondervan, 1990.

———. *Studies in the Fourth Gospel*. Grand Rapids: Eerdmans, 1969.

———. *The Gospel According to John*. New International Commentary on the New Testament. Rev. ed. Grand Rapids: Eerdmans, 1995.

Moyise, Steve. "Does the NT Quote the OT Out of Context?" *Anvil* 11 (1994) 133–43.

———. *Evoking Scripture: Seeing the Old Testament in the New*. London: Continuum, 2008.

———. "Intertextuality and Historical Approaches to the Use of Scripture." Pages 23–32 in *Reading the Bible Intertextually*. Edited by Richard B. Hays, Stefan Alkier, and Leroy A. Huizenga. Waco: Baylor University Press, 2009.

———. "Intertextuality and the Study of the Old Testament in the New Testament." Pages 14–41 in *The Old Testament in the New: Essays in Honour of J. L. North*. Journal for the Study of the New Testament Supplement Series 189. Edited by Steve Moyise. Sheffield: Sheffield Academic Press, 2000.

———. *Jesus and Scripture: Studying the New Testament Use of the Old Testament*. Grand Rapids: Baker Academic, 2010.

———. *The Old Testament in the Book of Revelation*. Journal for the Study of the New Testament Supplement Series 115. Sheffield: Sheffield Academic Press, 1995.

———. *The Old Testament in the New*. London: Continuum, 2001.

———., ed. *The Old Testament in the New: Essays in Honour of J. L. North*. Journal for the Study of the New Testament Supplement Series 189. Sheffield: Sheffield Academic Press, 2000.

Murray, John. *The Collected Writings of John Murray: Vol. 2: Select Lectures in Systematic Theology*. Cambridge: Cambridge University Press, 1977. Repr., Carlisle, PA: The Banner of Truth Trust, 2001.

Neusner, Jacob. *From Politics to Piety: The Emergence of Pharisaic Judaism*. Englewood Cliffs, NJ: Prentice-Hall, 1973.

———., W. S. Green, and J., eds. *Judaisms and Their Messiahs at the Turn of the Christian Era*. Cambridge: Cambridge University Press, 1987.

———. *Rabbinic Literature and the New Testament: What We Cannot Show, We Cannot Know*. Valley Forge, PA: Trinity Press International, 1994.

———., ed. *The Talmud of the Land of Israel: A Preliminary Translation and Explanation. Vol. 31: Sanhedrin and Makkot*. Translated by Jacob Neusner. Chicago: University of Chicago Press, 1984.

Neyrey, Jerome. "John 3–A Debate Over Johannine Epistemology and Christology." *Novum Testamentum* 23 (1981) 115–27.

———. *The Gospel of John*. The New Cambridge Bible Commentary. Cambridge University Press, 2007.

Nicol, Willem. *The Semeia in the Fourth Gospel*. NovTSup 32. Leiden: Brill, 1972.

Nielsen, Jesper Tang. "The Lamb of God: The Cognitive Structure of a Johannine Metaphor." Pages 217–56 in *Imagery in the Fourth Gospel*. Edited by Jörg Frey, Jan G. Van Der Watt, and Ruben Zimmermann. Tübingen: Mohr Siebeck, 2006.

Norquist, N. Leroy. Review of T. F. Glasson, *Moses in the Fourth Gospel*. *Lutheran Quarterly* 16 (1964) 72.

O'Day, Gail R. "Intertextuality." Pages 155–57 in *Methods of Biblical Interpretation*. Edited by John H. Hayes. Nashville: Abingdon, 2004.

O'Day, Gail R., and Susan Hylen. *John*. Louisville: Westminster John Knox, 2006.

———. *The Gospel of John: Introduction, Commentary, and Reflections*. The New Interpreter's Bible 9. Nashville: Abingdon, 1995.

———. *Revelation in the Fourth Gospel: Narrative Mode and Theological Claim*. Philadelphia: Fortress, 1986.

O'Grady, John F. "The Prologue and Chapter 17 of the Gospel of John." Pages 215–28 in *What We Have Heard from the Beginning: The Past, Present, and Future of Johannine Studies*. Edited by Tom Thatcher. Baylor: Baylor University Press, 2007.

Olbricht, Thomas H. "The Theology of the Signs in the Gospel of John." Pages 171–81 In *Johannine Studies: Essays in Honor of Frank Pack*. Edited by James Priest. Malibu: Pepperdine University Press, 1989.

Olson, Dennis T. *Numbers*. Interpretation. Louisville: John Knox, 1996.

Osburn, Carroll D. "Some Exegetical Observations on John 3:5–8." *Restoration Quarterly* 31 (1989) 129–38.

Pack, Frank. "The Holy Spirit in the Fourth Gospel." *Restoration Quarterly* 31 (1989) 139–48.

Painter, John. *John: Witness and Theologian*. London: S.P.C.K., 1975.

———. "The Signs of the Messiah and the Quest for Eternal Life." Pages 233–56 in *What We Have Heard from the Beginning: The Past, Present and Future of Johannine Studies*. Edited by Tom Thatcher. Waco: Baylor University Press, 2007.

Paschal, R. W. "Sacramental Symbolism and Physical Imagery in the Gospel of John." *Tyndale Bulletin* 32 (1981) 159–61.

Patte, Daniel. "Structural Criticism." Pages 183–200 in *To Each Its Own Meaning*. Edited by Steven L. McKenzie and Stephen R. Haynes. Louisville: Westminster John Knox, 1999.

Pazdan, Margaret. "Nicodemus and the Samaritan Woman: Contrasting Models of Discipleship." *Biblical Theology Bulletin* 17 (1987) 145–48.

Piper, Otto A. "Unchanging Promises: Exodus in the New Testament." *Interpretation* 11 (1957) 3–22.

Pomykala, Kenneth., ed. *Israel in the Wilderness: Interpretations of the Biblical Narratives in Jewish and Christian Traditions*. Leiden: Brill, 2008.

Poythress, Vern S. *God Centered Biblical Interpretation*. Phillipsburg, NJ: P&R, 1999.

———. "What Does God Say Through Human Authors?" Pages 81–99 in *Inerrancy And Hermeneutic: A Tradition, A Challenge, A Debate*. Edited by Harvie M. Conn; Grand Rapids: Baker, 1988.

Pryor, John. "John 3:3, 5. A Study in the Relation of John's Gospel to the Synoptic Tradition." *Journal for the Study of the New Testament* 41 (1991) 71–95.

———. *John: Evangelist of the Covenant People: The Narrative and Themes of the Fourth Gospel*. Downers Grove: InterVarsity, 1992.

———. "The Johannine Son of Man and the Decent-Ascent Motif." *Journal of the Evangelical Theological Society* 34 (1991) 341–51.

Reim, Günter. *Jochanan: erweitere Studien zum alttestamentlichen Hintergrund des Johannesevangeliums*. Erlangen: Verlag der Ev.-Luth. Mission, 1995.

Remus, Harold E. "Miracle." In *ABD* 4:845–69.

Rengstorf, Karl. "σημεῖον, συσσήμον." In *TDNT* 7:200–69.

Renz, Gabi. "Nicodemus: An Ambiguous Disciple? A Narrative Sensitive Investigation." Pages 255–83 in *Challenging Perspectives on the Gospel of John*. Edited by John Lierman. Tübingen: Mohr Siebeck, 2006.

Resseguie, James. *Narrative Criticism of the New Testament: An Introduction*. Grand Rapids: Baker Academic, 2005.

Richard, Earl. "Expressions of Double Meaning and Their Function in the Gospel of John." *New Testament Studies* 31 (1985) 96–112.

Ridderbos, Herman. *The Coming of the Kingdom*. Translated by H. de Jonste. Philadelphia: P&R, 1962.

———. *The Gospel According to John: A Theological Commentary*. Translated by John Vriend. Grand Rapids: Eerdmans, 1997.

Riga, P. "Signs of Glory: The Use of 'Sēmeion' in St. John's Gospel." *Interpretation* 17 (1963) 402–24.

Roberts, Rev. Alexander, Sir James Donaldson, and Arthur Cleveland Cox, eds. *The Ante-Nicene Fathers Vol. 1: The Apostolic Fathers with Justin Martyr and Irenaeus*. New York: Cosimo Classics, 2007.

Robertson, O. Palmer. *The Christ of the Prophets*. Phillipsburg, NJ: P&R, 2004.

Robinson, D. W. B. "Born of Water and Spirit: Does John 3:5 Refer to Baptism?" *Reformed Theological Review* 25 (1966) 15–23.

Romanowsky, John W. "'When the Son of Man is Lifted Up': The Redemptive Power of the Crucifixion in the Gospel of John." *Horizons* 32 (2005) 100–16.

Ronning, John. *The Jewish Targums and John's Logos Theology*. Peabody: Hendrickson, 2010.

Rowley, H. H. "Zadok and Nehushtan." *Journal of Biblical Literature* 58 (1939) 113–41.

Russell, Walt. "The Holy Spirit's Ministry in the Fourth Gospel." *Grace Theological Journal* 8 (1987) 227–39.

Sahlin, Herald. *Zur Typologie des Johannesevangeliums*. Asskrift: Uppsala Universitets, 1950.

Sakenfeld, Katharine Doob. *Numbers: Journeying with God*. International Theological Commentary. Grand Rapids: Eerdmans, 1995.

Sanders, James A. "The Stabilization of the Tanak." Pages 225–52 in *A History of Biblical Interpretation. Vol. 1: The Ancient Period*. Edited by Alan J. Hauser and Duane F. Watson. Grand Rapids: Eerdmans, 2003.

Sandmel, Samuel. "Parallelomania." *Journal of Biblical Literature* 81 (1962) 1–13.

Sarna, Nahum. *Exodus*. The Jewish Publication Society Torah Commentary. Philadelphia: The Jewish Publication Society, 1991.
Schechter, Solomon. *Aspects of Rabbinic Theology: Major Concepts on the Talmud*. Peabody: Hendrickson, 1998.
Schmidl, Martin. *Jesus und Nikodemus: Gespräch zur Johanneischen Christologie*. Regensburg: Pustet, 1998.
Schnabel, Eckhard. "Sanhedrin." In *NIDB* 5:102-06.
Schnackenburg, Rudolf. *The Gospel According to St. John*. 3 vols. Vol. 1: Translated by Kevin Smyth. Edited by J. Massingberd Ford and Kevin Smyth. New York: Herder and Herder, 1968. Vol. 2: New York: Seabury, 1980. Vol. 3: New York: Crossroad, 1982.
Schneiders, Sandra. *The Revelatory Text: Interpreting the New Testament as Sacred Scripture*. San Francisco: Harper, 1991.
Schofield, Alison. "The Wilderness Motif in the Dead Sea Scrolls." Pages 37-53 in *Israel in the Wilderness: Interpretations of the Biblical Narratives in the Jewish And Christian Traditions*. Edited by Kenneth E. Pomykala. Leiden: Brill, 2008.
Scholtissek, Klaus. "The Johannine Gospel in Recent Research." Pages 444-72 in *The Face of New Testament Studies: A Survey of Recent Research*. Edited by Scot McKnight and Grant R. Osborne. Grand Rapids: Baker Academic, 2004.
Schuchard, Bruce G. *Scripture Within Scripture: The Interrelationship of Form and Function in the Explicit Old Testament Citations in the Gospel of John*. SBL Dissertation Series 133. Atlanta: Scholars, 1992.
Schürer, Emil. *A History of the Jewish People in the Time of Jesus Christ*. Rev. ed. Translated by Sophia Taylor and Peter Christie. 3 vols. Peabody: Hendrickson, 1998.
Schweizer, Eduard. *Ego eimi: Die religionsgeshichtliche Herkunft und theologische Bedeutung der johanneishcen Bildreden, zugleich ein Beitrag zur Quellefrage Des vierten Evangeliums*. Forschungen zur Religion und Literatur des Alten und Neuen Testaments 56. Göttingen: Vandenhoeck & Ruprecht, 1939.
Selvaggio, Anthony T. *The Seven Signs: Seeing the Glory of Christ in the Gospel of John*. Grand Rapids: Reformation Heritage, 2010.
Sidebottom, E. M. *The Christ of the Fourth Gospel: In Light of First-Century Thought*. London: SPCK, 1961.
Slotki, Judah J. *Midrash Rabbah: Numbers*. London: Soncino, 1983.
Sloyan, Gerard S. *John*. Interpretation. Atlanta: John Knox, 1988.
Smalley, Stephen S. *John: Evangelist and Interpreter*. Carlisle, PA: Paternoster, 1978.
———. "'The Paraclete': Pneumatology in the Johannine Gospel." Pages 289-300 In *Exploring the Gospel of John. In Honor of D. Moody Smith*. Edited by R. Alan Culpepper and C. Clifton Black. Louisville: Westminster John Knox, 1996.
———. "The Johannine Son of Man Sayings." *New Testament Studies* 15 (1969) 278-301.
Smith, D. Moody. Introduction to *History and Theology in the Fourth Gospel*. 3d ed. By J. Louis Martyn. Louisville: Westminster John Knox, 2003.
———. *John*. Abingdon New Testament Commentaries. Nashville: Abingdon, 1999.
———. *The Composition and Order of the Fourth Gospel: Bultmann's Literary Theory*. Yale Publications in Religion 10. New Haven: Yale University Press, 1965.

———. "The Pauline Epistles." Pages 265–91 in *It is Written: Scripture Citing Scripture: Essays in Honour of Barnabas Lindars*. Edited by D. A. Carson and H. G. M. Williamson. Cambridge: Cambridge University Press, 1988.

———. *The Theology of the Gospel of John*. Cambridge: Cambridge University Press. 1995.

Smith, Robert H. "Exodus Typology in the Fourth Gospel." *Journal of Biblical Literature* 81 (1962) 329–42.

Soll, Will. "Descent, Descend." In *NIDB* 2:102.

Speiser, E. A. "Background and Function of the Biblical Nāśī." *Catholic Biblical Quarterly* 25 (1963) 111–17.

Strack, Herman, and Paul Billerbeck. *Kommentar zum Neuen Testament aus Talmud und Midrasch*. 6 vols. Munich: C. H. Beck, 1922–1961.

Stegner, William Richard. "Wilderness and Testing in the Scrolls and in Matthew 4:1–11." *Biblical Research* 12 (1967) 18–27.

Stendahl, Krister. *The School of St. Matthew and Its Use of the Old Testament*. Philadelphia: Fortress, 1954.

Stibbe, Mark. *John as Storyteller: Narrative Criticism and the Fourth Gospel*. New York: Cambridge University Press, 1992.

———. *The Gospel of John as Literature: An Anthology of Twentieth-Century Perspectives*. New York: E. J. Brill, 1993.

Streeter, B. H. *The Four Gospels: A Study of Origins*. New York: St. Martin's, 1956.

Sundberg, Albert C. Jr. "Response Against C. H. Dodd's View: On Testimonies." Pages 182–94 in *The Right Doctrine From the Wrong Text? Essays on the Use of the Old Testament in the New*. Edited by G. K. Beale. Grand Rapids: Baker Academic, 1994.

Talbert, Charles. *Reading John: A Literary and Theological Commentary on the Fourth Gospel and the Johannine Epistles*. New York: Crossroad, 1992.

Talmon, Shemaryahu. "The 'Desert Motif' in the Bible and in Qumran Literature," Pages 31–63 in *Biblical Motifs: Origins and Transformations*. Edited by Alexander Altmann; Cambridge: Harvard University Press, 1966.

———. "Wilderness." *IDB* 946–48.

Teeple, Howard M. *The Mosaic Eschatological Prophet*. Journal of Biblical Literature Monograph Series 10. Philadelphia: Society of Biblical Literature, 1957.

Tenney, Merrill C. *John: The Gospel of Belief*. Grand Rapids: Eerdmans, 1976.

Thatcher, Tom. *Why John Wrote a Gospel: Jesus-Memory-History*. Louisville: Westminster John Knox, 2006.

Thielman, Frank. *Theology of the New Testament: A Canonical and Synthetic Approach*. Grand Rapids: Zondervan, 2005.

Thomas, John Christopher. "Healing in the Atonement: A Johannine Perspective." *Journal of Pentecostal Theology* 14.1 (2005) 23–39.

Thompson, Marianne Meye. "John, Gospel of." In *DJG* 368–83.

———. "Signs and Faith in the Fourth Gospel." *Bulletin for Biblical Research* 1 (1991) 89–108.

———. "The Gospel According to John." Pages 182–200 in *The Cambridge Companion to the Gospels*. Edited by Stephen C. Barton. Cambridge: Cambridge University Press, 2006.

———. *The Humanity of Jesus in the Fourth Gospel*. Philadelphia: Fortress, 1988.

Tov, Emanuel. "The Septuagint." Pages 161–88 in *Mikra: Text, Translation, Reading & Interpretation of the Hebrew Bible in Ancient Judaism & Early Christianity*. Peabody: Hendrickson, 2004.

Tuckett, C. M. "The Son of Man and Daniel 7: Inclusive Aspects of Early Christologies." Pages 164–90 in *Christian Origins*. Edited by K. J. O'Mahony. Journal for the Study of the New Testament Supplement Series 241. Sheffield: Sheffield Academic Press, 2003.

Tull, Patricia K. "Rhetorical Criticism and Intertextuality." Pages 156–80 in *To Each Its Own Meaning*. Edited by Steven L. McKenzie and Stephen R. Haynes. Louisville: Westminster John Knox, 1999.

———. "Signs in the Old Testament." In *NIDB* 5:254.

Turnage, Marc. "Is it the Serpent that Heals? An Ancient Jewish *Theologoumenon* and The Developing Faith in Jesus." Pages 71–88 in *Israel in the Wilderness: Interpretations of the Biblical Narratives in Jewish and Christian Traditions*. Edited by Kenneth E. Pomykala. Leiden: Brill, 2008.

Vanderkam, James C. *The Dead Sea Scrolls Today*. Grand Rapids: Eerdmans, 1994.

Van der Watt, Jan. "Double Entendre in the Gospel According to John." Pages 463–81 In *Theology and Christology of the Fourth Gospel: Essays by the Members of the SNTS Johannine Writings Seminar*. Edited by G. Van Belle, J. G. Van Der Watt, And P. Maritz. Leuven: Leuven University Press, 2005.

———. "Knowledge of Earthly Things? The Use of ἐπίγειος in John 3:12." *Neotestamentica* 43 (2009) 289–310.

VanGemeren, Willem. *The Progress of Redemption: The Story of Salvation from Creation to the New Jerusalem*. Grand Rapids: Baker, 1988.

Vanhoozer, Kevin J. *Is There a Meaning in this Text?* Grand Rapids: Zondervan, 1998.

———. "The Semantics of Biblical Literature: Truth and Scripture's Diverse Literary Forms." Pages 53–104 in *Hermeneutics, Authority, and Canon*. Grand Rapids: Zondervan, 1986.

Vellanickal, Matthew. *The Divine Sonship of Christians in the Johannine Writings*. Rome: Biblical Institute, 1977.

Von Rad, Gerhard. *Old Testament Theology*. 2 vols. Old Testament Library. Translated By D. M. G. Stalker. San Francisco: Harper Collins, 1962. Repr., Louisville: Westminster John Knox, 2001.

Von Wahlde, Urban C. *The Earliest Version of John's Gospel: Recovering the Gospel of Signs*. Wilmington, DE: Michael Glazier, 1989.

———. "The Johannine 'Jews': A Critical Survey." *New Testament Studies* 28 (1982) 33–60.

Vos, Geerhardus. *Biblical Theology: Old and New Testaments*. Grand Rapids: Eerdmans, 1948. Repr., Carlisle, PA: Banner of Truth Trust, 2000.

Wagner, J. Ross. *Heralds of the Good News: Isaiah and Paul in Concert in the Letter to The Romans*. Leiden: Brill, 2002.

Wall, Robert W. "Intertextuality, Biblical." In *DNTB* 541–51.

———. "Reading the New Testament in Canonical Context." Pages 370–93 in *Hearing the New Testament: Strategies for Interpretation*. Edited by Joel Green. Grand Rapids: Eerdmans, 1995.

Watson, Francis. *Paul and the Hermeneutics of Faith*. London: T&T Clark International, 2004.

Wead, David. "The Johannine Double Meaning." *Restoration Quarterly* 13 (1970) 106–20.

———. *The Literary Devices in John's Gospel.* Theologischen Dissertationen. Vol. 4. Basel: Friedrich Reinhart Kommissionsverlag, 1970.

Wenham, Gordon J. *Numbers: An Introduction and Commentary.* Tyndale Old Testament Commentaries. Downers Grove: InterVarsity, 1981.

Westcott, Brooke Foss. *The Gospel According to St. John: The Authorized Version with Introduction and Notes.* London: John Murray, 1882.

Westphal, Merold. *Whose Community? Which Interpretation?: Philosophical Hermeneutics for the Church.* Grand Rapids: Baker Academic, 2009.

Wevers, John Williams. *Notes on the Greek Text of Exodus.* Society of Biblical Literature Septuagint and Cognate Studies Series 46. Atlanta: Scholars, 1998.

———. *Notes on the Greek Text of Numbers.* Society of Biblical Literature Septuagint and Cognate Studies Series 46. Atlanta: Scholars, 1998.

———. *Text History of the Greek Numbers.* Mitteilungen des Septuaginta-Unternehmens 16. Göttingen: Vandenhoeck & Ruprecht, 1982.

Williams, George H. "The Wilderness and Paradise in the History of the Church." *Church History* 28 (1959) 3–24.

———. *Wilderness and Paradise in Christian Thought.* New York: Harper, 1962.

Williams, Patrick. "Snake on a Stick." *Christian Century* 111 (1994) 223.

Williamson, H. G. M. "Samaritans." In *DJG* 724–28.

Wilson, Robert R. *Prophecy and Society in Ancient Israel.* Philadelphia: Fortress, 1980.

Wise, M. O. "Feasts." In *DJG* 234–41.

Witherington, Ben III. "Jesus as the Alpha and Omega of New Testament Thought." Pages 25–46 in *Contours of Christology in the New Testament.* Edited by Richard Longenecker. Grand Rapids: Eerdmans, 2005.

———. *Jesus the Sage: The Pilgrimage of Wisdom.* Minneapolis: Fortress, 2000.

———. *John's Wisdom: A Commentary on the Fourth Gospel.* Louisville: Westminster John Knox, 1995.

———. *The Christology of Jesus.* Minneapolis: Fortress, 1990.

Wright, Christopher J. H. *Deuteronomy.* New International Biblical Commentary. Peabody: Hendrickson, 1996.

———. *Knowing Jesus Through the Old Testament.* Downers Grove, IL: InterVarsity, 1992.

Wright, J. E. "Esdras, Books of." In *DNTB* 337–40.

Wright, N. T. *Jesus and the Victory of God.* Minneapolis: Fortress, 1996.

Yarchin, William. *History of Biblical Interpretation: A Reader.* Peabody: Hendrickson, 2004.

Young, Edward J. *My Servants the Prophets.* Grand Rapids: Eerdmans, 1952.

Zeitlin, Solomon. "The Titles High Priest and the Nasi of the Sanhedrin." *Jewish Quarterly Review* 48 (1957) 1–5.

Zumstein, Jean. "Intratextuality and Intertextuality in the Gospel of John." Pages 121–35 in *Anatomies of Narrative Criticism: The Past, Present, and Futures of the Fourth Gospel as Literature.* Translated by Mike Gray. Edited by Tom Thatcher and Stephen D. Moore. Atlanta: Society of Biblical Literature, 2008.

www.ingramcontent.com/pod-product-compliance
Lightning Source LLC
Chambersburg PA
CBHW070251230426
43664CB00014B/2493